CW00832204

1,000,000 Books

are available to read at

www.ForgottenBooks.com

Read online
Download PDF
Purchase in print

ISBN 978-1-330-19491-1
PIBN 10049741

This book is a reproduction of an important historical work. Forgotten Books uses
state-of-the-art technology to digitally reconstruct the work, preserving the original format
whilst repairing imperfections present in the aged copy. In rare cases, an imperfection in
the original, such as a blemish or missing page, may be replicated in our edition. We do,
however, repair the vast majority of imperfections successfully; any imperfections that
remain are intentionally left to preserve the state of such historical works.

Forgotten Books is a registered trademark of FB &c Ltd.
Copyright © 2018 FB &c Ltd.
FB &c Ltd, Dalton House, 60 Windsor Avenue, London, SW19 2RR.
Company number 08720141. Registered in England and Wales.

For support please visit www.forgottenbooks.com

1 MONTH OF
FREE
READING

at
www.ForgottenBooks.com

By purchasing this book you are
eligible for one month membership to
ForgottenBooks.com, giving you
unlimited access to our entire
collection of over 1,000,000 titles via
our web site and mobile apps.

To claim your free month visit:

www.forgottenbooks.com/free49741

* Offer is valid for 45 days from date of purchase. Terms and conditions apply.

English
Français
Deutsche
Italiano
Español
Português

www.forgottenbooks.com

Mythology Photography **Fiction**
Fishing Christianity **Art** Cooking
Essays Buddhism Freemasonry
Medicine **Biology** Music **Ancient**
Egypt Evolution Carpentry Physics
Dance Geology **Mathematics** Fitness
Shakespeare **Folklore** Yoga Marketing
Confidence Immortality Biographies
Poetry **Psychology** Witchcraft
Electronics Chemistry History **Law**
Accounting **Philosophy** Anthropology
Alchemy Drama Quantum Mechanics
Atheism Sexual Health **Ancient History**
Entrepreneurship Languages Sport
Paleontology Needlework Islam
Metaphysics Investment Archaeology
Parenting Statistics Criminology
Motivational

The Barber of Bıhunga, Ruwenzori.

FROM RUWENZORI TO THE CONGO

A NATURALIST'S JOURNEY ACROSS AFRICA

BY A. F. R. WOLLASTON

WITH ILLUSTRATIONS

LONDON

JOHN MURRAY, ALBEMARLE STREET, W.

1908

DEDICATION

To Youth there comes a whisper out of the West :
' O loiterer, hasten where there waits for thee
A life to build, a love therein to nest,
And a man's work, serving the age to be.'

Peace, peace awhile ! before his tireless feet
Hill beyond hill the road in sunlight goes ;
He breathes the breath of morning, clear and sweet,
And his eyes love the high eternal snows.

HENRY NEWBOLT.

1591656

PREFACE

IT is often complained that when a man has made a journey, whether it is across the Channel, or a mountain-range, or a continent, he thinks it his duty on his return to chronicle his achievement in a book. I confess that I have sometimes been of those who complain, but I generally read the books, rarely with little, often with great, enjoyment. *Qui s'excuse s'accuse* is a proverb which applies particularly to the writers of Prefaces, but I am assured, on no less authority than that of Mr. Murray, that the Preface or Apology at the beginning is as essential a part of a book as the Index or Guide at the end.

The idea of writing this book was first suggested to me by my friend, the late Professor Alfred Newton, of Cambridge. In a letter which reached me on the Congo a few weeks before his death, he wrote : 'I am rather like the poor girl in one of Dickens's books who exclaimed that " Africa is a beast," and accordingly have never been able to take any real interest in the country, finding nearly all African books of travel to be duller than any-

thing short of " Bradshaw." Yet the subject ought
to be highly interesting, and that I don't find it so I
set down to the want of style on the part of the
authors—most of whom take themselves so very
seriously, while the few who do not disgust one by
their flippancy. It is a very curious thing, and one
at which I have often wondered, for in a general
way most books of travel, whether by Englishmen
or foreigners, in other parts of the world, exercise a
charm upon me, and I feel sorry when I come to
the end of them. If you will write me some more
of your letters I may alter my opinion of the
" beast." '

Professor Newton died before he read many more
letters from Africa, but his suggestion germinated
slowly and bore fruit in the shape of the present
volume. Africa *is* a beast, it is true, but a beast of
many and varied moods, often disagreeable and
sometimes even dangerous to body and soul; but
withal she has an attraction which can hardly be
resisted, and when once you have come under her
spell you feel it a duty to uphold her reputation.
So I have attempted, for the benefit of those who
have a misconception of the country, to convey
something of the ' feel ' and smell of Africa as it
appeared to me on hot and hilly roads, on winding
waterways, and on cloud-girt mountain-sides. The
book contains no tales of thrilling adventures and

hairsbreadth escapes, nor are there records of 'bagged' elephants and lions. The first half of the book is occupied with the time spent by the British Museum Expedition in Ruwenzori, while the rest treats of the countries through which Carruthers and I passed on our way from Uganda to the West Coast. Though geographical research was not a part of the object of the expedition, many of the districts which we visited are almost unknown to Europeans, to Englishmen least of all, and are here described for the first time. I have avoided, as far as possible, the journal method of writing, and have merely introduced a thin thread of narrative to connect the description of one region with that of another. If I appear to give an unduly favourable impression of the Congo Free State in Chapter XVIII., it is because the other side of the case is the only one which is ordinarily presented to English readers.

The last part of a Preface is easier, and requires less explanation. I am indebted to the Editor of the *Westminster Gazette* for permission to publish parts of Chapters II. and IX., which originally appeared in that journal. Signor Vittorio Sella, who accompanied the Duke of the Abruzzi on his Ruwenzori expedition, has most kindly allowed me to reproduce the beautiful photograph which appears at p. 92. My thanks are due to Mr. R. B. Woosnam for permission to make use of the photographs at pp. 60, 90, and 158 ; to Mr. D. Carruthers for the photographs at pp. 78 and 162 ; and to Mr. F. A. Knowles, of Uganda, for the photograph at p. 168.

To my friend, Henry Newbolt, for his invaluable suggestions, for his kindness in reading the MS. and correcting proofs, and for the Dedication which he has written for this book, I will not here attempt to express my thanks.

In conclusion, I may say that if any reader finds one-hundredth part of the pleasure in reading that I have had in writing the book, I shall be well rewarded.

A. F. R. W.

CHELSEA, 1908.

CONTENTS

CHAPTER I

ENGLAND TO EAST AFRICA

CHAPTER II

NAIVASHA AND THE VICTORIA NYANZA

CHAPTER III

CIVILIZED UGANDA

CONTENTS

CHAPTER VII

CLIMBING IN RUWENZORI

CHAPTER VIII

CLIMBING IN RUWENZORI (*continued*)

CHAPTER IX

THE PLAINS OF RUISAMBA

CONTENTS

CHAPTER X

THE SEMLIKI VALLEY

CHAPTER XI

THE WEST SIDE OF RUWENZORI

CHAPTER XII

ANKOLE AND LAKE ALBERT EDWARD

CONTENTS

THE MFUMBIRO VOLCANOES

CHAPTER XIV

LAKE KIVU

CHAPTER XV

FROM KIVU TO TANGANYIKA

APPENDICES

LIST OF ILLUSTRATIONS

xix

INTRODUCTION

Ever since its discovery by Sir Henry Stanley in 1888, the great range of mountains in Equatorial Africa, known as Ruwenzori, or the 'Mountains of the Moon,' has attracted the attention of naturalists in all parts of the world, especially in Europe and America. The isolated position, and the great altitude attained by the forest-clad, snow-capped peaks, rising to nearly 17,000 feet, made it certain that a rich and peculiar Fauna and Flora must await the investigations of the explorer.

With a view to benefiting the British Museum (Natural History), I therefore determined, if possible, to be first in the field; but the task of raising sufficient funds for the purpose of sending out a large and properly equipped expedition to thoroughly explore all parts of the range took more time to achieve than I had at first contemplated. At last, however, this difficulty was overcome through the generosity of—

> His Grace the Duke of Bedford,
> The Earl of Dartmouth,
> Viscount Iveagh,
> Lord Strathcona and Mount Royal,
> The Hon. N. C. Rothschild,
> Sir Alexander Baird,
> Sir Ludwig Mond,
> Mr. W. A. Bell,
> Mr. C. Czarnikow,
> Mr. W. H. St. Quintin,
> The Trustees of the Percy Sladen Fund, and
> The Worshipful Company of Fishmongers,

who became subscribers to the Ruwenzori Expedition Fund on the understanding that the first set of the specimens collected should be presented to the British Museum. Mr. C. E. Fagan, Secretary of the British Museum (Natural History), kindly consented to act as treasurer to the fund.

Meanwhile, the services of four first-rate field-naturalists and collectors—viz.:

> Mr. R. B. Woosnam (leader ⎧ Late of the
>   of the expedition)   ⎨ Worcestershire
> Mr. R. E. Dent,   ⎩ Regiment,
> Hon. Gerald Legge, and
> Mr. D. Carruthers—

were secured, and to these was finally added Mr. A. F. R. Wollaston, who undertook to look after the health of the various members of the expedition, and to form botanical and entomological collections.

It would be a difficult matter to find any five people who could have carried out the work as successfully and as thoroughly as these gentlemen have done, and when a complete account of the zoological results is published in the *Transactions of the Zoological Society of London* this will be abundantly evident. The botanical results have already been published in a paper by Dr. A. B. Rendle and others, which appeared in the *Journal of the Linnæan Society*, January, 1908, vol. xxxviii., pp. 228-279.

The organization and equipment of this large expedition took many months to arrange, and before it had reached its destination and commenced work a number of the birds peculiar to the region had already been procured, and sent to the British Museum by Mr. F. J. Jackson, C.B., whose nephew, Mr. Geoffry Archer, paid a short visit to the north-eastern slopes of Ruwenzori in February, 1902.

The Ruwenzori range has now been investigated as completely as is at present possible ; unfortunately, the western heights, which lie within the Congo territory, had to be abandoned before they had been properly explored, owing to the hostility of the natives.

The collections formed are among the finest that have ever been sent to the British Museum, both as regards the number of species and the perfect condition in which they have reached this country; and, so far as the birds are concerned, they, no doubt, contain the great majority of the species which occur in Ruwenzori.

At present it is only possible to give some slight idea of what has been done, and the following is a list of the specimens which have been received :

404 *Mammalia* (twenty-three new species).
2,470 *Aves* (twenty-four new species).
135 {*Reptilia* *Amphibia*} (two new species).
31 *Pisces* (two new species).
12 *Crustacea*.
100 *Arachnida*.
1,015 *Coleoptera* (six new species).
33 *Orthoptera*.
25 *Neuroptera*.
47 *Hymenoptera*.
1,372 *Lepidoptera* (forty-seven new species).
130 *Hemiptera*.
23 *Homoptera*.
55 *Diptera*.
38 *Mollusca* (six new species).
66 *Vermes*.

Lastly, a very fine collection of dried plants

(including thirty-four new species and one new genus) was made, and numerous growing plants and seeds were sent home, and are now being cultivated at the Royal Botanic Gardens at Edinburgh under the care of Professor I. Bayley Balfour.

The close affinity between the Highland Fauna of Ruwenzori and that of the Cameroon is a very striking feature of the collection as a whole, and when the various groups have been thoroughly worked out, as will shortly be the case, a very valuable and important addition will certainly have been made to our knowledge of the Fauna and Flora of Tropical Africa.

W. R. OGILVIE-GRANT.

BRITISH MUSEUM (NAT. HIST.),
CROMWELL ROAD,
LONDON, S.W.

FROM RUWENZORI TO THE CONGO

CHAPTER I

ENGLAND TO EAST AFRICA

'Over the great windy waters, and over the clear-crested
    summits,
Unto the sun and the sky, and unto the perfecter earth,
Come, let us go——'
CLOUGH.

THE forest and mountain regions of Western Uganda
and the eastern districts of the Congo Free State
have long been an unknown land and difficult of
approach, but the few accounts that had been given
by travellers, and the remarkable birds and beasts
that they had brought back with them, excited the
curiosity of naturalists—not least among them the
authorities of the Natural History Museum at
South Kensington. The discovery by Sir Harry
Johnston of the okapi and other interesting forms
in the Semliki Valley, and the numerous new species
of birds obtained by Mr. F. J. Jackson's collector
in the unexplored range of Ruwenzori, pointed to
that district as being the most likely to produce

birds and beasts new to science. The improved facilities for reaching Uganda by railway from the coast, the tranquil state of the country, and (possibly) the rumour of other zoological expeditions being sent by foreign countries to the same region, determined the dispatch of an expedition in 1905. Funds were raised from various generous contributors, and in October the British Museum Ruwenzori Expedition left England, fully equipped with apparatus for obtaining zoological and botanical collections. The expedition was under the leadership of Mr. R. B. Woosnam, and with him were Messrs. R. E. Dent, D. Carruthers, and the Hon. G. Legge. A day or two before the expedition started I heard for the first time of its existence, and that they were in need of a doctor who would attend the other members of the party, and, when not so occupied, would assist in making collections of plants and insects. I at once went to see Mr. Ogilvie Grant, and it was arranged that I should start by the next boat, in four weeks' time. It was unfortunate that I had just obtained an appointment elsewhere, but the chance was too good to be thrown away, even if it had been Harley Street and ten thousand a year that I was leaving behind; so I incurred the wrath of my authorities, left them in a fortnight, and after two weeks of hurried preparations took ship from Genoa for Mombasa early in November.

I do not pretend to have the slightest knowledge

of fiscal questions, but I could not help wondering why it should be necessary to travel to a British colony by a foreign steamship line. It is true that the British India Company has a service to Mombasa, but this involves changing ship at Aden, with always the probability of spending a few days in that most disagreeable port, and the possibility of having a part of one's baggage lost or broken in the transhipment. There are three lines of steamships which have direct services between Europe and Mombasa: the Austrian Lloyd from Trieste, the Messageries Maritimes from Marseilles, and the German East African Line from Hamburg. The first of these lines is the best, but the last is the most convenient for passengers from England, as their intermediate boats call at Dover, enabling one to send heavy baggage without transhipment direct to East Africa.

The Reichs Post Dampfer *Markgraf* could not, even by stretching truth to the uttermost, be called a good boat. She was uncomfortable and unclean, she rolled abominably in the calmest sea, and stories were even told of her having turned turtle in port. It is to be hoped that she has done so ere this. The voyage through the Mediterranean and the Red Sea to the Indian Ocean is sufficiently familiar to a large proportion of Englishmen; the first sniff of the East at Port Said, however much polluted by the worst of European civilization, is always a pleasant thing to the inveterate wanderer, and it is agreeable enough, only a week after leaving a cold November fog in London, to lie in a deck-chair and watch the camels shuffling along the grilling banks of the Suez Canal, and the pelicans soaring high over Lake Timsah. The Red Sea was kinder than it often is, and Aden was reached without any more exciting adventure than the slaughter by a 'sporting' German of an unfortunate owl that perched one day upon the rigging. The bird fell overboard and was lost, but that did not seem to affect the spirits of the 'sportsman,' who was warmly congratulated by his friends on his good shooting.

From Aden, where the customary traffic in ostrich feathers and leopards' skins afforded us a few hours' diversion, the voyage down the east coast of Africa was dull in the extreme. Of ships we saw none at all, except the remains of a big French liner that had run ashore a few months previously near Cape Guardafui, and the few glimpses we got of the coast were of a bare and forbidding land. Our rather stiff and brass-bound fellow-passengers, most of them German officers going out to their East African colony, came undone in a quite unexpected way when we crossed the Line. For most of them it was their first voyage, and they submitted, with true discipline, to be ducked and soaped and shaved in quite the old-fashioned manner. It should be mentioned, however, that they washed away the taste of the soap in copious

Rubber-Vines.

To face page 4.

Botanic Garden, Entebbe.

libations to Neptune and Kaiser Wilhelm until the small hours of the following morning.

Late in the evening of the nineteenth day after leaving Genoa we sighted the lights of Mombasa, and the next morning at daybreak we steamed into the harbour, where there were three other steamers, all of them, to our disgust and to the delight of our companions, flying the flag of Germany. Nearly half a day was occupied in passing through the custom-house, thanks to the stiff-necked attitude of the Indian officials; but there was some compensation for the annoyance in watching the astonishing athletic feats of the Swahili labourers, who hoisted cases as big as grand pianos on to their heads, and trotted nimbly up the steep slope from the shore to the warehouses above. Mombasa is picturesquely situated on an island, with a small harbour, Mombasa Harbour, on the north, and a far finer harbour, Kilindini, a couple of miles or so to the south. It is a pity that the town was not built near to Kilindini Harbour, as only small vessels can enter Mombasa Harbour, while ships of large tonnage go to Kilindini, and land their passengers and cargoes a long way from the town.

The old town of Mombasa is a queer jumble of India and Africa and Southern Europe; men of every shade of colour between black and white may be seen in the streets, and almost every tongue is heard spoken. The old Portuguese fort, flying the red flag of the Sultan of Zanzibar, is a conspicuous building overlooking the harbour, but there is little else to see. The modern town, where are the new Government buildings, the cathedral, and the houses of the officials, lies on low ground on the seaward side of the old town. Some of the buildings are quite imposing, and the houses of the Europeans, most of them surrounded by large gardens, are comfortable dwellings with wide verandahs, well suited to the climate. There is a system of narrow-gauge tram-lines running along the main roads, with branches running off to every house. Each official keeps his private trolley, in which he is pushed by coolies to and from his daily work. No Englishman in Mombasa walks if he can possibly avoid doing so; indeed, if it be not impertinent for an outsider to sit in judgment on them, one would suggest that they do not take sufficient exercise.

There are two very indifferent hotels and an excellent club, where the members are as hospitable as Englishmen always are in tropical places. Outside the town are gardens of manioc and sweet-potatoes, and large plantations of coco-nut palms, with patches here and there of uncut forest. Hideous baobabs, with their stunted branches bare of leaves, and magnificent mango-trees laden with ripening fruit, were the most noticeable trees early in December; but, its sweltering climate notwithstanding, Mombasa has not the appearance of rich tropical luxuriance that is so characteristic of

Singapore and such places on the other side of the Indian Ocean.

But the true title to fame that belongs to Mombasa rests on the fact of its being the starting-point of the Uganda Railway. Work on the line was begun in January, 1896, and after innumerable difficulties had been overcome, and the colossal sum of nearly seven millions sterling had been spent on its construction, the railway was completed and opened for traffic to the Victoria Nyanza in 1902. But in spite of the great expense of keeping it in order, repairing bridges and viaducts, and so on, the railway was already paying more than its working expenses within a short time of its completion. It may safely be said, without exaggeration, that the Uganda Railway has completely changed the face of a great part of Equatorial Africa. Beautiful countries, which a few years ago were thought to be beyond the reach of any but the most venturesome explorer, can now be visited by anyone who can afford to take a railway ticket ; and the journey to the Victoria Nyanza, which meant a toilsome journey of three months with a big caravan from the coast, or even longer by way of the Nile, can now be accomplished in less than forty-eight hours. Instead of spending many weeks at the coast in collecting provisions, and servants, and porters, and (very likely) an escort for the journey, the modern traveller in East Africa installs himself comfortably with his belongings in a first-class railway carriage, and in a few minutes the train thunders across the high bridge over the strait which separates the island of Mombasa from the mainland, and the journey across the continent of Africa is begun.

At first for many miles the line goes curling up steep bush-covered banks, and looking back one sees beautiful views of the bays and creeks about Mombasa, the last glimpse of the ocean for a long time to come. This country along the coast is fairly well populated, and seemingly prosperous; villages and plantations were seen scattered at intervals in the remnants of forest, and the natives seemed fat and well-looking. But as we went ever higher and higher, the forest was left behind, and we entered on a country of unspeakable dreariness, where dust and thorn-trees between them possessed the land. Glimpses here and there of the old caravan road running straight ahead, mile after mile through this waterless desolation, banished any regrets that one might have felt for the old order of things. It was hard to believe that this was the East Africa of which one had heard so much, but according to fellow-passengers this was only the desert of Sinai—Taru was the name they gave it—and the Promised Land lay beyond. Meanwhile, seeing that I was a stranger in the land, these same fellow-passengers beguiled the tedium of the journey with stories of the lions which infest this region. There was the well-worn tale of the lion who overate himself and was driven along the road with a herd of donkeys, and the more credible story of the unhappy lion-hunter who slept at his post in the railway-carriage, and was carried out of the window and eaten by the very lion he went out to slay. One story-teller, with a greater gift of imagination than the others, even went so far as to point out the scratches made by the lion in its departure. Night fell during the course of these narrations, and my sleep was disturbed several times by the imagined tugging and roaring of lions, only to find that it was the sudden jolt of the train as it stopped, or the shriek of the engine as we started laboriously uphill again.

The sun rose over a very different scene. Dust and rocks and scrub were left behind; instead we looked for miles over rolling plains of short grass, which recalled very vividly the prairies of Manitoba. Scattered over the plain were various moving objects that looked like cattle, but as the light grew stronger we saw their hideous faces, and knew that they were herds of hartebeeste. I had always imagined before that the accounts I had read of the marvellous quantities of game to be seen from the line were either a mendacious advertisement of the railway to attract unwary globe-trotters, or else the reminiscences of travellers who had passed along that way before the railway was ever thought of; but it would be almost impossible to exaggerate the amazing swarms of game that are to be seen on every side. There is a strip of land a mile wide

on either side of the line in which it is forbidden to
shoot anything but lions and leopards, and the
other creatures seem to be perfectly well aware of
the protection that they have there. As we
approached the famous Athi Plains the country
literally swarmed with game ; it was like travelling
through a very well stocked cattle-run or a vast
zoological garden. Huge herds of stupid-looking
hartebeeste stared stolidly as the train went lumbering by, hardly taking the trouble to get out of its
way ; little groups of wildebeeste performed ungainly gambols, and seemed ever trying without
success to stand upon their heads. Burchell's
zebras, looking a silvery blue rather than yellow,
were feeding placidly in large herds, and family
parties of Thomson's and Grant's gazelles scampered
about everywhere. Two or three immense elands
kept loftily aloof from the common herd, and here
and there we saw an ostrich, looking like some
forgotten relic of an antediluvian age. If one
is fortunate there is always a chance of seeing
a rhinoceros, or a family of lions, or a herd of
giraffes, in some part or other of this wonderful
journey.

But more to be remembered than all the herds
of game on the Athi Plains was a glorious view of
the highest mountain in Africa, the great cone of
Kilimanjaro, rising out of the morning mists
100 miles to the south, its snows glittering in
the brilliant sunlight. From near Nairobi I looked

eagerly for a glimpse of Mount Kenya, but there was nothing to be seen save great banks of cloud, where the mountain lay hid.

A few miles before we arrived at Nairobi, the train was kept waiting to take up a small caravan, which was seen hurriedly approaching from a mile or so away. The party consisted of three blood-stained Europeans and a dozen or more equally blood-stained native porters, carrying on their heads loads of antelope meat. The porters perched themselves somewhere on various outside parts of the train, and the Europeans and the loads of meat were crammed into the compartment where I happened to be. They brought with them a cloud of flies such as no mortal Pharaoh could have tolerated for long, and I think we were all of us glad enough when this stage of the journey came to an end. So far as I could gather, they were prospective settlers, who had been in the country for some time waiting for land to be allotted to them ; they had spent a good deal of their capital in doing nothing for many months in a very expensive place, and, in order to save what remained, they shot game, the meat of which they sold to residents in Nairobi, and the heads and horns to tourists.

From these people, and from many others of the same kind whom I met in a few days spent at Nairobi and Naivasha, I heard all sorts of expressions of opinion, from the gloomiest to the most enthusiastic, about British East Africa and its future prospects and possibilities as a colony for Europeans. Everybody was agreed, even the most sanguine of them, that it was no place for a poor man. A capital of several hundred pounds at the least was regarded as an absolute necessity, and this at once puts the country on a different footing from such colonies as Canada or Australia or New Zealand. People in England are accustomed to hear East Africa spoken of as a 'white man's country,' but it can never really be a white man's country when the smaller trades and the labour are efficiently carried on by Indians and natives, whilst only the officials and the employers of labour are Europeans. And in any case the extent of healthy upland country suitable for permanent settlement by Europeans, after allowance has been made for native reserves, game reserves, and forests, is exceedingly limited. Great things were expected from rearing stock in some parts of the country, and a large consignment of sheep from Australia had just arrived ; but the experiment has not yet lasted long enough to show whether or not it will be a success. Africa is cursed with such a host of parasites, and so little is known of horse sickness, and red-water, and cattle disease, and the other ills that affect domesticated beasts, that one hesitates to predict a very brilliant future for the stock-breeder in East Africa.

The agriculturists were talking hopefully of cereals

Bridge-Building in Uganda.

To face page 12.

and coffee, but with the boom in the Canadian North-West and the low Atlantic freights, it is questionable whether their grain would pay them; while so long as Brazil alone grows more coffee than the world consumes, their beans could hardly find a profitable market. Potatoes and European fruit and vegetables do well in some districts, but the cost of transport by the railway is great, and the way is long to the nearest market, South Africa, which is on the way to growing these things in sufficient quantities for herself. If prosperity is to come to British East Africa, the means of it will probably be the cultivation of cotton. There are large districts where the soil and climate are well suited to the plant, and even in the cooler uplands it has been grown with considerable success. Most of the native tribes are capable of learning agricultural methods, and it is not unreasonable to hope that in a few years' time the colony will have become one of the great cotton-producing countries of the British Empire.

At that time (December, 1905) the settlement of land seemed to be in a state of complete chaos. There was a large number of prospective colonists waiting about in the country, and suffering from various forms of distress. Some of them had had land allotted to them, which had subsequently been taken away again; some had been given land which did not exist; and some had received grants of land which had previously been given to another. There were many who had applied months previously for land, and who had waited so long that, when at last it was allotted to them, their capital was gone, and they had not enough to pay down the sum necessary before taking possession. A great deal of the confusion was doubtless due to the transfer of the colony from the Foreign Office to the Colonial Office, which had taken place a few months earlier, and much was due to the weakness of the Survey Department, which was miserably undermanned, and had not nearly completed its work.

Apropos of the survey, it might not be out of place to mention the case of a surveyor whom I met in the Naivasha district. He had served as a trooper in South Africa, and had stayed in the country as a surveyor after the war. A spirit of adventure made him spend his whole fortune on the purchase of a passage to Mombasa, where he landed without a penny in his pocket. But there the Indian Penal Code, which prevails in East Africa, arrested him for his pennilessness and sentenced him to three months' imprisonment, with subsequent deportation to Bombay, of all places in the world. When his term was almost at an end, he was rescued from bondage by an official of the Survey Department, who was crying out for assistance, and sent to work —very successfully, I believe—on the survey of the country. It was an interesting object-lesson to have a glimpse, though only a passing one, of a new country in the making. Probably, if we but knew it, all our colonies have 'muddled through' like this in the beginning; the wonderful thing is that they do get into working order at last. 'Fortune brings in some boats that are not steer'd.'

CHAPTER II

'In the afternoon they came unto a land
In which it seemed always afternoon.'

TENNYSON.

To the west of Nairobi the character of the country changes completely. The open, rolling plains end abruptly at the foot of the Kikuyu Hills, and the line begins at once to ascend rapidly by steep gradients and wide curves, which afford an endless series of changing views of the plain below. There are some fine stretches of forest, where gangs of natives were busy cutting fuel for the railway, and a good deal of native cultivation. For mile after mile the train struggles painfully on, always uphill, mounting about 2,000 feet in five-and-twenty miles, until suddenly the engine whistles—it sounds like a sigh of relief—and in a moment we are plunging down from the Kikuyu Escarpment into the Great Rift Valley. One could wish to wait awhile upon the brink and take in the scene at leisure, but as we go racing downwards, over bridges and round apparently impossible curves, we get impressions of steep, well-wooded slopes, a broad vale of brilliant grass to right and left so far as the eye can see, and on the

16

other side the dark forest-covered ranges of the Mau. It looks indeed like a Promised Land, and it may be hoped that some day it will flow with milk and honey.

Of all the beauties of the Rift Valley, there is none that can be compared with the lovely and mysterious Lake Naivasha.

'She smiled, but the water stood in her eye,'

might well have been written of Naivasha, whose name in the native language means 'The Tear.' Almost always there is a smile of sunshine on her wide waters and on the broad pastures of her eastern shore, while on the other there is as often a black frown of thunder-clouds rolling over the Mau and a white cap of rain on the peak of Longonot. It is hard to believe that this is Africa, and within but a few miles of the Equator. Naivasha has been likened to many different places; one writer was reminded of a gloomy Irish lough—perhaps his first visit was in the wet season, or perhaps the resemblance was suggested by the snipe in the swamps; another was reminded of the Bay of Naples, and the view from Posilipo; but to my mind there is something of New Zealand in the air and in the scene as well. The great slumbering volcano, Longonot, its lava-covered slopes scored by the rains into a thousand gullies, might well be Tarawera, and though no geysers nor pink and white terraces have yet been found, there are jets of steam spouting through the scrub and

2

springs of boiling water. There is a mystery about this lake with its fresh water and no apparent outlet, hardly rising or falling in the heaviest rains or in the longest drought; and many stories are told of underground rivers and of water heard falling into vast caverns. There is a mystery, too, about the beginning of the lake; it is said that the grandfather of the oldest inhabitant remembers a time when there was no lake here, but these are problems rather for the geologist or the collector of folk-lore.

To the wandering naturalist, whether his bent be towards birds, beasts, butterflies, or plants, Naivasha is one of the happy hunting-grounds that he has dreamt of, but has never hoped to see. The margin of the lake is fringed with sedges, tall reeds, and papyrus. Beyond the papyrus is a marvel of water-lilies, pink and white and blue, but mostly blue. Where the shallows extend far into the lake, there may be near a mile of water-lilies. In the morning, when the breeze ruffles the water and breaks up the reflections, the green of the translucent upturned leaves, the blue of the flowers, the orange of the submerged stems, and the almost amethyst light of the water, together make a very opal of colour. One of the prettiest bird-sights I have ever had the good luck to see was here. In a little bay of lilies, standing on the shining leaves and preening their plumage, was a party of long-legged, black-winged stilts, winter emigrants from the North; round them was a wall of graceful bending papyrus, and overhead

House-Building in Ruwenzori.

To face page 18.

floated a snowy Caspian tern. Among the lilies and in the open water beyond were a myriad coots and grebes, ducks and cormorants, and further still were great fleets of pelicans. Overhead were circling and constantly crying a pair of sea-eagles, sometimes so high up that it was difficult to make out the two shouting specks against the sky, and sometimes so low that one could clearly see the brilliant black and white and chestnut of their plumage. It is said that there are no fish in Naivasha, but so vast a swarm of fish-eating birds would hardly come here if that were true. On a shallow sunken mud-bank is a long line of white, which shows a tinge of black and crimson as the great flock of flamingoes rises and flaps lazily away. Happily there are no crocodiles here, but hippos abound, and one may often catch a glimpse of nose and eyes as they lie in the shallows basking in the sun, or at night, when they feed, hear them crashing through the reeds.

It is only here and there that one can follow the water's edge; mostly the reeds are too thick and the ground too swampy for any but a water-buck to pass. Along the outside, where the grass meets the reeds, are big flocks of Egyptian geese, which spend the day in sleep, but make noise enough in the evening and early morning. Here, too, are black ibises, wary as curlews, and sacred ibises in small parties of two and three, always busily searching for food, exploring every inch of ground. Prettier and more confiding are the great white heron and the smaller buff-backed heron, which hardly take the trouble to move as one approaches ; they love to feed among the herds of native cattle, often perching upon the backs of the beasts, as one sees them do in Egypt. Crowned cranes, generally in pairs, stride conceitedly about within a dozen yards of one, evidently conscious of the law that protects them.

Of big game, though there is plenty in the district, one does not see very much on the eastern side of the lake. Here on the wide grassy flats and on the lower slopes of the hills immense flocks of goats and sheep find pasture. At the time of my visit there were driven into the 'boma' near the camp nearly 20,000 bleating animals every evening, to the accompaniment of much shrill whistling from the Masai boys who tend them. Ugly little savages are these Masai boys, clothed in little else than a long spear and round their necks a string of beads or empty cartridge-cases. It is a pretty sight to see a herd of the graceful little Thomson's gazelle (or Tommies, as they are locally called) mingling with a flock of sheep and goats, and following with the others when the boys whistle, or even needing a prod with the spear-point to make them move on faster. Whether they do it for amusement or for the sake of companionship, or for a better protection against their enemies, the prowling leopard and lion, who shall say ? Grant's gazelle, a somewhat larger animal with beautifully curved horns, is found here too ; but they are not so tame as the former, and go bounding away—bouncing is almost the word—as though they were made of springs. A few lumbering hartebeeste, hideous red brutes with all the ugly features of the cow and of the donkey combined, are seen here and there; they trot off until they are just out of range, then turn round and treat one to an inane stare.

One morning I came suddenly over a low hill right into the midst of a herd of zebras. Off they went, fifty or more of them, as fast as they could gallop, straight towards a newly strung wire-fence; either they did not see it or they were too much frightened to turn aside, but not one of them swerved; they all dashed through the fence, as though the wires were cobwebs, and so far as I could see not one was damaged in the least. Zebras may be seen from the railway literally in thousands on the Athi Plains, and again in the rolling grass country between Naivasha and Nakuru. At the Government farm a few miles from Naivasha experiments have been made in crossing zebras, but hitherto no very satisfactory hybrid has been produced. The pure-bred animal is difficult to tame and of very little use as a beast of burden; but a strong hybrid, capable of resisting the many diseases of the country, would solve the horse problem of East Africa, and would go far towards ensuring the prosperity of the colony.

Towards the south-east corner of the lake is an island, where I camped for a short time. The voyage of a mile or more from the mainland was made in the relics of a boat, which, from its appearance, must have been brought there by the first explorers twenty years ago ; it was never less than half full of water, which kept two boys busy baling with empty oil-cans, and the one and a half broken paddles threatened every moment to be reduced to none at all. Half-way across are two small islets, one a favourite breeding-place of herons and ibises, which nest there in hundreds, the other apparently a play-ground of the hippos, to judge from the trampled reeds and the crashing and gruntings which issued from it at night. As we beached the boat on a narrow spit of sand, we disturbed a pair of green-shanks, which whistled as they went away, and reminded me of many happy days spent searching for their nests in Sutherland. The island is an almost perfect crescent in outline, nearly a mile in length and a quarter of a mile across at its widest part, tapering away to a fine point at either end. From high ground in the middle there is a steep fall to the lake on one side, the inner curve of the crescent ; on the other side is a gentle slope covered with grass and shrubs to a fringe of swamp and reeds bordering the lake. On this sunny slope were hundreds of willow-wrens, singing (in December) as perfect a song as in an English woodland in June. The tangle by the lake-shore is the haunt by day of many water-buck, which swim over from the main-land and find there a sanctuary from their enemies, the lions and hyenas.

To anyone who finds amusement in building imaginary houses the island affords unending pleasure. There are at least a score of places where one would like to build a house and make a garden; the trouble would be in choosing the best among so many. When, in the time to come, Naivasha is the centre of a settled and prosperous land, and this is the Isola Bella of the lake, it is to be hoped that the happy man who comes to live here will build a house in keeping with the country, and not disfigure the lake with a German castle or a Moorish palace.

Beautiful as the days are, the nights are even better still. As the shadows lengthen and the sun goes down behind the Mau, a troop of baboons in the rocks begins to chatter before going to bed, and there is a stir amongst the geese beside the lake. Jackals, waking from their long siesta, trot over the plain and creep cautiously towards the camps of the natives. Something brown appears at the edge of the reeds; it is a water-buck. At first his head and horns alone are visible; then, after a wary look about him, he steps out from his shelter, and, stopping here and there to crop a tuft of grass, strolls off to a favourite salt-lick a mile away. Like the red-deer of Exmoor, the water-buck play havoc in an unfenced garden and cultivated land; they love to pull a root out of the ground, and then, after a single bite (and not always that), move on to another. The twilight goes quickly, and in half an hour it is black night. There is a croaking chorus of frogs down by the lake, and the 'konk' of herons overhead flying to their fishing. As we move towards the camp, our steps are perhaps a little quickened when we hear the unearthly howl of hyenas and the discontented grunt of a lion. It was a happy chance, for which I shall never cease to be grateful, that kept me for a few days at Naivasha. It is said of the blest of one nation that, when they die, they go to Paris; to others life is complete when they have seen Naples; for my part, had I never seen those two cities, I should have been content when I had seen Naivasha.

After leaving the lake the railway follows the Rift Valley almost due northwards for a long distance through a rich-looking grass country full of game, until, after many twists and turns, Nakuru with its beautiful lake is reached. This district contains some of the most valuable land in East Africa; a great part has been taken up by holders, great and small, and already one can see numbers of hideous corrugated iron buildings from the railway. Night fell as we climbed higher still on to the summit of the Mau range; but the increasing cold was a sufficient indication of the altitude that we had reached, very nearly 8,000 feet above the sea, and I was glad enough to cover myself with all the blankets that I had brought.

A few hours later I awoke from an evil dream, in which I thought I was being boiled at the bottom

of the crater of Longonot, threw off the blankets
(contributory causes of the dream), opened the
windows of the carriage, and thought I was dreaming again.   The yellow plains of grass, the rolling
hills, the herds of game, the pale blue sky, and the
'nip,' as of Europe, in the air—all were gone.
Instead were a level country brilliantly green, big
trees, scattered as in an English park, and a different
sun blazing out of a different sky.   Above all, the
smell of this proclaimed it another land ; there was
no longer the clean dry smell of the uplands, but
the heavy, sweet, intoxicating smell of luxuriant
vegetation.   This was the country of the Kavirondo,
and the most populous that we had passed through
since we left the coast.   Native villages, compact
little collections of round grass huts, enclosed within
a circular hedge of tall aloes, were seen on every
hand, and the inhabitants were busily occupied in
the fields or in tending their flocks of sheep and
goats.

The most remarkable peculiarity of these people
is their total lack of clothing ; the men are gaily
attired in ear-rings, and the women in strings of
beads and elegant coils of telegraph-wire about
their limbs.   Fortunately for the Uganda Railway,
the latter custom seems to be going out of fashion.
Some of the women affect a short tail made of some
sort of fibre, but the majority of them, both men
and women, are so magnificently proportioned, and
their skins are so clear and glossy, that one is quite

ready to forgive them for their disregard of the ordinary proprieties.

The approach by railway to the Victoria Nyanza is, it must be confessed, most disappointing. Instead of suddenly seeing, as you had rather hoped to do, a wide view of the greatest lake in Africa, stretching far into a boundless horizon, you become aware, without any emotion at all, of a narrow arm of dirty brown water, bounded by rough grass and papyrus. This was the beginning of the Kavirondo Gulf, a huge north-eastern arm of the Nyanza, and in a few minutes the first stage of the journey came to an end, when the train ran on to the pier at Kisumu or Port Florence, and a dusky official cried out—rather unnecessarily, seeing that I was the only passenger—' All changes!'

Africa is a land of surprises at every turn, so one is not in the least astonished to find lying alongside of the quay a perfect little ocean steamship. The white paint and the glistening brass-work, the electric light, and the Indian cook, made me think that this was a P. and O. liner eastward bound, rather than a little steamer on a remote lake, which fifty years ago no white man had ever seen. After the grime of the Deutsch Ost Afrika and the discomfort of the Uganda Railway, this was luxury indeed. While the steamer was being crammed full of cargo, I strolled along the shore and watched a party of Kavirondo fishermen at work. They use a long seine-net made of grass and papyrus stalks, which

Lobelia Giberroa, Ruwenzori (7,000 feet).

To face page 26.

they manage in the same way as we do. When the net comes into shallow water, the women wade out with large baskets of a fine mesh, with which they scoop up quantities of small fry. These little fish, prepared by the cook on board, were excellent, and not unlike whitebait.

The voyage down the Gulf was made in a succession of heavy thunder-storms, which came sweeping down from the hills on the south and east, the last foot-hills of the Mau range. It was astonishing how quickly the sea rose even in this land-locked gulf, but when we came near to open water there was such a heavy sea running that it was thought advisable, although the moon was full, to anchor for the night in the shelter of one of the many islands. It was curious to hear the hoot of an owl and the grunt of an otter, and all the while to feel the roll of a ship apparently at sea.

The voyage across the lake to Entebbe is not in any way interesting. For a short time the ship is out of sight of land, but generally the north shore is in sight, or some of the innumerable islands that lie along the coast. A few seagulls and cormorants, the only birds that I saw, made it hard to believe that this was not the sea. The only remarkable thing I saw was some heavy dark clouds, which rose rapidly on the horizon, and seemed to portend a sudden storm. However, there was no cause for alarm, as they were nothing more serious than immense swarms of flies, which have a habit of coming into the world all at the same moment. Their lives can be only very brief, a few hours at the most, after which they may be seen lying in myriads on the water, an easy prey for many hungry fish. We were afterwards very much troubled by these same clouds of flies on Lake Albert Edward. Uganda welcomed me with a smile of sunshine, and I landed at Entebbe on a glorious afternoon, when the roads and trees were steaming after the daily thunder-storm.

CHAPTER III

'I rather would entreat thy company
To see the wonders of the world abroad,
Than, living dully sluggardized at home,
Wear out thy youth with shapeless idleness.'
SHAKESPEARE.

IT is perhaps hardly necessary to state that Entebbe
is the administrative capital of Uganda; but, as it is
still omitted from many even of the most recently
published maps, it may be as well to remark that it
lies at the extreme north-west corner of the Victoria
Nyanza, and is consequently only a few miles north
of the Equator. The British officers who chose the
site for the future capital must have had an unusual
share of foresight and imagination, for they could
hardly have found a more beautiful spot. The town
—whose name in the native language means 'The
Chair'—lies near the end of a long and hilly pro
montory between two narrow inlets of the lake.
The landing-place is on the east side of the town,
and the way leads up by a steep high road, shaded
by immense forest trees, to a sort of level platform,
the seat of the chair presumably, behind which rise
two pointed hills. The greater part of the town

29

lies on this more or less level platform, excepting
some of the military lines, which extend on to the
hills above, and the Indian quarter, which is being
moved away from the town.

Considering that less than twenty years ago the
site of Entebbe was covered by dense forest, the
present condition of the place can be described as
little less than marvellous. Instead of growing up
haphazard, as so many new towns have done, because
a railway has passed that way or some one has happened to find gold, the plan of Entebbe has been
carefully thought out, and the result is as pleasing
a place as one could find anywhere. Broad roads,
with here and there wide open spaces, run between
the houses of the officials, which lie in large gardens.
Many of the giant forest trees have been left standing
in the gardens, and avenues of flowering trees have
been planted along the roadsides. The houses are
mostly fair-sized brick buildings with wide verandahs
and corrugated iron roofs ; the official red colour
that they are painted is inconspicuous, but one
would think that white would have been cooler.
The original Commissioner's residence stood at the
top of the steep rise from the lake, but it has been
sold to an enterprising syndicate to be converted
into an hotel, and the present Commissioner is building a new residence above the town. A gorgeous
club-house was being built, and the Europeans play
lawn-tennis, and on alternate days cricket and foot-
ball, so that, with excellent shooting to be had not

very far away, it cannot be complained that the Uganda officials have a very bad time.

One of the most interesting things to be seen in Entebbe at that time was the laboratory of the Royal Commission on Sleeping Sickness, under the charge of Lieutenants Gray and Tulloch,* R.A.M.C., where the disease was being studied with a view to discovering its nature, and, if possible, some means of treatment. Close at hand was the native hospital, filled with miserable wretches in various stages of the disease. It is sad to have to record that, though a great deal has been done towards checking the spread of sleeping sickness, no means of successfully treating it after infection has taken place has yet been discovered ; it is invariably fatal. The destruction that has been caused by this terrible scourge is almost incalculable ; enormous areas of the lake-shore and whole archipelagos, where there was a swarming population only a few years ago, have been rendered absolutely desolate by sleeping sickness. I visited a few islands and a strip of shore not far from Entebbe, and walked through large grass-grown villages, where scattered bones were the only signs of humanity to be seen. It has been computed that more than 200,000 people have died of the disease in Uganda alone during the last seven years, and this is probably well

* Lieutenant Tulloch contracted the disease himself during the course of his experiments, and died shortly after he returned to England, in the summer of 1906

within the mark. Apart from the appalling waste
of human life, it involves a very serious loss to
the State, which cannot afford to lose a large and
thriving population living along its main waterway.
One of the effects was to be seen in the increasing
difficulty of inducing porters and labourers to remain
at Entebbe, where they are afraid of catching the
disease. There is also the not inconceivable possibility of its being turned into an anti-European
weapon ; an unscrupulous agitator could easily per-
suade a half-educated people that the white men
were responsible for the disease, and that the obvious
remedy was to turn them out of the country. Happily,
only four Europeans have been attacked by sleeping
sickness in Uganda, though the number in the Congo
Free State is probably a good deal greater.

The forest on the slopes between the town and
the lake has been ingeniously converted into a
Botanic Garden. Many of the trees have been
cut down, and the thick undergrowth has been
cleared away, with the result that one can see the
splendid proportions of the trees that are left. As
a rule the trees in an African forest are crowded
so closely together, and their trunks are so much
obscured by a tangle of creepers, that one does not
realize what giants they are. In the cleared spaces
experiments are being made with cotton and various
kinds of rubber-producing plants ; some of these latter
promise to do very well. The Botanic Garden is
a very pleasant place for a stroll in the evening after

the rain, when the crowned cranes fly up into the tree-tops and shriek their evening chorus, and cloud after cloud of white egrets fly down to settle on the yellow-flowered ambatch-trees along the margin of the lake. Black-and-white kingfishers drop with a sounding splash into the water, seldom with success, and, if you stand very still, you may chance to see an otter hunting in the shallows. Noisy plantain-eaters and giant hornbills fly high up from tree to tree, and the monkeys wake up from their afternoon snooze. The vervet monkey is common, but far prettier is the little white-nosed monkey, a charming little creature with black and chestnut fur and a white nose. Occasionally one sees a colobus, a magnificent black monkey with white whiskers and white ruffs down its sides, and a long white, feathery tail. Shooting is forbidden in the immediate neighbourhood of Entebbe, and the birds and monkeys have become extraordinarily tame. It was here that I first heard and saw flying wild the common grey parrot with a red tail, that often calls so familiarly to the passers-by from a London basement; they are found wherever there is forest, right across from Uganda to the Atlantic, and now I can never hear one without being carried back in memory to a shady garden beside the Victoria Nyanza or to still evenings in the Congo Forest.

Another pleasant spot near Entebbe is the high ground above the town, whence one may see a view of lake and islands and forests that it would be hard to equal anywhere. Forty miles away on the southern horizon lie the Sese Islands, so brilliantly described by Sir Harry Johnston, and toward the east headland after headland and more islands, like the isles of Greece, as far as the eye can reach. Inland are dark green forests, flat plains of papyrus, and range upon range of grass-topped hills.

Entebbe is almost purely and simply a Government station. Of the Europeans who live there, there are not more than half a dozen who have no connexion with the administration. There are four European trading firms, only one of these being English, while the rest of the trade is carried on by Indian merchants. So far as I could find out, there was in the year 1905 only one genuine colonist in the whole of Uganda. There had been three or four others at different times, who had either died or had become bankrupt, until only one remained; but perhaps rumour exaggerated the tale.

Twenty miles north of Entebbe is Kampala, or Mengo, as it is variously called; strictly speaking, Kampala is the name of the Government part of the town, and Mengo the name of the missionary quarter and the part about the royal palace. There will no doubt be a light railway from Entebbe before long, but at present you go along a broad high road on a bicycle (if you have one), or by rickshaw, or by mule-cart—horses are few and far between in Uganda. It was my fate to go by rickshaw, drawn by two relays of four sturdy

The Eastern Slopes of Ruwenzori (9,000 feet).

To face page 34.

Waganda with infinite noise and fuss. Two Chinese or Japanese coolies would have covered the same distance in half the time, and in a dignified silence, but the native of Africa, particularly the semi-civilized variety inhabiting Uganda, on the rare occasions when he does do any work, wastes half his energy in proclaiming the fact to the world, and generally has the impertinence to demand baksheesh in addition to a liberal payment. This road is the beginning of the great highway from the Victoria Nyanza to Lake Albert and the Upper Nile. It is already possible to drive as far as Hoima, the capital of Unyoro, and in a short time tourists will be able to travel by rickshaw and steamer from Entebbe to Khartoum.

Kampala is built, like Rome, on seven hills, and a tour of inspection is not a thing to be undertaken lightly. The most striking feature of Kampala, and one which can be seen from many miles away, is the Protestant cathedral, with its two towers standing well upon the highest hill. The building, which is of native bricks and of timber cut in the forests hard by, and thatched with native grass, was constructed entirely by native workmen, and may fairly claim to be the greatest wonder of Uganda, if not of all Equatorial Africa. The name of Mr. Borup, the architect, who had, I believe, never built a church before, should surely go down to posterity as of one who has achieved a great and lasting work. Another, and perhaps the most interesting, sight of Kampala is the works of the Uganda Industrial Mission, where native carpenters may be seen doing very creditable joinery; a printing press worked by native boys turns out countless copies of *Uganda Notes*, and hand-driven ginning machines try to cope with the masses of cotton which come pouring into the place every day. As in East Africa, cotton is likely to be the most profitable product of Uganda; rubber and fibres are produced in some districts, but cotton promises to be the backbone of the future prosperity of the country.

When I arrived at Entebbe, I found that the other members of the Ruwenzori Expedition had started nearly a month before me, so I was naturally anxious to overtake them as soon as possible, but it was a full fortnight before I was able to get away. A good deal of the time was spent in waiting for the next steamer to bring the remnants of my baggage, which had gone astray between the coast and the lake; the rest of the time was occupied in making preparations for the journey. To anyone whose time hangs heavy on his hands, and who has never tried it, I can confidently recommend the organizing of a caravan, on however small a scale, as an absorbing, if somewhat irritating, occupation. You must think of every imaginable contingency which may arise, from the breaking of a leg to the burning of a saucepan, and be prepared to meet it. How much flour, how much sugar, how much rice does a man consume in a day? How long will a tin of jam last, or a pound of tea? These are questions that sound simple enough, but how many people can answer them? Then there is the momentous question of cooking-pots and pans. My cook enumerated a long list of things that he said were necessary. I divided the score by two, and the result was happily approximately correct. When all these things have been collected together, comes the most difficult task of dividing them into 60-pound loads, and so arranging them that one has to open as few loads as possible at each camping-place—not to open one box for the flour, another for the salt, another for the tea, and so on. Tent ropes and pegs must be looked at to see that they have not been devoured by white ants, and buckets and water-bottles to make sure that they do not leak.

. Meantime there was a cook and a boy and porters to be engaged. Applicants for the first two places presented themselves in dozens within an hour or two of my arrival, but as I had no knowledge of the Swahili or Luganda tongues, I found it difficult to make a choice from among so many. So I decided that the first duty of a boy was to call one early in the morning. In the first six days six successive boys failed to call me within an hour of the appointed time, but on the seventh morning one Maliko, the probationer of the day, called me at four o'clock instead of at five, and won the coveted post. Early rising was, I think, his one virtue—indeed, it became with him almost a vice, and I often called down maledictions upon his head in the small hours of the morning, but I owe him much for long miles covered in the cool of many days. With the aspiring cooks I had more difficulty. I could not sit down and eat a dinner made by every several cook; it would have been expensive, and might even have delayed my departure. But there was a way out of it. I have a weakness for well-baked bread with good crusts, so I gave to each prospective cook a portion of flour and some yeast, with instructions to bring back a loaf of bread on the following day. Some never came back; no doubt they ate their loaves. Others brought back their loaves, because neither they nor anyone else could eat them. But one, a harassed-looking youth, who rejoiced in the name of Bidimungubu, brought back a loaf of such excellence that, I am ashamed to say, I devoured a great part of it then and there. Biddy was appointed cook, but I regret to say he was a fraud. Two days after leaving Entebbe, when I had finished the supply he (said he) had made before starting, he perpetrated the most miserable attempt at bread-making that I have ever had the ill-luck to meet; it was something between Australian damper and the fladbrod of the Lapps, without the good qualities of either.

Engaging porters is a trying and interminable business. If you want, say, fifty porters, there is no difficulty in getting forty-five, but the last five are as shy and as hard to gain as the last few runs of a cricketer's century. Afterwards I found it a good plan to give out that I wanted twice as many porters as I really had need for; then, if there was a surplus, it was possible to weed out some of the feebler brethren. Then they must all be taken in a body to the Collector and be registered, but it is quite likely that before they get so far as that they will refuse to go unless they are paid a rupee more than they had agreed to accept. In the Congo Free State there is a regular tariff for certain distances, or for so many days' journey; but in Uganda you must make the best bargain you can, and the porters are well aware of the fact.

But there came a day when the tale of porters was complete, and all the stores, down to the veriest tin-opener, were packed up, and on Christmas Eve I went 'on safari' at last.

CHAPTER IV

TRAVELLING IN UGANDA

'For weary is work, and weary day by day
To have your comfort miles on miles away.'
CLOUGH.

IT was in the pocket of an old coat that I found
them—a hundred grimy cowries from the Indian
Ocean strung on a piece of banana fibre and polished
and worn smooth by innumerable fingers. *Cyprœa
annulus* is their scientific name ; ' simbi ' is what they
are called in Uganda. The sound and the smell
and the 'feel' of them, as I took them up, carried
me far away from the chill and gloom of the English
' summer ' to a ' cleaner, greener land,' and reminded
me of a thousand scenes and incidents under a
blazing African sky. These shells are the popular
currency in Uganda, and except in a few places,
where the people are wealthy enough to have rupees,
are universally used. Their value is not great—a
thousand, or in some places eleven hundred, go to
one rupee—and their bulk is considerable ; so it often
happens that on a long journey one has to take
several porters laden only with money. I do not
know if one shell, the thousandth part of a rupee,

commonly buys anything, though I have paid boys at the rate of one shell apiece for beetles. From three to ten shells will buy an egg, and one string of a hundred shells, having a value of about a penny farthing, is the usual price for a chicken. These prices sound cheap enough, but the Uganda egg is bad ninety-nine times out of a hundred, and the chicken is generally no bigger than a blackbird. It has been suggested that the African fowl lays bad eggs, but I believe that there is no scientific authority for this statement. In the towns and big stations one has little or no use for these shells; it is when one goes on a journey—'on safari,' to use the local expression—that they begin to become important for the daily business of buying food.

In spite of its many attendant drawbacks, there are perhaps worse ways of travelling than with porters in Uganda, always provided that you are not in a hurry, and are content to take two weeks over a journey that an express train would cover in as many hours. The most important part of this manner of travelling is the start, which can hardly be made too early. If there is a moon and the road is good, it is a pleasant thing to start off at one or two o'clock in the morning, and finish the day's march about the time when people at home are beginning to think of breakfast. It is cool up to eight o'clock, and the porters march along without stopping to rest under every tree, as they like to do when the sun is high. Even when there is no moon one starts at the first glimmer of dawn, and the march is finished and tents are pitched before midday.

The pleasantest hour of all the day is the hour just before and just after sunrise, when thin wisps of mist float upwards from the marshes, when every leaf and every blade of grass glitters with a hundred drops of dew, and the air is filled with the songs of birds. There are many people who believe that it is only in Europe, and especially in England, that birds can sing, but I have heard in Uganda and in the neighbouring parts of the Congo State such a morning chorus of birds as can only be equalled at a May sunrise at home. Ibises fly screaming from the papyrus swamps, turtle doves purr in the tops of the acacias, thrushes sing in the banana groves, and a host of others in the long grass and thick undergrowth. By eight o'clock the dew has disappeared, the birds are silent, and the sun is high enough to make itself unpleasant. Then begins the most tiring part of the day; the clear sky of the early morning becomes a coppery furnace; there is never a patch of shadow to relieve the dull brown and green of the grass and papyrus and thorn-trees, and the stony road under foot becomes almost intolerably hot. The porters, who up till now have been ahead out of sight and smell (I shall never learn to tolerate the peculiar bouquet of the African), and, if possible, forgotten, are discovered lurking by the roadside and trying to take shelter from the sun

Lobelias, Senecios, and Helichrysums, Ruwenzori (10,000 feet).

Vegetation at 11,000 feet, Ruwenzori.

To face page 42.

under meagre bushes or tufts of grass ; some say that they are sick, and others that their loads are too heavy ; generally the truth is not in them, but in all cases they must be urged onwards. If the 'niampara,' or headman, is a person of authority with the porters, one can go ahead at a more reasonable pace than the usual two and a half miles an hour and wait for them at the camping-place, but as often as not he is as lazy as the laziest porter, and if left alone they will come strolling in at four or five o'clock in the afternoon. Some of these niamparas, who of course carry no loads, have an evil habit of playing upon a whistle (of the 'penny' variety) as they walk along. On my first journey I put up with it for a day or two, and then bought the instrument at an exorbitant price ; but the next day the niampara was playing upon a larger and even shriller whistle, and I had to submit to music for the rest of the way.

'A very little little let us do' might be taken as the guiding principle in life of the Uganda porter. So long as he can carry the lightest load at the slowest possible pace for the shortest possible distance, he is content. The only thing that he does willingly and without encouragement is to eat, and this he does whole-heartedly, and, as a rule, with a magnificent array of teeth. There are stories told of porters' capacity for food, some of which are perhaps not true, but I have myself seen fifteen porters who had just finished consuming three antelopes and one hippopotamus, the latter skin and

all, in the space of two days.   On another occasion
I was travelling for a short distance with seven
porters; one evening, about nine o'clock, there
arrived food for thirty porters, but by five o'clock
the next morning there was not a scrap remaining,
and my precious seven did a long and very hot day's
march without being any the worse for it.

Throughout the greater part of the country the
scenery is not very striking.   One mile is very much
like another, great papyrus swamps alternating with
low hills covered with scrubby trees and tall elephant-
grass.   Along the principal roads of Uganda the
papyrus swamps have been bridged, or, rather, cause-
ways have been driven across them, so that one has
no longer to plunge up to the neck in the morass,
and spend, perhaps, a whole day in going half a
mile, with the loss of many loads.   Under the cause-
way are culverts, through which the clear black
water runs into a deep pool below, where white and
blue water-lilies grow in the shadow of the tall
papyrus.   In very dry seasons the natives set fire
to the swamps, and a more dreary sight than a mile
of burnt and charred papyrus stalks, with a glimpse
of black mud and water at the roots, and here and
there a blackened palm-tree, can hardly be imagined.

Over the hills that separate one swamp from
another the road goes, like a Roman road, straight
ahead, no matter how steep it may be.   In Uganda
the roads are usually wide, as wide as a country lane
in England, but owing to the native habit of always

walking in single file there is only one very narrow track, often more like a gutter than a track, where one can walk, and this meanders like a cow from side to side of the road, and is always ready to trip up the booted traveller, who walks on rather a wider base. On either side of the road is a dense growth of tall elephant-grass, or ' mateitei,' which grows from 10 to 15 feet in height, and effectually blocks out any view of the surrounding country. Much as he loves and admires all things that grow out of the earth, I do not think that even Sir Harry Johnston could find a good word to say for elephant-grass. It is the ugliest and the rankest and the hottest form of vegetation I have ever met, and in countries where there are not, as in Uganda, broad roads, but one has to walk along the native path, a tunnel a few inches wide, the horrid stuff is constantly hitting you in the face, knocking your hat off, and pulling your pipe out of your mouth, until you wonder why you were ever fool enough to leave home. But, like many other disagreeable things, it has one compensating feature : it shows that the soil is good, and where there is elephant-grass there is probably abundant food for yourself and your porters.

In the districts where elephant-grass is happily absent, the road will be bordered with short grass— that is to say, not more than waist-high—with a beautiful mixture of flowering plants, sunflowers, coreopsis, orchids, a little prickly aloe with a scarlet flower, and a hundred others. These flower-gardens go far to relieve the monotony of the road, and to make one forget for a while the roasting sun that is blazing fiercely down upon one's head. Sir Harry Johnston describes how he used to find afternoon tea prepared for him at the top of weary hills by thoughtful chiefs ; many a time would I have cheerfully undertaken the cares of office of Special Commissioner and Commander-in-Chief for the sake of a cup of tea on those interminable hills.

Incidents and excitements are few and far between. Sometimes there is a rumour of big game, and sometimes of a leopard or a lion, but as a rule the news is a month old at the least. There are native caravans to be seen on the road almost daily, generally porters laden with hides or bales of cotton on their way to Kampala, and very rarely one meets a European. On my first journey from Entebbe to Toro, a distance of twelve days, I met one European, a most genial missionary, who gave me a delicious pineapple and a quantity of useful phrases in the local dialect, of which I was woefully ignorant. I cannot suppose that a clergyman of the Church of England would teach me any expression that was not strictly Parliamentary, but the effect of these when uttered to my porters on the following day was positively magical. Coming back along the same road a few months later, we met at different times three Englishmen, two Germans, and one Frenchman ; the road was crowded with Europeans.

One day I was walking along the hateful road, wondering why such a miserable country had ever been made, when of a sudden I heard a distant jödel. I thought I must be dreaming, or had sunstroke, or a sudden attack of fever; but it was a real jödel, as good as ever I heard in the Alps. On it came, up the hills and down into the hollows, and soon I met an ordinary Uganda porter striding along with a load upon his head and jödelling to himself as happily as could be. I should have liked to shake him by the hand, and ask him where he learnt to do it, but I did not want to interrupt the tune, so I passed him with a silent blessing. Perhaps he was with the Duke of the Abruzzi, and learnt it from his guides, or perhaps he got it from Mr. Douglas Freshfield's guide the year before. As the sound went dwindling away into the distance, I had only to shut my eyes and find myself in green meadows redolent of cattle and wildflowers, or on a snow-peak with all the Alps about me, instead of plodding along a hot and lumpy road, through as dreary a country as ever was made.

Dull and monotonous though most of the days are, there is always a happy moment in every day, and that is when you come in sight of the camping-ground, and, if the porters have marched well, the tent is pitched and a fire burning. Along most of the roads in Uganda there have been made at intervals of ten or fifteen miles regular camping-places, usually within reach of a village with sufficient cultivation to provide food for porters. The camping-place consists of a cleared compound surrounded by a reed fence, in which are a large rest-house, made of mud and thatched with grass, for the European traveller and his baggage, a small cook-house, and numerous mud or grass houses for the porters, sometimes within and sometimes outside the fence. If the rest-house is clean—some are very much the reverse—it is probably a good deal cooler there during the day than in the tent, which need only be used for sleeping. Supposing that a fairly early start has been made, and there is no necessity to travel very quickly, one tries to arrive in camp by twelve o'clock at the latest, so as to avoid marching through the hottest hours of the day. These hours are spent by the porters, and sometimes by the European too, in sleep. Every self-respecting Uganda porter carries a sleeping-mat, which he rolls up, with his property inside it, and ties on to his load. Arrived in camp, he unfurls his mat, stretches himself upon it in a shady place, and is soon asleep.

This is the quietest hour of the day or night, and one can read or dream in peace for a time, and forget the petty worries of African travel—they are none the less annoying because they are so small. But it is over all too soon; the camp wakes up about four o'clock, and the noise and wrangling begin once more. Many of the porters perform quite an elaborate toilet after the midday siesta.

Tree-Heaths and Giant Groundsels (*Senecio*), Ruwenzori (12,500 feet).

Lobelia Deckenii, Ruwenzori (12,000 feet).

You see gentlemen, who have been content with the scantiest rag about the loins in the morning, come out in the afternoon clothed in white samite— a sort of low-necked night-shirt affair—and go off to flirt with the ladies in the village. Their ablutions are not a very serious business, except as regards their feet, which they wash with extreme care, as who would not that walked barefoot in a country where 'jiggers' abound? It is not an uncommon thing, and always a pleasing sight, because they are quiet when they are doing it, to see one half of the caravan extracting jiggers from the feet of the other half. Then there are the sick to be attended to. A black man is always sick if he thinks there is a chance of getting medicine. It is astonishing how they like even the nastiest medicine, and what prodigious doses they will consume. Every white man, be he lawyer or parson or soldier, is to them a doctor, and I doubt if he does much more harm in his practice than members of the most learned profession themselves.

In the midst of these occupations one probably receives a visit from the chief of the neighbouring village. If he is a person of no great consideration, he receives payment for the 'present' of food that he has brought with him and takes his departure. But it is more likely that he is an important person, or considers himself so—and few of them are lacking in self-importance—in which case he comes

4

attended by his brothers and cousins and children
and a troop of menials, and for the time being he
takes possession of the camp.   He plants himself
in a chair—luckily they always bring their own—
at the entrance to your tent, while the attendants
squat at his feet and proceed to take stock of your
possessions.   You offer him tea and cigarettes ; he
consumes half of your precious store of sugar, and
tries to take the whole box of cigarettes.   Then he
asks every conceivable impertinent question that
he can think of, and after telling you what a big
man he is, and how many hundreds of pounds he
receives from the Government, he condescends to
accept a rupee or two in exchange for his presents
and retires.   There are authors who have written
nothing but praise of the manners of these worthies,
but, in my experience, to mention them in the same
day with the meanest Oriental would be an insult
to the latter, while they are boors compared with
Soudanese or Arabs of the same social standing.
Whatever they may have been a few years ago, it
is to be feared that contact with Europeans has had
a bad effect on their manners.

   When the chief and his following have departed,
there are probably sounds of strife and wrangling
among the porters, who declare that the quantity
of food is insufficient, or that some one has been
given too big a share ; but their differences are
settled somehow, and you have time for a stroll, and
perhaps a chance of shooting a partridge or a

guinea-fowl before sunset, when the nightjars begin to swoop and flicker over the grass, and you come home to dinner. In places where there are very many mosquitoes you must dine by daylight, and get into the mosquito-net soon after sunset; but that does not very often happen, and you can generally sit out of doors under the stars and watch the picturesque groups of porters as they sit eating and always talking about their camp-fires. One dinner in camp is very much like another, and I can only remember one that stands out from amongst the rest. It was Christmas Day, almost the first day that I was on the road, and, like royalty, I had music in the shape of a drum and a flute to entertain me at my feast. Maggi, prepared with water that oozed with difficulty out of a swamp, was not the *delectable consommé* that the label claimed it to be; the curried *cuckoo* (Swahili for chicken) was an osteo-logical monstrosity, and the lukewarm Crosse and Blackwell's Christmas pudding out of a tin would have vanquished the stoutest heart. The best part of the dinner was a blue water-lily stuck in an empty bottle, with which I decorated the table in honour of the day. But dinner (in Africa, at all events) is only a preface to tobacco and a book and bed. There are probably few people that ever lived who would have been more out of place in Mid-Africa than Mr. Pepys, but I found him a most constant and faithful companion, who never failed me.

Hardly a moment, it seems, after you have been lulled to sleep by the murmur of mosquitoes and the mutterings of the porters, the boy comes and shakes you into wakefulness; in ten minutes the tent is down, and the daily round has begun again.

CHAPTER V

'And then I looked up toward a mountain tract,
That girt the region with high cliff and lawn.'
                                        TENNYSON.

As one travels westward from the Victoria Nyanza
across Uganda, the country becomes daily poorer
and less populated. The rich elephant-grass country
of the kingdom of Uganda is left behind, and the
road traverses the rocky highlands of Unyoro. The
latter is more picturesque; there are more flowers,
and occasionally one can see a distant view of hills
and valleys; but one day's march is very like another,
up hill and down dale yesterday and to-day and
to-morrow. Indeed, I found it so wearisome that
I registered a vow never to return through Uganda,
but to go straight on until I came to the sea on the
other side; as a matter of fact, I did return by the
same route, only to make preparations for the journey
to the sea.

I was glad enough when, after nearly a fortnight's
march, we arrived at Toro, the capital of the Western
Province of Uganda, and the most westerly British
post. Like many other places in Africa, Toro is
known by a variety of names. Strictly speaking,

Toro is the name of the province ; Fort Portal (formerly Fort Gerry) is the name of the hill where the Government station and police lines are ; Kabarole is the hill of the Church Mission station, and Kasagama's is the King's hill. Sickness among the porters delayed me for a few days at Toro, and I was hospitably entertained by Mr. Haldane the Collector and Mr. Knowles the Sub-Commissioner of Toro and Ankole. Major Powell-Cotton had arrived there a few days before with his wife, and was just setting out for a six months' okapi hunt in the Congo Forest.

Fort Portal is built upon a hill, on the top of which is the ' boma,' a square enclosure bounded by a deep square trench and lines of eucalyptus-trees, and containing the collector's office, guard-house, and stores. On the slope of the hill are the two or three houses of the officials and the police lines, orderly rows of round, white-washed mud huts. There is a detachment of about 150 Uganda police under the charge of a British non-commissioned officer, and very soldierly they look in their dark-blue jerseys and putties and white breeches. On either side of the road that leads up to the fort is a row of Indian stores. What sort of business they can all do it is hard to imagine ; possibly some of the rubber and ivory from the Congo leaks out in this direction. A mile to the south, across a valley where flows a beautifully clear stream, is Kasagama's palace, perched on a hill

Mount Luigi di Savoia, Ruwenzori : from the Upper Mubuku Valley.

To face page 54.

commanding a fine view of his kingdom. Close by is the C.M.S. station of Kabarole, near enough to keep a watchful eye on Kasagama. There are a hospital and a resident doctor and nurse at Kabarole, in addition to the teaching staff of the mission. Still a mile farther south is the large Roman Catholic Mission of the White Fathers, most notable for the excellence of the vegetables which they grow, and for the scented avenues of eucalyptus-trees about the mission. There is a large and thriving population, immense plantations of bananas, and (it need hardly be said) miles of elephant-grass.

On the whole, one could find many worse places, in Uganda at all events, to live in than Toro. It is high up, more than 5,000 feet above the sea, and comparatively cool—in fact, I found it much too cold on coming there afterwards from the roasting plains near Lake Albert Edward—and you can sleep every night without a mosquito-net, a far more blessed dispensation than one would imagine. The unlimited supply of clear fresh water is perhaps an even greater advantage than the absence of mosquitoes. There is always the chance of slaying a leopard or a lion, if one is anxious to do so, and some of the best elephants in Uganda are to be found within a day's march. Some of the country round about Toro is exceedingly beautiful. A few miles to the east is a belt of glorious tropical forest, full of gorgeous flowers and birds and monkeys, and

with a mountain torrent, the Mpanga River, rushing through the midst. An hour's walk to the north
of Toro takes you to two lovely little crater-lakes,
full of wild-duck and water-lilies, and if you walk
a few miles farther still you come to one of those
wonderful surprises of which Africa is so fond.
The road, which has been ascending slowly but
surely all the way, suddenly disappears at your feet,
and you seem to be standing on the edge of the
world. It is another of the great African escarp-
ments, the Eastern edge of what has been called the
Albertine Depression. At the foot of the escarpment, 3,000 feet below, are woods and yellow plains
and the Semliki River winding through the distance.
Far beyond are the pointed hills of the Congo watershed, and shimmering in the haze to the north are
the waters of Lake Albert.

But the greatest glory of Toro is the superb view
of Ruwenzori which may often be seen from there.
Although Toro lies within a very few miles of the
north-eastern end of the range, it is often completely
hidden from sight ; in fact, I was myself for many
days within a short distance of the mountains, and
could not even have suspected their existence, but
frequently they may be seen for days together filling
up the western view from Toro—a mighty wall of
forest-covered ridges, which mount higher towards
the south and dwindle away towards the northern
plains like a headland in the sea, deep valleys filled
with trees and shadows, in the far distance a towering

mass of jagged rocks crinkled against the sky, and overtopping all can just be seen two snow-clad peaks. The highest group of peaks lies farther to the west, and cannot be seen from Toro.

While we are here, within sight, as it were, of Ruwenzori, it may be a good opportunity to say something about the history and geographical position of what was until recently the least known mountain region in Africa. Like many other places of which but little is known, Ruwenzori has been the subject of all manner of extravagant guesses and ill-founded statements. The name, which is the mis-spelt corruption of a native word of very doubtful meaning, is entirely unknown by the people living on any side of the range; it is true that there is a village near the north-east corner of Lake Albert Edward called Runsororo, but this can hardly have any connexion with the name of the mountains. There is certainly a better historical authority and, to my thinking, more of romance about ' The Mountains of the Moon,' but Ruwenzori seems to have been generally accepted, and, after all, it is not an ill-sounding name. It is common to speak of it as a mountain, but it is in reality a range of mountains with at least five distinct groups of snow-peaks. It has been described as the highest mountain in Africa, at least 20,000 feet high, and with an extent of thirty miles of glaciers; its height, as determined by the Duke of the Abruzzi, is slightly less than 17,000 feet, so that both Kilimanjaro and Kenya are higher than

Ruwenzori, and ten miles would more than cover the extent of glaciers.

Another mistake that has frequently been made is to describe Ruwenzori as the 'great African water-shed' and the 'Congo-Nile water-parting.' As a matter of fact, all the water that runs from Ruwenzori finds its way eventually into the Nile system. The streams that flow from the western slopes of the range join the Semliki River, which runs into Lake Albert, whence flows the Nile. The waters from the south flow into Lake Albert Edward, and those that come down the eastern valleys flow into Lake Ruisamba, whose waters flow into Lake Albert Edward and thence into the Semliki River. From the escarpment described earlier in this chapter, the streams in front of you, as you look over the edge, run straight away to Lake Albert, while the streams behind you make an almost complete tour of Ruwenzori, and travel nearly 200 miles to reach the same destination. The length of the range from the most northern spurs to the last foot-hills on the south, which correspond almost exactly with the Equator, is about seventy miles, and the breadth from east to west is, roughly speaking, about twenty miles. The first European to see Ruwenzori was probably Sir Samuel Baker, who saw what he called the 'Blue Mountains to the south' during his explora-tion of Lake Albert in 1864; but it was not until 1887, when Stanley came from the Congo on the Emin Relief Expedition, that the mountains were definitely recognized as a snow range, and for very nearly twenty years more they remained as little known and as mysterious as ever.

After several days' delay at Toro, I eventually dragged my porters away, sick and convalescent and malingering, and set out almost due south for the camp of the expedition in Ruwenzori. It was a great relief to change the direction and no longer to march with the sun burning one's back through all the long hours of the morning. This is a point quite worthy of the attention of other travellers in Africa ; if possible, go into the country at the west and travel eastwards rather than in the reverse direction. Not only was the direction changed, but the climate seemed to be changing too ; the nights became colder and the mornings chilly enough to keep the porters late abed. There were no regular camping-places along this road, and the porters built for themselves little beehive-shaped shelters of sticks and grass. When they were slow at turning out in the morning, I went the round of those huts and prodded with a stick, like a douanier searching for contraband, through the flimsy grass walls, until I felt something soft and fleshy, and then it was astounding to see how they skipped out through the rabbit-hole opening.

Whether it was that the porters had committed many and grievous sins in Toro, which must be expiated, or because they felt that they were coming into a strange and fearful land, I do not know, but for some cause or other they were taken at about this stage of the journey with a strong access of religious fervour. About half of them were Christians, and it was curious in the evening to hear the droning of prayers instead of the usual quarrellings and sounds of strife. The headman was chief priest among them, and his nasal, monotoning voice, growing always flatter and flatter, irresistibly suggested the savour of incense and the atmosphere of a cathedral in Italy or Spain. Some of them had books, with which I held a class in catechism, and they were not a little impressed by the apparent skill with which I read a language, which they knew I could not speak. The great majority of them were Roman Catholic, and in this connexion it might not be out of place to mention an incident which occurred some months later. I was walking along the road towards Entebbe one morning when I met three people, a White Father and two native boys—one carrying a water-bottle and the other a small parcel. The missionary was on his way to visit a native chief about a week's journey distant; his change of raiment was in the small parcel, and his food, he told me, he always obtained at the villages where he slept. We exchanged tobacco and good wishes and went our different ways. A few miles farther on I met a caravan of some thirty porters laden with the usual impedimenta of travel—tent, bed, cooking apparatus, stores, and so on ; then three cows and a flock of sheep and goats ; and then some half a dozen

Upper Mubuku Valley.

To face page 60.

boys carrying guns and rifles and pushing a bicycle (it was uphill) ; and lastly a member of the Church Missionary Society, who was able to give me the latest news from Europe, and told me many interesting things about the country.   It is far from my wish to suggest that I am less in sympathy with one mission than with another ; I was always treated with the utmost kindness by missionaries of every denomination, both when I was with the British Museum Expedition and subsequently, and the splendid work that many of them do must be obvious to every one, but it was impossible to help thinking that one stood a considerably better chance of getting to the root of the matter than did the other.

The character of the country was changing with almost every mile as we went south ; undulations became steep hills, and valleys and swamps became clear mountain streams.   The delight of drinking and washing in pure water instead of in the boiled mud, to which one was beginning to get accustomed, is a thing of which it is difficult to speak calmly. At the Wimi River, a beautiful torrent with steep wooded banks, I came unexpectedly upon a family bathing-party of yellow baboons, of all sizes from that of a mastiff to a small terrier ; they ran about on the rocks and barked in the most alarming manner, and I was not at all sorry that the river was between us.   There was something rather mysterious about this road ; the hills we were crossing were unmistakably mountain foot-hills, and the streams were unmistakably mountain streams, but though the sun blazed and there was never a cloud in the sky, early and late a thin haze hid everything a mile or two away from view. At another time of the year, when I was walking along the same road, I saw the most glorious views of Ruwenzori, and could hardly believe that I had seen nothing before.

But the mountains did at last disclose themselves, and in so magnificent a fashion that I was almost glad that they had remained hidden so long. We were camped a few miles up the biggest valley of the east side of the mountains, within a few hours of the end of the journey, when I was roused early from my bed by the cry of ' Gamballagalla !' (the Uganda name of Ruwenzori), and on coming out from the tent I saw a sight which was reward enough for the longest journey. What had seemed the night before to be a mere gap in the low hills was seen to be a noble mountain valley with steep grass-covered slopes and wooded ridges. Above was a bold buttress of sheer black crags, and beyond these towered a snow-peak. Poised almost upon the topmost pinnacle was the setting moon, a few days past the full. Whilst we looked the moon sank out of sight, and a rosy flush spread over the ice and snow. A few moments more and the snow had vanished like a puff of smoke ; a flood of sun-light turned the black crags to a flaming orange, and the grass in the valley glittered with a million drops of dew. I rubbed my eyes and wondered whether the snow-peak had been a reality or a dream, as I remember doing once before in Switzerland. I was walking over through the snow from Martigny to the valley of Chamonix one day in winter, and just as I began to go downhill towards Argentierre, I saw first one black rock and then another, and soon every pinnacle and aiguille of Mont Blanc, rising from a heavy bank of clouds, seemed towering over my head. For perhaps two minutes they continued clear, and then they vanished as swiftly as they came, leaving only a lasting memory of my first view of Mont Blanc.

My doubts were dispelled a few minutes later, when we waded across the Mubuku, biggest of all Ruwenzori rivers, waist-deep, and so cold that it could only have come from a high mountain region.

There must be very few places in the world where one can walk in a couple of days from hot plains grilling under the Equator to a land of Alpine frosts and snows, where sun-helmets and mosquito-nets give way to furs and blankets, and the camp fire serves no longer to scare away the lions, but to warm the shivering traveller. I have seen snow-capped peaks in New Guinea within 100 miles of the Line, but dense forests and the cannibalistic propensities of the natives make their exploration impossible without an armed escort. But it can be done in Ruwenzori, and the first part of it, which is as far as we shall get at present, seemed to me, after the many weary miles left behind, one of the most enchanting walks of my life. The path wound slowly up the wide valley through woods and fields and large gardens of bananas, crossing here and there a small tributary stream. There was a crisp freshness in the air that was unspeakably delicious, and the roar of the Mubuku, close beside the path, sounded like a triumphal march. The valley narrowed suddenly, and, turning a sharp bend, we came in sight of our journey's end, the camp of the British Museum Expedition, perched high up on a ridge before us. After an hour's climb up the steepest hill they had ever seen, which they protested that they never would be able to get up, the porters put down the loads they had carried for some 250 miles, and, after a good deal of cheering and dancing, departed down the hill more quickly than they came.

CHAPTER VI

THE EAST SIDE OF RUWENZORI

'A wanderer is man from his birth.
    He was born in a ship
    On the breast of the river of Time;
    Brimming with wonder and joy
    He spreads out his arms to the light,
    Rivets his gaze on the banks of the stream.'
                        MATTHEW ARNOLD.

THE four members of the British Museum party had arrived some three weeks earlier, and were already well established when I joined them. The spot selected for the camp was about as perfect a one as could have been found. At the top of a steep ridge between two narrow valleys, where the ridge itself merged into the main valley wall, was a tiny space, perhaps a quarter of an acre in extent, of fairly level ground. On this space were three native huts, the village of Bihunga, and the camp of the expedition, which consisted of a large grass hut, two or three lesser huts, and a few tents. There was so little room to spare that if one had tried to pitch another tent, it would assuredly have fallen over the edge into one of the valleys below. The natives were inclined to take alarm at the advent of so many strangers, but they soon overcame their shyness, and gained considerable profit from our sojourn amongst them. There was a grand view across and down the Mubuku Valley to the plains about Lake Ruisamba, though the lake itself could not be seen, and beyond that a sea of rolling hills far into the middle of Uganda. In the opposite direction the view of the higher valley and the heart of the range was cut off by a projecting spur, which rose about 1,000 feet above Bihunga, and acted as a welcome shield against the cold wind which often blew down the valley from the snows. The other members of the expedition had already made considerable progress with the collections, and had obtained several hundred skins of birds and small mammals. The usual plan was to go out early in the morning, and shoot enough birds to keep the collector occupied for the rest of the day ; the late afternoon was devoted to setting traps for rats and mice and other small animals. The expedition had been supplied with some very large traps for catching lions and leopards, but these, though they were useful afterwards for catching hyenas on the plains, caught nothing in Ruwenzori except one small native child, who incautiously put her foot into one and was held tight, and screaming, with no worse damage done than a slight scratch. Her anxious parents dressed the wound with an unspeakable mixture, and the result was that for several weeks she was my solitary patient.

The natives soon discovered that they could make an appreciable addition to their incomes by hunting, and bringing in beasts of various sorts. Hyraxes, gigantic rats, bats, mice, worms, beetles, chameleons, and snakes came pouring into Bihunga when once it was found that there were people mad enough to pay for such follies. The care with which they secured the captive beasts, and the air of mystery and importance with which they produced them, were always a source of amusement. If it could by any means be avoided, they would never hold a beast in their hands, but always bind a string of banana-fibre round its neck, and attach that to a stick, or else they wrapped the creature in elaborate parcels of banana-leaves, which they opened with a great display of caution and pretence of fear. The moment of unpacking the parcel was always an exciting one, as you never could tell what might be produced; a mouse might make a sudden dash for liberty, or a swarm of beetles or crabs come scurrying out, or a few chameleons would come strolling out, looking fearfully bored, or half a dozen bats would flap out into the sunshine. One of the most curious things that was brought was a single small beetle tied to a stick by a most ingenious harness about its middle; it was a common species of which we had many specimens, but it was bought and put to death for the sake of its harness, and now, I hope, it adorns the National Collection.

My business was to make collections of plants

and insects, and so long as the weather continued fine these provided me with plenty of occupation. Bihunga is just at the upper limit of the elephant-grass zone, and above this, below the beginning of the mountain forest, is a belt of cultivated land. The population being very small, and the slopes of Ruwenzori very big, it is unnecessary to cultivate any single piece of ground for long, so, as soon as the land shows any signs of deterioration, a fresh piece is cleared of grass and trees, and the old is neglected, and soon becomes an almost impenetrable wilderness.   It is in these patches of old cultivated ground that the greatest numbers of flowers are found growing.   Clumps of white and yellow daisies and helichrysums are scattered between thickets of purple-flowered acanthus and bushes of a papilion-aceous kind with yellow flowers and long black seed-pods, and tall white clusters of dombeya.   Here and there stood stiff and upright giant lobelias (*L. giberroa*, see illustration, p. 26), and clambering through the shady places was often found a gorgeous red and yellow gloriosa lily.   A tall pink begonia, growing about 2 feet high, looked very familiar, and thickets of brambles and beds of nettles gave a curiously English air to some of these flower-gardens. Almost more remarkable were the number and variety of ferns of every sort and size, from the smallest asplenium to a tree-fern 12 or 15 feet in height.   These latter are, of course, nothing in comparison with the monsters of Australia or New

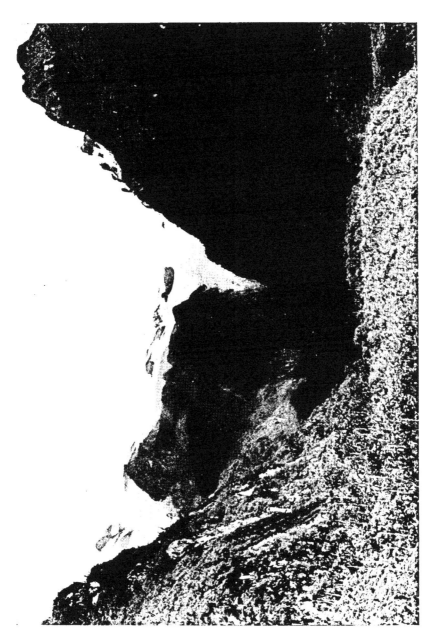

The Upper Mubuku Valley, looking North (from 13,000 feet).

To face page 68

Zealand, but a mass of them covering a steep bank beside a mountain stream is a very beautiful sight. Where there were so many flowers, and so great a variety of them, one would naturally expect to find a great number of butterflies, but they were disappointingly few, and most of them were sombre and inconspicuous ; however, they atoned somewhat by their rarity for their lack of beauty.

It has been remarked above that the view of the upper valley above Bihunga was cut off by the ridge on which the camp was set. From the summit of this ridge a new world was seen unfolded. The valley, which had become narrowed by the Bihunga ridge, widened again into a broad basin filled with forest and intersected by small subsidiary spurs that sloped down from the greater heights above. Through the middle of the forest the white streak of the Mubuku, hundreds of feet below, could be seen and heard roaring through its rocky bed, and across the valley the huge mass of Portal Peaks towered to 12,000 feet and more. Over the head of the valley rose ridge after ridge of forest and rocky peaks, and in the farthest distance could be seen a glistening slope of snow. It may, perhaps, be objected that I insist too much upon the views from one place or another. In a country where the greater part of one's time is spent dawdling along narrow tracks hedged in by walls of grass and bushes, whence nothing can be seen but the back of the man in front of you, or groping blindly through tunnels of forest, the views acquire an importance which can hardly be realized in a country built upon a smaller scale. It is the views seen or hoped for (too often the latter) which alone make travelling tolerable in Africa, and I shall venture to record them without further apology.

After toiling up the steep ascent on one side of the spur, it was a delight to plunge down on the other into the cool forest below. There was a narrow track, used sometimes by the natives on their hunting expeditions, which always lured one on through the forest. Anyone who loves walking in a wood knows how hard it is to turn back ; there is always something a little farther on—a turn in the path, or a stream to be crossed, and an enticing hill beyond. Sunbeams reaching the ground here and there, mysterious shadows, and the desire to see yet a little more, always beckoned one on from tree to tree, even after almost every turn of the path had become familiar.

The trees in this Ruwenzori forest are not of very great size, hardly bigger than forest-trees in England, but the greater density of the foliage, and the thick undergrowth, and the tangle of vines and creepers which envelop the trunks, together produce a dampness and darkness that are quite foreign to an English wood. Except in the early morning and late afternoon the forest is strangely silent ; the rustle of heavy falling leaves (it is always autumn in the forest) and the hush of the wind in the trees are the only sounds to be heard. Rarely, as you move quietly along the path, 'konk, konk, konk,' like the cry of a raven grown musical, sounds overhead, and if you stand still enough and peer upwards you may see a beautiful green turaco* sidling up and down a branch with wings and tail outspread, and performing the most quaint antics for the entertainment of another. Sometimes a small antelope leaps up with a shrill bark almost at your feet, and shows a momentary flash of brown as it disappears into the thicket, or there is a crashing and swaying in the upper branches as a troop of black monkeys take alarm, and, chattering and whistling, swing themselves off into safety. Sometimes the slow progress that one makes is suddenly hastened by meeting an army of large black ants with formidable jaws, that come streaming along the path. If, as it generally happens, one is walking heedlessly along with thoughts in the trees rather than on the ground, a sudden biting at many points is the first warning that one has of the enemy's approach, and boots and garments have to be hurriedly torn off before the last invader is captured and slain. Wandering on and on, you see at length a glint of light through the trees in front, the forest ends abruptly, and you come out into the broad sunlight. The change is almost startling in its suddenness and degree; you feel that you have been translated in a moment from

* *Turacus emini.*

Africa to a southern English county. From the edge of the wall of forest a hill slopes steeply upwards, covered with deep bracken, and here and there scattered trees, which look from a short distance for all the world like oak-trees; swallows and martins are hawking in the air, butterflies are fluttering about the flowering trees; and over all is the watery pale-blue sky of a northern climate. With the least effort of the imagination, one would say that this was one of the higher parts of the New Forest, or a woodland in Somerset or Devon.

Wherever we went from the camp at Bihunga, it was necessary to mount or descend at least 1,000 feet, with the result that we thought nothing of going up 2,000 or 3,000 feet along a forest ridge in the morning in pursuit of birds or plants. After spending several days scrambling up and down the steep hill-sides, it was sometimes a pleasant change to go down into the valley and stretch one's legs upon level ground. It was like going down from Montanvert to Chamounix, but instead of walking through pine-woods in the level valley, we took shelter from the sun in groves of tall bananas. I always think that sunlight comes more beautifully through the leaves of Spanish chestnuts than through any other leaves, and next to them in order come the leaves of the banana; they are just transparent enough to temper the sunlight and produce a small degree of shade and coolness without any suggestion of darkness or gloom. There are always plenty of butterflies among the bananas, and many flowering plants are found between the stems—clumps of white balsams, pink and white crinum lilies, and scarlet-flowered cannas. The thud of raindrops on the leaves is very pleasant to listen to, and the 'sound of going,' when a sudden storm of wind strikes a large plantation, is like the rush of the sea upon a shingly beach.

The expedition remained encamped at Bihunga for very nearly four months. During nearly a month of that time—that is to say, throughout January—the weather was almost uniformly fine. Day succeeded to day of bright sunshine and cloudless skies; it was neither too hot by day nor too cold by night, the average maximum and minimum temperatures being about 74° F. and 58° F. Birds nested, butterflies were on the wing, and the hillsides were ablaze with flowers. One began to think that this was one of the most beautiful places in the world, and blest with the ideal climate, until one day without any warning the sky filled with clouds and the rain descended. Thenceforward, with the exception of a few occasional fine days, the weather was almost continuously wet, until we left the mountain valley in the middle of April. The sun might shine for an hour or two in the early morning, but with a very disagreeable regularity a white bank of clouds would come softly rolling up the valley about nine or ten o'clock, and in a few minutes the mountains were cloaked in mist, and everything would be soaked with moisture. This added very materially to the difficulty of making collections, for not only was the time in which collecting was practicable very much shortened, but the work of drying skins and plants was made almost impossible.

During the spell of fine weather in January we were visited by an Austrian climber, Herr Grauer, and three members of the Church Missionary Society, who were on their way back from an expedition to the head of the Mubuku Valley, where they had made an attempt to 'climb Ruwenzori.' Although they only succeeded in reaching the summit of one of the higher ridges, not the watershed, of the range, the point reached by Herr Grauer's party, about 15,000 feet, was the highest that had been attained up to that time. It was unfortunate that we could not take advantage of the fine weather in the same month; both of the expeditions that we made to the centre of the range were unavoidably delayed until after the wet weather had set in. Herr Grauer stayed with us for several days, which he occupied chiefly in removing from his person the mud of Ruwenzori, of which he could not say bad enough things, and, as we subsequently found out for ourselves, his description was in no way exaggerated. Visitors and excitements were rare at Bihunga, and we were all sorry when our delightful friend departed.

So far as it is possible to judge from our own

View from the Camp at Bujongolo, Ruwenzori (12,500 feet).

To face page 74

experience, and from the reports of other travellers and the very untrustworthy information supplied by natives, there is generally a short dry season in January and a longer period in June and July, and possibly in early August, when the greater part of Ruwenzori is comparatively free from rain. Throughout the rest of the year, though there are occasional fine days, it may be said that the rainy season is almost continuous.

The few incidents that varied the monotony of our sojourn at Bihunga were, as a rule, furnished by the four-legged rather than by the two-legged inhabitants. There were a great many chimpanzees in the forest; their 'nests,' light platforms of sticks built in the forks of high trees, were frequently found, and often at night one would hear their cries near the camp; it was a most melancholy sound, like the wailing of children in distress. They are shy animals, and are not very often seen; but on one occasion we had an excellent view of a small family party, a baby with its two parents, feeding on the fruit of a tree below the camp. With the help of field-glasses it was easy to see the almost painfully human gestures of the old ones, as they helped the little one to move from branch to branch, and fed it with berries. Although they are most commonly found in the tropical forests at a lower level, chimpanzees wander about a great deal and go far up the mountains in search of food; we found traces of them at a height of nearly 10,000 feet in Ruwenzori, where they had been feeding on the berries of a podocarpus.

Sometimes there was a visitation of lions. One morning a boy came in with a very scared face, saying that he had just seen a very big lion in the grass down in the valley, and shortly afterwards the mutilated remains of a large wild boar, off which the lion had been dining, were brought in; it was remarkable that only the hind-quarters of the animal had been touched : there was not a mark on its head or back to show that it had been killed by a blow. On another occasion a party of lions elected to spend a 'week-end' pig-hunting in the valley. Between Saturday and Monday they killed four wild pigs within half a mile of the camp, and, according to those who were there at the time, the shrieking of the unhappy victims was most terrible to hear; there was no moon at the time, and the vegetation was too dense to make lion-hunting by candle-light an attractive amusement for anybody except the lions. Leopards, although they were but seldom seen, were always with us, and, if one may believe the word of the goatherd, they showed a nice discrimination in disregarding the sheep and goats of the natives in favour of ours.

The natives, who belonged to the Bakonjo tribe, were invariably friendly, and, as well as being naturalists, were useful to us as porters and as providers of some of our food. They live in neat round huts built of grass stems on a framework of wooden posts, with a roof of bamboo poles, and divided into four or five rooms within, and thatched, both roof and walls, with banana-leaves ; there is generally a projection from the roof, 3 feet or 4 feet wide, forming a sort of porch over the doorway. When the walls begin to give way, or the house becomes for some other reason uninhabitable, it is not uncommon to see the roof, supported on a dozen pairs of black legs which appear beneath it, moving about the hill-side to be fixed on to a new wall elsewhere. It was amusing to watch the population emerging from the huts in the morning. After a great deal of crowing and clucking, some one inside would take the trouble to open the door and let out a dozen or twenty chickens, followed by as many sheep and goats ; after a short interval five or six children would appear, then the women, and last of all, slowly and deliberately, the lords of creation. The greatest number that I counted, exclusive of live-stock, was seventeen from one hut ; considering that there is always a fire burning in the house, and that the close-fitting door, the only apparent means of ventilation, is always tightly shut when the family retires to rest, it is difficult to understand why they ever come out alive at all.

The men spend a good deal of their time in hunting monkeys and small antelopes and hyraxes ; these latter (the conies of the 'stony rocks') are very eagerly sought for, both for their meat, which is considered a great delicacy (we found it rather tasteless and tough), and for their skins, which are sewn together to be made into a sort of short mantle. Cultivation is almost entirely carried on by the women and children, and they are very skilful in coaxing crops to grow on slopes so steep that the whole field is in danger of sliding down into the valley below. At the upper limit of cultivation— that is, about 7,000 feet—they grow chiefly a dwarf bean, a kind of millet grass, and a large arum ;* this latter has a large white root, which is exceed- ingly poisonous if it is eaten raw, but it is not unpleasant boiled or roasted, and the leaves (see illustration, p. 198) make quite a passable spinach. Sometimes the natives from the lower slopes brought up large bunches of sweet bananas, and if they could not all be eaten before they had passed the stage of ripeness, a way was found after some experiment of putting them to a good use. The recipe may as well be given here, and perhaps some one will make a fortune out of it. Wash your hands. Take bananas, as many as possible, and place them, skin and all, into a large basin or other vessel. Press the bananas very vigorously with the hands, and keep on pressing and kneading until all the juice has been squeezed out of them. Add a few hand- fuls of fine dry grass, and with the help of this wring out all the juice from the pulp, which may be given to the chickens. Make a funnel of a piece of banana-leaf lightly packed with grass, and through

* *Collocasia.*

Mosses on the Heath-Trees, Ruwenzori (10,000 feet).

To face page 78.

this filter pour the liquid into another vessel. This is 'mubissi,' pure banana-juice, a favourite drink of the people of Uganda. Over a slow fire let the 'mubissi' simmer gently for several hours, and then allow it to cool. This is Ruwenzori syrup. It is about the consistency of treacle, and has a quiet taste of honey and banana, with a suggestion of sunshine and a suspicion of acidity. When well made it is excellent.

Owing to the difficulties of the language of the Bakonjo, we could only communicate with them through our Uganda boys, with whom they had some words in common, and so we were unable to find out any of their tribal customs and legends—if, indeed, they have any. We were invaded once by a primitive orchestra of some ten or a dozen young men, who played each upon two pieces of wood of different lengths, with the shorter of which they struck sharp blows upon the longer. The rhythm was intricate and difficult to follow, but they kept time admirably, and without the accompaniment of groans and howls the effect would not have been unpleasing ; it recalled some of the 'music' that may still be heard in the Scottish Highlands. The occasion was the death of a father of the tribe, which had taken place some weeks before ; in the meantime the people had allowed their hair to grow, and now the end of the time of mourning was being celebrated with music and dancing and a general shaving of heads. Although it cannot be said that

they are a musical race, the Bakonjo were possessed of a saving sense of humour.   One of our
party had brought with him a gramophone.   I confess to a rooted dislike of the gramophone considered
as a musical instrument, but it must be admitted
that the machine was often a source of amusement.
The kind of humour that incites the white man to
mirth had very little effect on the natives, but there
was a certain song, a deplorably sentimental ditty
about Jerusalem and choir-boys, so far as I can remember, and with a tune well suited to the sentiment, which never failed to produce a shout of
laughter from the black people.   Sometimes, when
the instrument was performing out of doors, it was
most entertaining to watch a native stalk it carefully
from behind, and make a hasty dash for covert,
when he came within range of the full blast of the
funnel.

Excursions to the higher parts of the mountains,
of which some account will be given in the following
chapter, interrupted the regularity of our sojourn at
Bihunga, which, while it was sometimes monotonous,
never became dull.

CHAPTER VII

CLIMBING IN RUWENZORI

'Questa montagna è tale,
Che sempre il cominciar di sotto è grave
E quant' uom più va sù, e men fa male.'

DANTE.

BEFORE inviting the patient reader to accompany me on our attempts to reach the heart of Ruwenzori, I will briefly record the expeditions that had been made with a similar purpose by previous travellers. The first ascent that was made in the range was in 1889, when Lieutenant Stairs, of Stanley's Emin Pasha Relief Expedition, reached a height of 10,677 feet on the western slopes. So far as I can unravel the complication of native names, this ascent must have been from one of the valleys north of the Butagu. In 1891 Dr. Stuhlmann ascended to a height of 13,326 feet in the Butagu Valley on the west side of the chain; and though he did not reach the snow, he obtained fine photographs of the highest peaks. In 1895 Scott Elliot ascended to about the same point in the Butagu Valley and made excursions into four valleys on the eastern side of the range, reaching the watershed in two different places, but in neither valley did he reach

the snow level.   The next expedition was that of
J. E. S. Moore, who was the first to reach the snow
and to demonstrate beyond doubt the existence of
glaciers in Ruwenzori.   Moore climbed to the summit of one of the ridges of Ingomwimbi or Kiyanja
or (as it is now called) Mount Baker, at a point
close to the rock reached subsequently by Herr
Grauer's party.   In the same year (1900) Sir Harry
Johnston succeeded in arriving almost at the same
point as Moore, and in 1903 Mr. and Mrs. Fischer
climbed to the foot of the Mubuku glacier, but did
not ascend farther.   Mrs. Fischer was the first, and
is hitherto the only, European woman to visit the
snows of Ruwenzori.   But it was not until 1905
that a really serious attempt was made by a party
of mountaineers to solve some of the problems of the
range. Messrs. Douglas Freshfield and A. L. Mumm,
with the guide, Moritz Inderbinnen, of Zermatt,
spent several days in November at the head of the
Mubuku Valley trying to force a way to the summit
of one of the ridges, but the abominably wet weather
made mountaineering an impossibility, and they
were compelled to beat a retreat.   The party, whose
mountaineering experience is too well known to
need mention here, was equipped with everything
necessary for making explorations, and had they not
been misled most unfortunately by the statements of
previous travellers into selecting one of the wettest
months of the year for their expedition, there can be
little doubt but that they would have been completely

successful. In January, 1906, Herr Grauer and a party of missionaries, as has been already stated, reached the summit of one of the ridges, which they erroneously thought to be the watershed of the range, at a height of 14,813 feet.* At the end of the same month R. B. Woosnam, during the course of a bird-collecting excursion, climbed alone to Herr Grauer's highest point.

It was not until the latter half of February—that is, some time after the beginning of the rainy season—that we were able to make an excursion up the valley. The object of the expedition was primarily to collect specimens ; Woosnam and Dent were in quest of birds and mammals, and I went to collect plants, but we had at the back of our minds the idea of getting up something if an opportunity should occur, and we accordingly took with us all the apparatus that we could collect. This consisted of about 25 feet of Alpine rope and a pair of crampons, which we had obtained from Herr Grauer, and an old ice-axe, which Mr. Freshfield had left behind him at Toro ; not a very complete equip-ment for attacking a group of unknown mountains. The British Museum had not considered the remote possibility of exploration in fitting out the Ruwenzori Expedition, and I had left England in too much of a hurry to be able to get more than the bare necessaries of travel. The lack of a light tent, that

* Corrected height, determined by H.R.H. the Duke of the Abruzzi.

we could carry ourselves, necessarily limited our excursions to such as we might make from the highest camp to which our porters would consent to go, and that, as will be seen, was not very far.

It was in one of the rare intervals of sunshine that we set out full of hope for the upper regions, but we had not gone far before we were drenched through to the skin, a condition to which one soon becomes accustomed in Ruwenzori. Above the bracken-covered slope, described in the last chapter, the path proceeds along a narrow, knife-edged ridge with a sheer drop of almost 1,000 feet to the Mubuku torrent on one side, and a steep slope to a large tributary stream on the other. This ridge is apparently the remains of a gigantic moraine, through which the Mubuku has cut a deep U-shaped trough. On the crest of the ridge, at an altitude of rather less than 9,000 feet, is an immense erratic boulder, called Vitaba or Nakitawa, as big as two four-roomed cottages rolled into one. It is a favourite camping-place of the natives, and, except when a strong wind is blowing, its overhanging sides afford a fair amount of shelter. Evidences of former glaciation become increasingly numerous above this altitude, but there are some, in the form of ancient moraines, etc., at a much lower level, according to Scott Elliot even so low as 5,200 feet.

One of the most remarkable features of Ruwenzori is the abrupt change that is often seen from one

Kiyanja (King Edward Peak) from Bujongolo.

To face page 84.

kind of vegetation to another. Above the tropical forest, which extends to about 8,000 feet, is a more or less constant zone of bracken and giant heath-trees, and above this, with at first a sprinkling of Podocarpus* and other large trees, begins the zone of bamboos, which are found growing up to 11,000 feet, though their densest growth occurs between 9,000 and 10,000 feet. After leaving the big rock, Vitaba, the track plunged almost at once into the bamboos, and the difficulties of the march began. It was hard enough for the unburdened European to struggle and wriggle between the unyielding stems, but how the Bakonjo, with one hand supporting the loads on their heads and the other grasping a big stick, managed to find a way through passed all understanding. A semblance of a path had been made by cutting out a bamboo here and there, but the cut stems, which generally found their way across the track, and the fallen leaves mixed up with mud on a steep slope, made the going about as bad as can be imagined, and progress was deplorably slow.

There is a small crater lake high up in the bamboo forest, which two of us visited one day. There was not even a vestige of a track leading anywhere near it ; in fact, it was a place that the natives studiously avoided, and those whom we took with us could hardly be induced to approach it. The bamboos were so thick that we could not force

* *Podocarpus milanjiana.*

a way through them, and cutting was too slow a process, so the natives adopted the plan of bending the bamboos down and walking over the top of them, which rather unusual method of procedure we followed for some time.   Our guides, who professed to know the way, were as ignorant as we were ourselves, and with the additional difficulty of rain and fog, it was by the merest chance that, after several hours of toilsome scrambling, we came suddenly on the lake at an altitude of about 9,800 feet.   It was almost circular, and about 400 yards across.   If it is—as there can be little doubt that it is—a crater lake (the banks are very steep, and at a distance of 1 yard from the edge we were unable to reach the bottom with a long bamboo pole), it is the highest crater lake in Ruwenzori.   The next visitor to the lake, if ever another has the energy to venture there, will find the remains of a quaint little shrine of branches decked with leaves and flowers, which our guides erected to conciliate the evil spirits of the place.

After struggling for miles through the dense jungle of bamboo, where all sense of direction was quickly lost, it was a relief beyond measure to come out occasionally on to tolerably level ground, where one could at all events get a glimpse here and there through the fog and rain, even though it meant exchanging the slippery slopes for swamps and sloughs, where the easiest path was knee-deep in mud and water.   ' The way was also here very wearisome, through dirt and slabbiness.   Nor was there on all this ground so much as one inn or victualling house wherein to refresh the feebler sort.   Here, therefore, was nothing but grunting, and puffing, and sighing.   While one tumbleth over a bush, another sticks fast in the dirt; and the children, some of them, lost their shoes in the mire, while one cries out, " I am down," and another, " Ho! where are you ?" and a third, " The bushes have got such a fast hold on me, I think I cannot get away from them." '   The description is so true that one is tempted to believe that, if he had not been there himself, John Bunyan must have met some one who had travelled to Ruwenzori.   But, unlike his little band of pilgrims, we did not come to ' an arbour, warm, and promising much refreshing,' called ' The Slothful's Friend.'   The end of our day's journey was a steep black precipice, 400 or 500 feet high, called Kichuchu.   At the foot of the precipice, which in one place was slightly overhanging, we found a small space, a few yards only in extent, of comparatively dry ground.   It quaked ominously, like thin ice, at a heavy tread, but one does not employ the ordinary standards of wet and dry in such places. There was not room enough to pitch a tent, so we unfurled our beds and laid them close to the foot of the cliff, and as far as might be from the constant cascade of water, which splashed into pools from the overhanging rock.

The most notable feature of the camp at Kichuchu

was the nocturnal chorus of the Ruwenzori ghosts. It was always said by the natives that there were devils high up in the mountains, and anyone of a superstitious turn of mind who has slept or has tried to sleep at Kichuchu could well believe it. So soon as it became dark, first one and then another shrill cry broke the silence ; then the burden was taken up by one high up on the cliff overhead, then by others on either side, until the whole valley was ringing with screams. Various theories were advanced to account for it : frogs, owls, and devils were amongst the suggestions, but the natives declared that the noises were made by hyraxes, and we discovered afterwards that they were right. It is possible that each actual cry was not very loud, but the steep hill-sides and the bare wall of the cliff acted as sounding-boards, which intensified the noise to an incredible extent. It was one of the most mournful and blood-curdling sounds I have ever heard, and it caused an uncomfortable thrill, even after we had been assured that it had not a supernatural origin.

The upper Mubuku Valley—that is to say, from Kichuchu (9,833 feet) to the foot of the Mubuku glacier (13,682 feet)—is built in a series of gigantic steps of from 500 to 1,000 feet in height, between which lie tolerably level terraces of from one to two miles in length. The first of these steps is made by the cliff at the foot of which lies the rock-shelter of Kichuchu. The path leads up a

sloping rift in the rock face, in some places so well
sheltered that the dust of ages lies thick upon the
ground, but more generally it is nothing but the
bed of a stream, and is exposed to the drippings
from the rocks above. A climb of about an hour
brings one to the first great terrace. There is a
small area of swamp, but this terrace is chiefly
remarkable for the wonderful luxuriance of the
heath-trees, which attain here their greatest growth.
A heath-tree is a thing entirely unlike any of the
trees of England; the reader must imagine a stem
of the common 'ling' magnified to a height of
60 or 70 or even 80 feet, but bearing leaves and
flowers hardly larger than those of the 'ling' as it
grows in England. Huge cushions of many-coloured
mosses, often a foot or more deep, encircle the
trunks and larger branches, while the finer twigs
are festooned with long beards of grey lichen, which
give to the trees an unspeakably dreary and funereal
aspect. This first terrace was perhaps the most
difficult and tiring part of the whole ascent, for not
only did the heath-trees grow very close together,
but the ground beneath them was strewn with the
dead and decaying trunks of fallen trees, some of
them hard as bog oak, and others ready to crumble
at a touch, but all of them covered with a dense
carpet of thick moss, which necessitated a careful
probing before any step forward could be taken.
The way in which our Bakonjo porters, encumbered
as they were with awkward loads, hopped nimbly

from one trunk to another made one feel thoroughly ashamed.

As we ascended the steep slope at the other end of the terrace the heath-trees became rather less dense, and in the intervals between them appeared a few helichrysums, tall senecios with clusters of yellow flowers, and a beautiful little blue violet (*Viola abyssinica*) very similar to the English dog-violet. At the top of this slope, about 11,800 feet, the climber enters upon a new world, or, to speak more truly, it is a tract that seems to be a relic of a long past age. One would not be in the least surprised to see pterodactyls flying screaming over-head (they must have been noisy creatures, I think), or iguanodons floundering through the morasses and browsing on the tree-tops. But there are no living creatures to be seen or heard; it is a place of awful silence and solitude. It is an almost level meadow or 'swampy garden,' as Sir H. H. Johnston called it, a mile or more long, and several hundred yards wide. Out of the moss, which everywhere forms a dense and soaking carpet, grow thick clumps of helichrysum with white and pink flowers, and standing up like attenuated tombstones are the tall spikes of giant lobelias (*Lobelia deckenii*). Groundsels (*Senecio adnivalis*) grow here into trees 20 feet high, St. John's wort (*Hypericum*) is a tree even higher, and brambles (*Rubus doggetti*) bear flowers 2 inches across, and fruit as big as walnuts. Through the middle of the meadow the Mubuku

The Upper Mubuku : Kiyanja in Distance.

To face page 90.

meanders over a gravelly bed, as perfect a trout stream in appearance as one could wish to see. On either side are steep rocks and slopes covered with heath-trees looming like ghosts upwards into the everlasting fog. At its upper end the meadow is bounded by an almost precipitous wall, over which the Mubuku falls in a splendid cascade.

A slippery scramble in pouring rain brought us to the top of the last great step in the valley, and soon afterwards to our camping-place, Bujongolo (12,461 feet). It should be remarked that 'camping-place' is a very flattering description of a space about 10 feet square under the shelter of an over-hanging cliff, and surrounded by huge blocks that had fallen therefrom. Our porters found refuge in all sorts of queer holes and crannies amongst the rocks. There was not space enough to pitch a tent, and we were a miserable little party as we sat huddled round a fire of sodden heath logs, which produced only an acrid and blinding smoke. Not for the first time did I bless the inventor of the Wolseley valise, when I crept into mine and tried to accommodate my bones to the bumps of our rocky floor. Our successors at Bujongolo, more blessed with means and men than we were, cut down many of the trees to build a platform, upon which they pitched their tents and made a fairly comfortable camp for their six weeks' stay.

The cliff overhead is the haunt by day of large fruit-eating bats (*Rousettus lanosus*), which measure about 2 feet across the wings. At sunset they come flapping out, and for a second or two afford a chance of a difficult shot before they disappear through the heath-trees towards the valley below. To judge from the number of their tracks, which we found about the camp and far up the mountain-sides almost to the snow level, leopards and another smaller cat were fairly common, but we never chanced to see one. Our first night at Bujongolo I shall never forget by reason of an earthquake, the most severe I have ever felt, which awoke me from a troubled sleep. Every moment—it seemed to last for minutes instead of, probably, for a few seconds only—I expected to see the cliff, which made our roof, come crashing down to put an untimely end to our travels.

Vittorio Sella, Photo.

The Highest Peaks of Ruwenzori, from the Slopes of Kiyanja.

To face page 92.

CHAPTER VIII

CLIMBING IN RUWENZORI (*continued*)

'When I would get me to the upper fields,
 I look if anywhere
A man be found who craves what joyaunce yields
 The keen thin air,
Who loves the rapture of the height,
And fain would snatch with me a perilous delight.'

T. E. BROWN.

A SHORT distance above Bujongolo, where it flows
through a deep and narrow gorge, the Mubuku
takes a sharp bend to the right (north), and at the
same time the valley widens out into the third and
last of the great swampy terraces, at an altitude of
rather less than 13,000 feet. As one comes out
from the last of the heath forest at the bend of the
valley, there is suddenly unfolded a glorious view of
mountains and snowfields. In the middle of the
view towers up the beautiful peak Kiyanja,* thought
by Sir Harry Johnston to be the highest point in the
range, with two glaciers on its flanks. To the right,
at the head of the valley, the great Mubuku glacier†
thrusts its long nose almost down to the valley floor,

* Named by H.R.H. the Duke of the Abruzzi ' King Edward
Peak,' a part of the Mount Baker massif.
† Moore Glacier.

and on either side are jagged peaks with steep black precipices and gentler slopes of snow. During all the eight or nine days that our two expeditions to Bujongolo together counted, I do not suppose that the mountains were visible for half as many hours; but the place was so grim and solemn, and so almost unearthly in its setting, that the scene is far more firmly impressed upon my memory than many that I have seen a hundred times more often. The lower slopes were covered with lobelias* and senecios and helichrysums, and the inevitable moss. Here was found one of the most striking, and not the least interesting, of the many new birds that were dis-covered by the expedition. This was a sunbird (*Nectarinia dartmouthi*) of a dark metallic green colour shot with a wonderful iridescent purple. Two feathers of its tail were prolonged several inches beyond the others, and upon its breast, almost hidden by the wings, were two tufts of short crimson plumes. To see one of these little birds perched upon a tall blue spike of lobelia, fluttering his wings and flirting his long tail, was one of the prettiest sights imaginable. Sunbirds and large swifts, which live in the steep rocks like the Alpine swifts in Europe, were almost the only living things to be seen.

* The lobelia that grows from 12,000 feet almost to the snow level had been wrongly identified in former collections with a species found on Kilimanjaro. Dr. A. B. Rendle finds that it is a distinct species, and has named it *Lobelia wollastoni*.

The first expedition that we made from Bujongolo was to the head of the Mubuku glacier, in which we followed, with some few variations, the route taken by Herr Grauer's party a month earlier. A mile or more of ploughing through swamp took us to the end of the level terrace, beyond which we mounted at first over an old moraine covered with a forest of senecios, and then over smooth, glacier-worn rocks coated with moss and oozing with water, and up through a curious tunnel, formed by a huge block jammed across a gully, to the foot of the glacier (13,682 feet). We had often noticed far down in the valley below that there was no great difference in the volume of the Mubuku from morning to evening, as there is in the glacier-fed streams of Europe, and the reason was apparent when we came to the Mubuku glacier. Both early and late there was never more than the merest trickle of water flowing from this glacier. The reason, which has been pointed out by Mr. Freshfield,* is that in Africa, as in other tropical and subtropical regions, notably the Sikkim Himalayas, the glaciers lose most of their substance by evaporation. It was pleasant to think that a part of that tiny stream would perhaps find its way into the great river, which goes swirling past the temple of Abu Simbel and carries fatness to the fields of Egypt. We scrambled up a few hundred feet of loose and rotten rocks, more dangerous than difficult, and then took

* *Alpine Journal,* vol. xxiii., p. 48.

to the glacier near the top of the ice-fall, where it
was necessary to cut a few steps among the séracs.
From the top of the ice-fall we made a wide detour
across the glacier to avoid the risk of an avalanche
from a little hanging glacier on our right—the
remains of recent avalanches were scattered all
about us—and thence an hour's walk up an easy
snow slope took us to the top of the ridge and the
rock, which Herr Grauer had named King Edward's
Rock (14,813 feet).* Meantime the clouds, which
had been drifting about the peaks as we ascended,
settled down in a thick pall, and by the time that
we gained the ridge we were unable to see fifty
yards in any direction. Our predecessors had supposed that they had reached the watershed at that
point, and, seeing nothing ourselves, we saw no
reason to doubt the fact. It was discovered subsequently that it was not the watershed, but only
a ridge connecting a big Eastern buttress with the
main chain. A momentary glimpse through the
clouds that day would have solved many questions;
but though we stayed and shivered for two hours in
a bitter north wind, our patience was wasted and
our labour in vain. The camera and a dozen un-
exposed plates seemed to grow unduly heavy before
we reached camp that night, and I confess to having
thought with longing and regret of a certain cheerful
guide, who loves to relieve 'monsieur' of his superfluous baggage towards the end of a long day.

* Now named 'Grauer's Rock

Looking up the Mubuku Glacier.

To face page 96.

On the following day soon after sunrise Woosnam and I set out for Kiyanja. Instead of following the Mubuku Valley up the wide terrace to the glacier, we turned off towards the west up a small tributary stream, and soon found ourselves in difficulties. Slopes, which from a little distance looked smooth and easy enough, were found on closer acquaintance to be cut up with gullies and water-courses, and clothed in the most disheartening vegetation that ever resisted the footsteps of a climber. We could not complain much about sinking at every step almost to the knees in moss and black slime; but through the moss grew, as high as one's head, a tangle of 'everlasting' bushes as stiff and wiry as broom, through which we had to force our way as best we could. The tall, upright spikes of the lobelias seemed to offer a sure support, but they generally crumbled away at a touch and sent one sliding down the slope again, while the stems of the senecios were too slippery with moss and moisture to be of any use in hauling oneself up the hill-side. It would have been hard work enough anywhere to make much headway over ground of that sort, but at an altitude of about 14,000 feet, where we had not been long enough to have become acclimatized, and where the slightest exertion was a labour, it only needed a word from one to the other of us and we had beaten a retreat. Luckily the word was not spoken, and, after we had lightened our burdens by leaving behind us cameras and all but the most

necessary food, we struggled on with less difficulty.

At a height of about 14,500 feet all our difficulties
were practically at an end; we had passed beyond
the limit of the lobelias and the bushy 'everlastings,'
though another species (*Helichrysum stuhlmanni*)
was found up to 15,000 feet, and the senecios were
getting fewer, until at 14,800 feet they ceased
altogether. Rocks, partly moraine and partly blocks
that had fallen from a high cliff on our left, began
to replace the moss and mud—a most welcome
change. Very fortunately we had had a clear view
of the mountain earlier in the day, and had mapped
out the course that we proposed to take, noting
certain prominent landmarks. Had we not done so,
there would have been nothing for us to do but to
stay where we were or retrace our steps, as the
clouds were low down on the mountains when we
came to the foot of the rocks. However, we groped
our way blindly forwards, and luckily recognized a
big wall of granite rock, which had shown up con-
spicuously pink from below. Here, in order to
make certain, if possible, of finding our way back
through the fog, we filled our pockets with 'everlasting' flowers, which we scattered, like Hänsel
and Gretel, every few yards as we went along.
Often as I had maligned the 'everlastings' before,
I blessed them that day; they undoubtedly saved
us from a night out on the mountain-side, if not
from worse things. After climbing up a few hundred

feet of steep but easy rocks, we came on to a small glacier,* bare and dry in its lower part, but covered with an increasing depth of snow as we went higher. A black mass before us loomed huge through the fog, and seven hours after leaving camp we stood on the peak, which seems from below to be the summit of Kiyanja (see illustration, p. 84). We built a small cairn, and, to keep ourselves warm, hurled huge boulders down the steep eastern face of the mountain into the Mubuku Valley. It is an attractive amusement, but not one to be recommended in regions more populous than Ruwenzori.

We waited as long as it was safe to do, if we were to get back to camp that night, and were just preparing to descend when a warm slant of sunshine pierced the fog, the clouds boiled up from below, and we looked right down the Mubuku Valley, and saw the river winding away over the yellow plain of Ruisamba and the blue hills beyond. It was like one of the rare glimpses that one gets from the Alps of the Lombard Plain, but it lasted only for a moment before it was blotted out again. Then there came a clearing on the other side, towards the north and west, and we saw that we had missed the real top of our mountain† (15,988 feet), which rose perhaps 150 feet higher than the point that we had reached, and was connected with ours by an arête of snow. It was disappointing to have missed it, but it was too late then to go on further.

* King Edward Glacier.   † King Edward Peak.

Towards the north-west was a big snow-peak*
about 400 feet higher than ours, forming a big
western buttress of the range; and further away,
apparently three or four miles to the north-west,
appeared two beautiful sharp-pointed snow-peaks,†
which seemed to be about 1,000 feet higher than
our peak, and must be unquestionably the highest
peaks in the range. Our estimate of their heights
proved to be approximately correct; H.R.H. the
Duke of the Abruzzi climbed them in the following
June, and found their heights to be 16,815 feet
(Margherita Peak) and 16,749 feet (Queen Alex-
andra Peak). The peaks were seen rising out of
a dense bank of clouds, which lay between us and
them, so that it was impossible to tell in what way
they were connected with the other peaks of the
range. All too soon the clouds enveloped us
again more densely than before, and it was fully
time to start back towards Bujongolo. Thanks to
our trail of 'everlasting' flowers, we lost no time in
the descent, and we staggered into camp just as
darkness set in, after one of the most tiring days
I have ever experienced.

At this point, even at the risk of wearying the
reader with topographical details, it may be as well
to recapitulate some of the theories which had
been held as to the highest peak of Ruwenzori.
Dr. Stuhlmann, during his explorations in the

* Savoia Peak, 16,339 feet.
† The two peaks of Mount Stanley.

Semliki Valley, obtained photographs from the west side of a double-topped snow-peak which he rightly believed to be the highest in the range. Sir Harry Johnston, who believed that Kiyanja (the peak that we first ascended) was the highest peak, saw also from the Lower Mubuku Valley another twin-topped snow mountain to the north-east of Kiyanja, which he named Duwoni, and of which there is a beautiful illustration in his book.* Arrived at the head of the valley, he concluded that the peak, which rose to the right of the Mubuku glacier, was the Duwoni which he had seen from afar. Mr. Douglas Freshfield, who visited Ruwenzori in 1905, obtained a clear view of the range from a distance of about thirty miles to the east, whence he saw and identi fied the reverse of Dr. Stuhlmann's two-topped highest peak. He also saw from the Lower Mubuku Valley Sir H. H. Johnston's two-topped Duwoni, and concluded that it was one and the same thing with the high peak of Dr. Stuhlmann. Like Sir Harry Johnston, Mr. Freshfield also believed † that Duwoni was the peak which rose immediately above the Mubuku glacier on its north-east side. It was abundantly proved by the view which we obtained from Kiyanja that the two high snow-peaks seen to the north-west could not be identical with Duwoni, which lay to the north-east of Kiyanja, while at the same time we had no doubt that the

* 'Uganda Protectorate,' p. 158.
† *Alpine Journal*, vol. xxiii., p. 188.

two north-west peaks were those which Dr. Stuhlmann had photographed from the west side, and
that they must be the highest peaks in Ruwenzori.

  Our next course obviously was to climb the peak
on the north-east side of the Mubuku glacier, and
see whether it was actually the Duwoni of Sir
Harry Johnston.   But the exigencies of natural
history collecting kept us down at Bihunga, and it
was not until the supply of new birds and beasts
showed signs of running short that we were able,
several weeks later, to devote a few days to another
mountain excursion.   At the time of our second
journey up the valley the way was, if possible, in
even worse condition than it was before, and the
rock-shelters, not even excepting Bujongolo, made
no pretence of being anything else than sodden
water-holes.

  On April 1 Woosnam, Carruthers, and I set out
for the supposed Duwoni peak.   We followed
Herr Grauer's route until we came to the Mubuku
glacier, where, instead of taking to the glacier near
the top of the icefall, we turned off up the rocks to
the right, and, following a steep and unpleasantly
wet gully, came on to the southern ridge of our
peak.   Snow-covered slopes below the crest of the
ridge afforded easier going, and in rather less than
six hours from the start we came to a rocky point
about 100 feet high, up which we scrambled, and
stood on the top of the peak.*   Meantime, it is

* Now named Wollaston Peak, 15,286 feet.

A Native Hut near Lake Ruisamba.

To face page 102.

hardly necessary to remark, the clouds had been about us almost from the start. Another top* of the same mountain, apparently of the same height as ours, and about a quarter of a mile distant to the north, showed up once or twice, and we saw occasional glimpses down the valley to the east; but though we waited for three hours on the top, the clouds never broke for a moment towards the north-west and west, the directions in which we hoped to see the highest peaks, so that our labour was once more in vain. A heavy fall of snow, which melted as it fell, made the descent over the rocks difficult and dangerous, and the gully was converted into a rushing ice-cold torrent. Could anyone have seen us, we should have presented a sorry and bedraggled spectacle as we floundered with many a fall homeward through the swamps by candle-light that evening.

After a day of comparative rest, in which I find from my diary that I 'stayed in bed most of the day reading "Don Quixote," and trying to dodge the water that fell from the rocks above,' we made another expedition to Kiyanja, in the hope of obtaining a better view of the range than on the previous occasion. There was a great deal more snow than before, so much so that on the glacier near the top we sank to the knees at every step, and progress was accordingly very slow; but in other respects the conditions were the same as on

* Now named Moore Peak, 15,269 feet.

the day of our first ascent—that is to say, we were
enveloped in clouds all the time, and except for one
moment, when the true top of Kiyanja loomed hazily
through the fog, we saw no view whatever.

I have been asked why it was that on neither
occasion did we attempt to make the short ascent
that lay between us and the true top of our peak.
The answer is sufficiently obvious. For a party
equipped as we were with only a single ice-axe and a
piece of rope too short to be of the slightest use, and
numbering only one member who had any experience of ice and snow, to wander in dense fog along
an unknown ridge of an untrodden mountain, with
invisible slopes on either side, would have been
contrary to the truest principles of mountaineering,
and would have been only to court disaster.
Moreover, though we had, as a matter of fact,
ascended higher by several hundred feet than any
of our predecessors in Ruwenzori, and had been the
first to reach the watershed of the range above
the snow-line, we were not actuated by any lust of
establishing 'records.'

The conclusions that we drew from the occasional
and fragmentary glimpses which we obtained of
various portions of the range were in the main
accurate, and I should like here to correct a mis-
representation of them that was published in the
*Geographical Journal.** H.R.H. the Duke of the
Abruzzi, in his lecture before the Royal Geographical

* Vol. xxix., p. 131.

Society, says : ' Mr. Wollaston . . . informed me
of the existence of two snow-peaks higher than
Kiyanja, and north-west of it. He could not tell
me how these peaks were connected with Kiyanja,
confining himself to an opinion, which proved
erroneous, that they were situated west of the
watershed. This information contradicted that
which I had previously derived from Freshfield,
and left me uncertain as to how to reach the highest
peaks. Should we follow the Mubuku Valley, or
the Butagu Valley, on the Semliki side, which had
been taken by Stuhlmann ? If the highest peak
was, in fact, divided from Kiyanja by a deep valley,
and if the passes leading to it from the Mubuku
Valley were impracticable, how could we transport
our camp across the range ? , In this case the better
course might be to take the Butagu Valley. But to
reach the latter we must make a circuit round the
southern flank of the chain. . . . Of the two
alternatives, we chose that which involved the
shorter journey, to ascend the Mubuku, and de-
termine on the spot whether we must cross to the
Semliki side.' The opinion that I expressed was
not that the two high peaks were ' to the west of
the watershed '—it was exceedingly improbable that
such high peaks should be away from the watershed—but that they stood on the west side of the
range, and sloped steeply down into the Semliki
Valley. They are, as a matter of fact, the most
western peaks in the range. I said further that if

the party proposed to reach the highest peaks from the Mubuku Valley, they would probably find it necessary to cross the range by the low pass to the south of Kiyanja, and skirt the base of that mountain on the Semliki side, and that was exactly the route that the Duke's party followed.

Now that the peaks and glaciers of Ruwenzori have been explored and named (some of them for the third and fourth time), it is unlikely that the range will often be visited. Tourists, who go to Lake Victoria, will think twice before they venture on a three weeks' march across country; and if that be not enough, the atrocious climate, and the chance of seeing nothing when you get there, will keep away all but the most enthusiastic and determined mountaineers. Those climbers to whom the comforts of the club-hut or of the mountain hotel are a necessity will certainly be well advised to give a wide berth to Ruwenzori. Instead of creeping stealthily downstairs in the small hours to drink hot coffee, and start by lantern-light with well-laden guides over dry rocks or snow, in Ruwenzori you must rouse up your slumbering boys, coax a reluctant fire into sufficient life to thaw your unpalatable food, and then, laden with your various impedimenta, plunge into a morass, where you are wet through before you have gone 50 yards. I have often wondered in the Alps why one is fool enough to go stumbling over moraines by candle-light at one o'clock in the morning; but one goes on doing it, and hopes to continue doing it for many years to come. Floundering through Ruwenzori swamps is very much the same sort of thing, though far more disagreeable ; but I confess that if a chance occurred again of falling into one of those moss-covered mud-traps, or of being tripped up by a helichrysum, I would welcome it without a moment's hesitation. Fixed ropes and 'pitons' have not yet appeared in Ruwenzori, nor do I think that they are ever likely to, as the climbing is nowhere difficult ; the main difficulty lies in approaching the peaks. The empty sardine-tin and the broken bottle are still strangers in the land, and long may they continue to be so.

The attempts that we made to penetrate into the heart of the range were hopelessly handicapped, as I have suggested above, by lack of means and equipment. We were not in any sense a climbing party, and our excursions were made during the course of other occupations. A strong party, who could afford to take with them one or two European porters, ought to have no difficulty in making a complete survey of the range. They would have to 'rough it,' and forego most of the comforts of civilization for a time ; but the fascination of being in an almost unknown world, and the strange beauty of the scenery, would be more than compensation enough for the unpleasantness. There still remains a considerable amount of good exploring work to be done from the western valleys of the range and on the southern peaks, and it would be pleasant to hope that it may be done by Englishmen.

CHAPTER IX

THE PLAINS OF RUISAMBA

'A sudden little river crossed my path
   As unexpected as a serpent comes.
   No sluggish tide congenial to the glooms;
This, as it frothed by, might have been a bath
For the fiend's glowing hoof—to see the wrath
   Of its black eddy bespate with flakes and spumes.'
                              ROBERT BROWNING.

I HAVE never been in prison, so I do not know
what it feels like to come out again, but I can
imagine that the sensations of a liberated prisoner
are not very different from those that we felt on the
day we left Bihunga. During the last six weeks
that we were there, there were, perhaps, six more or
less fine days. At the best our horizon was not a
very wide one ; with the steep valley walls on either
side and a high ridge at our backs, there was only
one narrow gap, through which the distance could
be seen, but more often than not heavy rain
descended upon us from above and dense clouds
rolled up the valley at our feet, so that life became
gloomy and monotonous enough.

At the foot of the valley, instead of crossing the
Mubuku to its left bank, we turned off to the south-

east over a low spur, and after two or three miles'
walk we were practically clear of the mountains and
on comparatively level ground. The change was as
pleasant as it was striking and sudden. After
having been cooped up for months in a narrow
valley, where every step taken was a labour, to feel
the firm smooth ground under your feet again was
as delicious as is the first walk on shore after a long
sea voyage. To exchange forests and thickets and
elephant-grass for a broad plain covered with short
grass and scattered bushes was no small benefit, but
the greatest joy of all was to see a wide expanse of
sky once more. On every side, except on our
right, where the eastern ridges of Ruwenzori fell
steeply to the plain, the land was low and stretched
far away into a distant horizon, which gave one a
most exhilarating sense of freedom. Twenty miles
away to the south-east lay the glistening waters of
Lake Ruisamba, and beyond that was seen the
outline of the Ankole Hills. As an instance of the
extraordinary clearness of the atmosphere at that
season (April) I may mention that, on the day after
we came out from the Mubuku Valley, we saw most
distinctly one of the Mfumbiro volcanoes, which lie
to the south of Lake Albert Edward, fully
120 miles distant. A few weeks later, after the
beginning of the dry season, it was seldom possible
to see from one side to the other of Lake Ruisamba,
a distance of some ten or twelve miles.

As we approached the lake the land became

flatter and flatter, and finally a dead level extending for several miles on its northern side. This country reminded me most forcibly of the Fenland of East Anglia. The sedgy grass, the scattered bushes, the occasional water-holes, the distant hills, which were not unlike the hills about Newmarket, and the glorious vault of sky, made one think of Wicken or Burwell Fen; given a windmill or two and a distant church tower, the illusion would have been complete.

After a few days' march in a southerly direction, and crossing two rivers, the Nyamwamba and Mukoki, we halted and formed our second base-camp near a village called Muhokya.* We had intended to go on to the neighbourhood of Lake Albert Edward, but as there is a large tract of country in that direction without fresh water and where food is very difficult to obtain, it would have been unsuitable for a long stay. The last of the eastern streams of Ruwenzori comes down a pretty valley near Muhokya, and where it debouches on to the plain, there is a large area of cultivation supporting a very considerable population. These people resisted the advance of Captain Lugard a few years ago, so much so that his Maxim gun played an important part in their pacification; but though we found them less agreeable to deal with than other natives of Uganda, we had no real trouble with them. Their chief characteristics were corpulence, laziness, and a love of music, if the sound of

* Also called Mokya and Muhochi.

The Plains of Lake Ruisamba.

To face page 110.

drums may be called music. There was a rumour, whilst we were at Muhokya, that the Commissioner of Uganda was going to pass through the place, and the people were required to build a rest-house for his caravan. Sometimes there were as many as a hundred men 'at work' on the building. Their 'work' consisted chiefly in sitting on the ground and eating bananas to the tune of an everlasting drum, which continued night and day. The house had been in the hands of the builders for six weeks when we left the place, and was then about half finished.

The natives divert the waters from the stream in numerous small irrigation channels, and raise very fine crops of bananas and mealies on the rich alluvial soil. There are many square miles of land of a similar character to that near Muhokya, and if it were possible to conduct some of the waters of the Nyamwamba and other streams further north over the plain, it would become one of the richest districts in Uganda. This country has that curious park-like appearance which is characteristic of so many parts of Africa, notably about Lake Albert, Lake Albert Edward, Tanganyika, and parts of Nyassaland. Mr. J. E. S. Moore's theory* that it denotes a country, which is in a stage of transition between being submerged under water and being clothed with forest, seems to be the correct explanation. From our camp near Muhokya, which stood on

* 'To the Mountains of the Moon,' chap. xxiii.

rising ground, we could see it in its various stages from the papyrus belt surrounding Lake Ruisamba through broad meadows of salt grass, where only a few euphorbias grew, to thickets of euphorbia and acacias, then a more or less uniform wood of acacias with occasional euphorbias, and furthest of all from the water a dense forest of various trees growing in the sheltered valleys. About the middle of May the acacias began to flower, and in a couple of days the whole country-side was a mass of white-blossoming trees, which from a little distance looked exactly like hawthorns, and the air was laden with delicious scents.

Soon after we were settled at Muhokya we thought of calling upon our nearest neighbour, the Belgian in command of the Congo post Kasindi, at the north end of Lake Albert Edward, and incidentally of gathering information about the Semliki Valley and the west side of Ruwenzori, which we proposed to visit later. Accordingly, Woosnam and I set off early one morning in April by the light of a waning moon, and were already well on our way when the sun rose. A few miles from Muhokya we came to Kikarongo, a circular lake, once a crater, about half a mile wide. The water is slightly salt, and is greatly appreciated by the hippos, who come here in large parties from Lake Ruisamba to bathe. The lake is shallow for a few yards only, and then deepens rapidly, so the hippos, who do not like deep water, never go very far from the shore. On a still day it is an amusing pastime to sit by the lake and watch the great brutes enjoying themselves. For a moment nothing is to be seen, then suddenly a score or more of huge heads burst through the surface with loud snorts, and squirting jets of water through their nostrils. They stare round with their ugly little pig-like eyes, yawn prodigiously, showing a fearful array of tusks and a cavernous throat, and sink with a satisfied gurgle out of sight, to repeat the performance a minute or two afterwards. Sometimes one stands almost upright in the water, then he rolls over with a sounding splash, showing a broad expanse of back like a huge porpoise; or a too venturesome young bachelor approaches a select circle of veterans, who resent his intrusion and drive him away with roars and grunts. There is something irresistibly suggestive of humanity about their ungainly gambols, only bathing-machines are wanted to complete the picture.

Another remarkable feature of Kikarongo is the extraordinary quantity of fish it contains. For several yards from the shore the shallow water is a seething mass of small fish a few inches long, most of them in a dying condition, and the majority of them (from some cause that I was unable to discover) blind in one or both eyes. Mr. Scott Elliot, who visited the place in 1894, found a stream running into the lake;* but, though I walked

* 'A Naturalist in Mid-Africa,' p. 127.

round it twice, I could not find a trace of water flowing either into or out of the lake ; so it may be that the water, which was formerly fresh, is now becoming too salt for the fish, but it is impossible to say for certain. Whatever the cause may be, they are dying in tens of thousands, and their bones are piled in some places a foot high all round the lake, where they provide occupation for a host of marabouts and black and white crows. When a breeze is blowing, the wise man passes to windward of the lake.

Beyond Kikarongo the country opens out into a wide plain of short grass—that is, grass about waist high—and scattered euphorbias. On our right hand were the last dwindling spurs of Ruwenzori, and on our left, beyond the plains, lay the dark green papyrus swamps at the end of Ruisamba, and far beyond that again the rising hills of Ankole. On all sides of us were swarms of small antelopes, the commonest being Thomas' cob and reedbuck. The former is a graceful tawny creature with horns like a big gazelle and a conspicuous white throat. He strolls off quietly, and stares at us as we pass within fifty or sixty yards. The reedbuck is smaller, of a sandy-grey colour, and with short horns that curve forwards. He leaps up from the grass where he has been lying, dashes off in great bounds, almost turning somersaults as he goes, then stops short, turns round, and whistles shrilly at us. This is (or was at that time) a game reserve, so that the animals

A Bakcnjo Mother.

To face page 114.

are never molested, and they have little fear of mankind, though they see plenty of them in the native
porters, who come along this way bringing loads of
salt from Katwe to Toro.   Near Katwe, the last
village on the Uganda side of the boundary, are
some small salt lakes, separated by a short distance
only from Lake Albert Edward.   One of these lakes
is very rich in a good kind of salt, and is a large
source of revenue to Kasagama, the King of Toro.
We met several porters dawdling along with
their long packages of salt, stopping to rest under
every tree by the wayside, and whenever we asked
them how far it was to Katwe, it was always four
hours farther on.

   The sun was well overhead, beating fiercely down
upon us when we crossed the Equator, and the road
was monotonously long and straight, only swerving
here and there to avoid one of the many craters,
some filled with bushes and some with salt water,
that lie scattered over the land.   There was a bit of
rising ground away ahead of us, from which we
hoped to see the end of our journey; but it was
always a mile away, and it seemed as if we should
never overtake it: however, we reached it at last,
and all the weariness of the walk and the heat were
forgotten.

   Through a V-shaped gap in front of us there
gleamed a stretch of bluest water—our first view
of the Albert Edward Nyanza: it was like one's
first glimpse of the Atlantic down a coombe in

Cornwall. We went on a few yards and saw what must be by far the fairest view in Africa. At our feet lay the great blue lake, with its bays and islands and canoes, stretching for sixty miles into the southern haze. Beyond, out of the haze, towering up for 13,000 feet, rose the huge cones of the Mfumbiro volcanoes. On our right—that is, the west—the nameless blue mountains of the Nile and Congo water-parting sloped steeply into the lake. On our left flat lands by the lake-shore and a belt of forest gave way to range upon range of the hills of Ankole, where two racing thunderstorms threw black shadows on the brilliant distance. Behind us rose abruptly the mighty mass of Ruwenzori—not the topmost snows, which lay hidden far behind, but forest-covered heights and tremendous precipices, with two deep gorges hewn into the very heart of the mountain.

The few miles down a gentle slope to Katwe, with this glorious view constantly changing before us, were quickly covered, and we halted for a short time in the village near the lake-shore, looking in vain for some little shelter from the sun. The headman of the place and most of the population came out to greet us, and we asked them for bananas; but Katwe produces nothing but salt, so they could not help us beyond escorting us past the old British fort,* long since abandoned, and pointing out to us the track to Kasindi, which could be seen

* Fort George.

a few miles to the west. The heat down there was intense, beating down mercilessly from above and upwards from the sandy salt soil; indeed, Katwe has the reputation of being the hottest place in Uganda, which I can very well believe, and we were not a little glad when we found ourselves near our journey's end.

But here an unexpected difficulty confronted us. The little river Nyamkassam, which forms the boundary at present between Uganda and the Congo State, though usually fordable with ease, was that day swollen by some sudden storm in Ruwenzori, and had become a deep, rushing torrent. We searched the bank for a possible crossing, and made a considerable noise to attract the attention of some one on the opposite bank, until the white figure of the Belgian officer in command of the post appeared and shouted to us to come across. We splashed through the more or less shallow overflow until we came to the ordinary bed of the stream, ten yards or so of racing water, too deep to wade and far too swift for us to swim across. On the other bank stood the Belgian with his army of about forty rather ragged-looking scoundrels, but efficient enough soldiers, as we found out afterwards. He suggested our going round by the lake, which meant a walk of two hours more, or waiting until the waters subsided, which might have kept us where we were for a day, or perhaps a week. Neither of these proposals commended itself very strongly to us, so we asked for a rope, which was brought by the soldiers in fragments of various sizes and thrown across. Some of the army swam across higher up the stream and held on to our end of the rope, by which we passed across our guns, water-bottles, clothes, and other impedimenta—all, indeed, but our hats. Then I tried to follow in the same way, but a few yards from the bank the rope broke, and had not the military contingent at my end of it held on fast, I should have gone sailing down to Lake Albert Edward at twenty miles an hour. After that it was better to follow Woosnam's more prudent example and swim across higher up, where the river was wider but not quite so swift, though swift enough for a moderate swimmer. We emerged on the Congo bank dripping and blushing under our sun-helmets, and introduced ourselves to Lieutenant B——, of the Belgian regiment of Grenadiers, clad in a spotless white uniform. He looked astonished enough at the sight of his strange visitors—we heard afterwards that our mysterious appearance was known all over the Congo—but instead of locking us up as suspicious persons, he took us in and entertained us most hospitably.

The post of Kasindi looked, like so many of the Congo posts, a very temporary affair—very different from the substantial British posts in Uganda. But Lieutenant B——'s quarters were a haven of refuge to us that day. A bottle of champagne, supplied to the Congo posts as 'medical comforts,' was found and opened, and we spent a most cheerful evening with our host, who even surrendered to us his easy-chair and his bed—about the greatest sacrifices a man can make in those climates. 'Reveille,' admirably sounded by a black bugler, roused us at dawn, and we were soon on our twenty-five mile walk back to Muhokya, taking with us a most kindly recollection of Congo hospitality.

A curious feature of the Ruisamba country is a number of deep ravines leading from the valleys in the hills above, down into the plain below. To judge from their steep sides and tortuous course, they can only have been formed by water ; but though we arrived there before the dry season had set in, there was never a sign of running water in any one of them. It would be interesting to know if they were formerly the beds of streams which have disappeared through a change of climate, or, if not, what is the cause of their present dried-up condition. They are now filled with a very dense vegetation, including several flowering trees and creepers, which we found afterwards on the edge of the Congo forest, and they were one of my most profitable hunting-grounds for butterflies. In the pursuit of butterflies in these ravines, there was always a chance of stumbling unawares upon a sleeping leopard or a buffalo, but I was lucky in never meeting either of them ; an angry bark and a scuffling in the undergrowth would sometimes make me look out for the nearest climbable tree, but it was never anything more dangerous than an agitated bush-buck. When two of the party were out shooting one day one of them shot a partridge, which fell within a few feet of an unseen buffalo. Instead of charging, as is the unpleasant habit of buffaloes, the great brute was as much astonished as they were, and had the grace to retire, or the numbers of the expedition might have been seriously diminished.

The Ruisamba plains seemed to us, who had been so long in the mountains, to be excessively hot, and as the land became parched with the dry season, the heat grew more intense ; but it was saved from becoming oppressive by the almost daily thunderstorms, which hardly ever failed us. In the early afternoon we could generally see two or three storms scudding across the plain from the east, their course marked by a whisp of rain-cloud, and a dark line of waving grass and trees. Soon we could hear one rushing through the plantations below, and in a minute it would be upon us with a burst of wind, which threatened to carry the tents and everything bodily away, and then came a deluge of rain, which meant hurriedly slackening the tent-ropes to prevent them from straining the pegs out of the ground. In ten minutes or a quarter of an hour the storm had passed, the rain dried up in an incredibly short time, and we could look forward to a calm evening in which to pursue our various occupations of shooting small birds for the collection, or partridges and guinea-fowl for the pot, or of catching moths by lamplight. The skies of mid-Africa are an unending joy, not less by night than by day. I have seen as many as seven thunderstorms going on at once, and I can hardly recall a single night when there was not a flicker of lightning to be seen low down over some part of the horizon.

There are two birds, which will live in my memory long after I have forgotten everything else about Muhokya. One is the Bateleur Eagle, which may be called the first-class cruiser among birds ; for power and swiftness of flight there is none that can compare with it. With its long wings and curious stunted tail it looks more like a huge bat than a bird as it sails high overhead, never flapping its wings, but giving just an occasional tilt from one side to the other. One moment it is here and the next it is a speck almost out of sight across the plain. The other is a very remarkable species of Nightjar,* in which some of the feathers of the wing, particularly the second primary, are enormously lengthened : the longest that was measured had a length of 21 inches. These birds sleep during the day in warm places on the hill-sides until sunset, when they fly down to the low ground about the lake. The long feathers trailing out like streamers behind them give the birds a most unnatural appearance, as if they had four wings ; but though one would expect the long feathers to be rather an encumbrance than other-

* *Cosmetornis vexillarius.*

wise when the bird is chasing insects, it can turn and twist in flight as quickly as a peewit.

Although we were so close to Ruisamba, we did not explore the lake very much, chiefly on account of the extraordinary discomfort of the native canoes, which are very small dug-outs and hardly capable of holding more than one person. It would be worth while to take a collapsible boat to Ruisamba, and explore the lake carefully from end to end, and navigate the river between it and Lake Albert Edward—a thing which, I believe, has never yet been done. On its west side the lake is surrounded by a dense barrier of papyrus, through which the natives have cut narrow tunnels to the open water for their canoes. The people live almost exclusively by fishing, and the fish that they sometimes brought us were the best that we got from any of the great lakes.

About the end of May there came a message from Mr. Knowles, the Sub-Commissioner, inviting us to go to Toro to meet the Duke of the Abruzzi, who was expected to arrive there on his way to Ruwenzori. Some of the party were away shooting in the Semliki Valley, so it fell out that I was the only member of the expedition available to accept the invitation. The necessity of walking along a blazing hot and thirsty road for sixty miles and back again might have been welcomed as an excuse for declining in another country, where society was plentiful ; but after several months of camp life one

A Group of Bakonjo Porters.

To face page 122.

would readily have walked as far or farther to meet even a less interesting personage than the distinguished Italian explorer. The Duke arrived at Toro on May 29, and was greeted by the whole population, including King Kasagama and his private band of musicians, who produced some of the most blood-curdling discords I have ever had the misfortune to hear. The other members of the expedition and the caravan of 400 porters, 'boys,' and escort, strolled in at intervals throughout the day. On the following day all the Europeans in the place, seventeen in all, counting the Italians, assembled to meet the Duke. Ladies on bicycles from the English mission, and men in clerical collars, looked strangely out of place in those surroundings; the French Fathers certainly had the advantage of them in their long white robes. The two Italian guides, Pettigax and Ollier, were a good deal astonished to find in so remote a place an European, who could talk to them about their own mountains and valleys. I met them again at Courmayeur last summer, and spent a delightful week climbing with Ollier, who never tired of talking about Africa and Ruwenzori. The expedition had seen a perfectly clear view of the whole range from Butiti* the day before they arrived at Toro, and had distinctly identified Dr. Stuhlmann's two-topped peak as the highest in the range; but, not being able to judge from that distance how far

* About eighteen miles east of Toro.

to the west that peak really was, the Duke was still inclined to the opinion that it was the same as Johnston's Duwoni. We had many conversations on the subject, but I think he was still a little sceptical, though very much interested, about the view which we had seen from Kiyanja.

The expedition stayed for three days at Toro, and started for Ruwenzori on June 1. I travelled with them until the following day, when they turned off into the mountains at Butanuka.

During the following weeks of fine weather, when we were still quite close to Ruwenzori, I confess to having felt many a bitter pang of envy. I used to walk almost daily to a spot from which I could see the snows and wished myself among them ; but the mountains were in the best possible hands, and the completely successful result of the Duke of the Abruzzi's expedition is now a matter of history.

Without making any invidious comparisons, it may be remarked that, if the Colonial Administration had spared a tenth part of the assistance, which they lavished on the Italian expedition, to make smooth the way for an expedition sent out by a department of their own Government, we should have been grateful. Though the local causes are of course different, it is the same spirit, which in India prompts us to assist the expeditions of foreigners, who wish to explore the high mountain regions about Thibet, while at the same time refusing permission to our own countrymen.

CHAPTER X

THE SEMLIKI VALLEY

' Son of the old Moon mountains African!
Stream of the Pyramid and Crocodile!
*   *   *   *   *
'Tis ignorance that makes a barren waste
Of all beyond itself.   Thou dost bedew
Green rushes like our rivers, and dost taste
The pleasant sunrise.   Green isles hast thou too,
And to the sea as happily dost haste.'

KEATS

IT may be open to doubt whether travelling in Africa has an altogether good effect on one's character, but at all events you can hardly fail to acquire the virtue of patience. Those happy people (or are they not really unhappy?) whose lives are determined by the legal or academical term, or by the daily nine o'clock train, would suffer many a rude shock in a country, where ' sasa ' (now) may possibly mean to-day or to-morrow, where you are lucky if the promises for ' kaishu ' (to-morrow) are fulfilled within a month, and where the place that is said to be ' mbali kidogo' (a little way off) is anything from twenty to a hundred miles distant.

Our experience in getting away from Muhokya was in no way exceptional. We had intended to

stay there for perhaps a month on our way round to
the west side of Ruwenzori, but means and men,
provisions and permission to travel, had tarried by
the way, and it wanted but a few days of three
months before we eventually quitted the place. A
few matches applied to the grass walls of our houses
completed the work of the white ants, which had
devoured all but the merest shell of the supporting
framework of poles, and in five minutes there was
nothing to bear witness to our long occupation of
the camp. Instead of following the level but very
roundabout route, which we had taken before by
Kikarongo and Katwe, we struck almost due westward across the hills, the southern outliers of
Ruwenzori, which separate the plains of Ruisamba
from those about the Semliki Valley. From the
summit of the hills a very striking and, at the same
time, instructive view was seen of Lake Ruisamba,
and of its connexion with the Albert Edward
Nyanza. For some reason best known to themselves, the people, who at different times have made
maps of this region, have represented Ruisamba as
merely a great backwater of Lake Albert Edward,
connected with the north-east corner of the latter
lake by a short but narrow strait. As a matter of fact,
Ruisamba is nothing of the kind, but a totally distinct
lake, whose waters flow into Lake Albert Edward
by a large river some ten miles long, which winds
at first through a flat marshy country and afterwards
between steep and rugged banks. Another curious

error which persists about the lake is the name Ruisamba, which is quite unknown to any of the inhabitants of its shores : they call it variously Dweru, Kafuru, and Bulima in its different parts, but never Ruisamba. However, it has, like Ruwenzori, a pleasing sound, and may well be adopted.

A steep descent through a partly cultivated country on the farther side of the hills brought us down to the level plains, which lie between the waters of the Nyanza on the south and the heights of Ruwenzori on the north, and are only separated from the plains of the Semliki Valley by one low ridge—a long south-westerly spur of Ruwenzori. This district is one to which a considerable import-ance attaches at the present moment, by reason of the fact that the ownership of it is uncertain. When this part of Central Africa was divided up, the thirtieth parallel of longitude was taken as the boundary between Uganda and the Congo Free State. Thus Uganda claimed the east and part of the north shore of Lake Albert Edward (in-cluding Katwe and its valuable salt lake), nearly the whole of Ruwenzori, and the Lower Semliki Valley ; while the west side of the Nyanza and the Upper Semliki Valley were recognized as a part of the Congo Free State. Unfortunately, a more recent and more accurate survey has discovered that the thirtieth parallel actually lies some ten or twelve miles to the east of where it was formerly thought to be.   Consequently, if we abide by our agreement, we give up to the Congo Free State the whole of our share of Lake Albert Edward and almost the whole of Ruwenzori.   It is very much to be regretted that so excellent a natural feature as the main ridge of Ruwenzori, or, better still, the Semliki River, was not selected as the boundary in the first instance.   An artificial boundary, such as one following a parallel of longitude, besides being expensive in its construction and maintenance, must inevitably come into conflict with native customs and tribal distributions, and would be an endless source of annoyance.   The salt lake at Katwe, to which the King of Toro has an ancient title, would be cut off from his dominions, and that would almost certainly lead to trouble and complications.   If the Semliki River were taken as the frontier, we should lose a certain amount of territory on its left bank near Lake Albert; but the gain in the ease of administration would more than compensate for the loss. In any case (but this savours, perhaps, too much of the jingo mountaineer!) it is to be hoped that after having lost Kilimanjaro to the more successful diplomacy of the Germans, we shall succeed in keeping the Mountains of the Moon within the British Empire.

The temporary boundary between the two States is the little River Nyamkassam, which flows from Ruwenzori into the north end of Lake Albert Edward —the same stream which we had found overflowing

Scene at a Funeral, Semliki.

To face page 128.

its banks three months previously. On this occasion the water was low, though very cold (some of its springs rise very high up in Ruwenzori), and our caravan crossed without any difficulty. The Belgian post of Kasindi, which was before on the river bank, had been moved a few miles farther west on to higher ground near the Lubilia River, a much more suitable place for a permanent post. Arrived there, we were met by an unexpected difficulty. The natives in the Semliki Valley, which we must traverse in order to approach Ruwenzori from the west side, had recently been indulging in raids, and had attacked one or two caravans, and the Belgian officer at Kasindi decided that we must not start without an escort. There were not soldiers enough in the post for any to be spared on escort duty, and there seemed to be every chance of our experiencing the usual delay of weeks before anything could be done; but for once good fortune came our way in the shape of a Belgian *sous-officier* and a dozen native soldiers *en route* for Fort Beni, in the Semliki Valley.

The Belgians have constructed a road down the Semliki Valley from Lake Albert Edward to Fort Beni, and thence through the forest to the Aruwimi district; but whatever it may have been at the time when it was first made, we found it in a state of the most miserable disrepair, due partly to neglect and partly to the destructive habits of elephants. From Kasindi a few hours' march in a north-westerly direction took us over a low ridge to Karimi, in the Semliki Valley, where there was formerly a Congo post, but now the only relics of their occupation are the long lines of papye-trees which the Belgians always plant about their houses. The papye (called elsewhere papaw, pawpaw, and papoia), which grows in most tropical countries, bears a fruit that has many of the good qualities of the melon and the apricot combined, the only fruit (to my mind) that is worth eating in Central Africa. They are good in Uganda, better in the Congo, and best of all in the Semliki Valley.

In this upper part of its course the Semliki is a clear stream, seventy or eighty yards wide, running between low banks fringed with tall reeds, at a ràte of about three miles an hour. It reminded me at once of the Ouse between Huntingdon and St. Ives. We stopped for a day at Karimi, waiting for our escort and a supply of food for our porters; and while some of the party occupied themselves with fishing in the river, others took advantage of the permission, which the Congo authorities had most generously given us, to shoot big game in a reserved district. Records of African big-game shooting may be, and, if the truth must be told, often have been, records of indiscriminate slaughter. Fortunately for our sportsmanlike instincts, the beasts in the Semliki Valley were wary and not too numerous, so that Carruthers and I had a hard day's work in making our bag of two cobus and one water-buck. I do not think I am more bloodthirsty than the ordinary mortal, possibly I may be even less so, but I confess to feeling a thrill of exultant satisfaction when a successful shot has crowned a long stalk, in which one has crawled and wriggled to find concealment behind a tuft of grass, or, standing up, has tried to assume the air and appearance of an acacia-tree. In the course of my first stalk I came across a family hunting-party of half a dozen meerkats—charming little creatures like mongooses, with stripes across their backs. They stood bolt upright on their hind legs to get a good view of me, and were as much interested in me as I was in them. Needless to say, they distracted all attention from the object of the chase, a big water-buck, which caught sight of me and departed, showing a less confiding interest in humanity than did the meerkats. However, a successor to him was found not far distant, and I soon experienced the joy of my first 'head'; the thought of it is treasured with the memories of my first trout and my first snow mountain.

From Karimi a long day's march brought us to the Lumi River, the first considerable tributary that the Semliki receives from the west of Ruwenzori. Here the officer of our escort took most elaborate precautions to guard against a night attack, which he felt confident would be made upon us. He informed us that a few weeks previously he had been attacked there at night by some five hundred natives, and that with eleven soldiers he had repulsed them with a loss of forty-six killed. He showed us a small hole in the river bank, the grave (so he said) of the forty-six, so there could be no doubt whatever of the truth of his story! The survivors did not come to avenge their dead that night, and except for the challenge of a sentry when a wandering water-buck came too close to the camp, we slept in peace at the Lumi River.

To the north of the Lumi River the character of the country changes somewhat; the acacias diminish in number, and tall borassus palms are conspicuous. The gentle undulations of the Upper Semliki Valley become steep hills with rocky slopes, not unlike parts of Unyoro, with streams in the valleys bordered with strips of forest, outliers of the great Congo Forest. After twelve or fifteen miles we descended again into the valley, crossed the Semliki in big dug-out canoes to its left bank, and climbed up a steep slope to the Belgian post, Fort Beni, where we were greeted by our friend Lieutenant B——, and were installed in a comfortable brick house, which seemed almost palatial after our cramped quarters of the last few months. Fort Beni was established about twelve years ago as an eastern frontier post of the Congo State, and it was expected that it would become a place of some importance; but the unruly habits of the natives who live between it and the nearest Congo waters have never been cured, and with the establishment of the new posts at Irumu in the Ituri district and at Rutshuru to the south, Beni has taken a secondary place. There is a garrison of about a hundred native soldiers, drilled and trained by a Belgian *sous-officier* under the command of one officer, who at the same time fills the offices of chief of the post, magistrate of the district, priest (for the purpose of marriages and funerals), doctor, and all the other multifarious parts which a white man fills in Africa. The post is well laid out with wide roads planted with avenues of papies, lemons, and guavas. There is a good garden, which provides vegetables for the officers' table, and a large plantation of castor-oil plants, which provide fuel for their lamps and medicine for the soldiers' children. The natives have been taught to make exceedingly good bricks, of which the officers' houses, stores, and soldiers' quarters have been built.

Standing as it does some three hundred feet above the Semliki, Fort Beni commands a fine view across the valley towards Ruwenzori, of the open country in the direction of Lake Albert Edward, and of the great forest to the north and west. The Semliki Valley may be roughly divided into three parts of more or less equal length. Starting from its outlet from Lake Albert Edward, it runs for some forty miles or more through a fairly level country of grass and scattered trees. Near Fort Beni it enters a more hilly country, whose irregularities cause occasional falls and rapids, and at the same time it enters the forest, a continuation of the

great Congo Forest, which overflows, so to speak,
the Congo-Nile watershed and extends eastward as
far as Ruwenzori.   After passing through the forest,
the Semliki flows through country like that about its
first part; this becomes flatter and more treeless as
Lake Albert is approached, until the river finally
loses itself in the vast papyrus swamps at the head of
that lake.   The Semliki Valley is in no place of very
great width.   To the east it is bounded throughout
the greater part of its length by the long ridge of
Ruwenzori, from which it is never many miles
distant, while farther north its eastern limit is formed
by the Lake Albert escarpment.   Its western
boundary is made by the steep mountains which
flank the west side of Lake Albert Edward, and
then, as they run northwards, dwindle rapidly into
the low hills of Mboga, which form the almost im-
perceptible water-parting of the Nile and Congo.
From its left side the Semliki receives no tributaries
of any importance, while from the right there flow
into it several large mountain torrents which drain
the slopes of Ruwenzori.   The highest peak of
Ruwenzori cannot be more than from fifteen to
twenty miles east of Fort Beni, but though we
stayed there for ten days we only saw the mountains
once, and then but for a few minutes; they seemed
to rise to an incredible height, and looked like a
phantom range looming through the morning mists.
Though our view was but short, there was time
enough to identify with certainty the highest peaks,

To face page 134.

The Semliki River, near Fort Beni.

and to verify the existence of the discredited 'Saddle Mountain.'*

A few miles to the north of Beni, after it enters the forest, the Semliki runs through some broken, hilly country, which interrupts the placid course of the stream and forms a series of magnificent rapids. Guided by the thunder of the water, which can be heard at a distance of many miles, we wandered by devious tracks through the forest, and after burrowing through a tunnel in the dense undergrowth, at length came out at a spot where the whole volume of the river plunged headlong over huge boulders through a channel which was in some places not ten yards wide. It is presumably owing to these rapids that crocodiles, which swarm in the Lower Semliki and in Lake Albert, do not ascend higher. They are not found at Fort Beni, where some of our party used to bathe daily in the river, to the great delight of the populace, and they are absent from Lake Albert Edward.

There is a large population and a wide area of cultivation along the edge of the forest. There are many indications of the forest having extended in

---

* Viewed from Beni, Mount Speke is seen a little to the north of Mount Stanley, and it presents very much the appearance of a great saddle. There can be no doubt that this is what the earlier Belgian travellers, who saw Ruwenzori from the west side, described as 'Saddle Mountain.' Later explorers thought that the Belgians referred to the highest peak (Mount Stanley), and concluded that 'Saddle Mountain' was non-existent.

recent times a great distance farther to the south than it does at present. Every year, as the land outside the forest becomes exhausted, more trees are cut down, and fresh clearings are made, and so slowly but surely the forest is encroached upon and dwindles. The villages at the edge of the forest are usually small—ten or a dozen huts at the most, arranged often in the form of a square, enclosing an open space, which is commonly used for drying maize and millet and other kinds of food. One side of the square is often occupied by the club-house, which is larger than the other huts, and built upon unthatched walls, so that the gossips inside the club have a clear view of all that goes on outside. In the club-houses the men-folk of the village seem to spend a good deal of their time ; tobacco and pipes are kept for the use of the community, and there is usually a pot of food simmering on the undying fire. In some of these houses we found luxurious seats made of reeds, constructed almost exactly on the model of a kind of garden-seat commonly seen in England. But the more usual form of chair is made of a straight piece of wood, which breaks into three branches at one end (see illustration, p. 144). The black possessor of one of these easy-chairs is a proud man, and he often succeeds in looking comfortable when he reclines upon it, but to the European anatomy the chair is a source of grief and pain.

After coming from Uganda, where the natives are not allowed to carry weapons, it was strange to us to see all the people going about armed. The majority of them carried spears, while a good many carried a short bamboo bow and a quiver full of arrows made of reeds pointed with curiously fashioned tips of metal. The tedium of our delay at Beni was enlivened (if it may be said without disrespect to the departed) by the death of Kilongozi, the big chief of the district. Many of his vassals had assembled several days before in anticipation of his death, and as soon as the event was announced it was greeted with a chorus of shrieks and wails, which resounded throughout the country, and continued, with brief intervals, for several days.

The chief was buried beneath the floor of his house, about which his subjects, to the number of more than a thousand, congregated in a dense throng. During the first day they were fairly quiet, and contented themselves with dancing slowly to the tune of the inevitable drums and with firing off guns at intervals. On the following days, inspired by the 'pombe,' which they drank in immense quantities, they were rather more boisterous in their grief. The women, and some of the men, attired themselves in a sort of very short ballet-dancer's skirt made of banana leaves, in which they performed some very quaint and intricate dances. Sometimes the women would stand aside, and the crowd of men, dividing into two opposite parties, would perform a war-dance or mimic battle, shrieking and howling like lunatics. Fortunately, etiquette forbids the wearing of spears and knives at a funeral, and harmless reeds were carried instead, or there might have been accidents. There were hundreds of drums and trumpets of ivory or antelopes' horns and whistles of various sorts in the crowd, and the deafening din which they produced was still in progress when we left Beni.

CHAPTER XI

' Speak as they please, what does the mountain care?
  Ah, but a man's reach should exceed his grasp,
  Or what's a heaven for? All is silver-grey
  Placid and perfect with my art: the worse!
  I know both what I want and what might gain,
  And yet how profitless to know, to sigh
  " Had I been two, another and myself,
  Our head would have o'erlooked the world!" No doubt.'
                        ROBERT BROWNING.

IT is easy to be wise after the event, and to point
out the weak spot in a scheme which has been tried
and found wanting. We protested against being
accompanied by an escort on our expedition to the
west side of Ruwenzori; but Lieutenant B——
insisted on the necessity of it, and we submitted
with a good grace. The Belgians claim in theory
to administer the left-bank of the Semliki right up
to Ruwenzori; but in practice their control stops
with the river, beyond which they never venture,
except to travel along the road by which we had
come from Lake Albert Edward. The natives
inhabiting the east bank of the river and the west
slopes of Ruwenzori are, in the Belgian phrase,
' *révoltés* '—that is to say, they refuse to recognize

139

the authority of, or to work for, the State. It is not improbable that the few exploring or semi-military expeditions, which had passed through their country in the last twenty years, had treated the natives with more harshness than consideration ; but, whatever the cause, the present attitude of the natives toward black soldiery is that of the bull to the proverbial red rag. The responsibility for this deplorable state of things rests with the Belgians, who are content to tolerate the existence of a warlike and hostile race living within a few miles of a garrisoned post, which they have occupied for years. With regard to our expedition, they ought either to have allowed us to go to Ruwenzori as a perfectly peaceable party without any escort, or they ought not to have allowed us to go at all. Personally I feel sure that, had they followed the first of these two courses, we should not have had any trouble with the natives, but we were not given the chance of putting it to the test : *hinc illæ lacrimæ.*

After less than the usual period of delay—about a week—we set out with our escort of thirty black soldiers, commanded by a Belgian *sous-officier*, and about one hundred of our Toro porters, of whom more than sixty were laden with food for themselves and their companions. The mere fact that it was necessary to carry food for our people augured ill, considering that we were on our way to a thickly populated and (presumably) cultivated country. From the river our course lay almost due east, a

The Semlıkı Rapids.

To face page 140.

direction which corresponds almost exactly with the line of the edge of the great forest. A wave, so to speak, of the great Congo-Semliki Forest, thirty or more miles wide, flows across the Semliki Valley towards Ruwenzori, becoming narrower as it approaches the mountains, and for a few miles flows up the slopes and becomes continuous with the mountain forest. Near the river the population is very scanty, and the few huts which we passed were deserted; but as we came closer to the mountains the land looked more fertile, and the population was correspondingly greater. The sight of our armed and uniformed guard was too much for the unhappy people, who fled from their villages and collected in crowds on the hill-tops, where they waved their spears and shouted defiance from a safe distance. In one village they seemed disposed to dispute our passage, but a couple of shots fired over their heads sent them off to join their fellows on the high ground. It was rather disconcerting to see one gentleman, not a dozen yards from me, taking a careful aim with bow and arrow; luckily I saw him before his preparations were complete, and he disappeared like a shadow in the long grass.

Arrived near the foot-hills of Ruwenzori, we camped in the only available open space in the forest that could be found, which happened to be a field of ripening beans. The inhabitants of the neighbouring huts had all fled, with the exception of an aged man and woman, who were promptly secured by the Belgian with halters round their necks, for no apparent reason that we could elicit from him. These miserable old people travelled with us for a day or two, and were then liberated. That night at the bean-camp was memorable for one of the heaviest thunderstorms I can remember, accompanied by a deluge of rain, and for the nocturnal attentions of the natives. So soon as it became dark, there began a chorus of yells and a symphony (or rather a kakophony) performed on drums and whistles and war-horns, which lasted at intervals until daylight. Now they were on one side of the camp and now on another, and often so close that they must have been within a few yards of the sentries; but the darkness was so intense that it was impossible to see them, and the rain so damped their ardour that they did not summon up courage enough to attack us. It was not a very propitious beginning to an expedition which had designs on the lives and liberties of nothing bigger than birds and butterflies.

The point for which we were aiming was the valley of the Butagu, the river which drains the waters from the highest peaks of Ruwenzori, and is the biggest river on the west side of the range. Owing to an error, we went too far to the north and crossed the Russirubi,* another big stream whose valley has never yet been explored. Though we

* So called in Dr. Stuhlmann's map. The natives, whom we questioned, called the river 'Paka.'

lost two valuable days in so doing, we were able to define very clearly the exact boundary of the great Semliki forest, and to see how, a little farther north of the Russirubi, it became continuous with the mountain forest. The foot-hills of Ruwenzori on the west side descend almost as abruptly into the level plain as do the walls of the valley of the Rhone above its entrance into the Lake of Geneva, and the mountain valleys open in as modest and un-assuming a manner there as they do in Switzerland.

Turning south towards the Butagu Valley, we passed for hours through magnificent banana 'shambas,' which could be seen extending for miles along the foot of the hills and out into the plain. Many of these shambas had been long neglected, and had run wild, and their extent was obviously far in excess of the needs of the present population. It was difficult to account for the diminution in the numbers of the people, unless it was a result of the raids, which the Manyuema from the Congo and the Kings of Toro and Unyoro from our own territory used to make into the Semliki Valley, but those are supposed to have ceased many years ago. We induced a few people to come down from the hills and talk to us ; but they were very shy, and, con-sidering our military display, they can hardly be blamed for not believing that we had the peaceable intentions which we claimed to have. Our next performance was quite enough to convince them to the contrary, and to put an end to any hopes which we might have had of making friends with them. At an altitude of about 6,000 feet in the Butagu Valley we came to a small cluster of huts on fairly level ground, where we decided to camp. Surrounding the huts was a small banana shamba, and outside that some cleared ground which would have made an excellent camping-ground; but in spite of protests more forcible than polite, our chief of escort cut down the bananas, which he said might shelter an enemy, and camped among the huts, which his soldiers naturally looted. Needless to say, the inhabitants had all fled, except one small child, who was taken on up the valley as guide! On the following day we climbed up by almost invisible tracks through the forest, which clothes the right (north) side of the Butagu Valley, to Kakalongo (7,100 feet), where there were a few scattered huts and a good deal of cultivation. It was manifestly out of the question to try and take our whole caravan higher than this point, so it was decided to make a camp there for as long a time as our food-supply would last. The slaughter by the escort of the only cow in the valley, in mistake (so they said) for a buffalo, was another incident which no doubt aggravated the hostility of the natives towards us.

The Butagu Valley is V-shaped and exceedingly steep-sided, the left bank especially being almost precipitous, so that there is hardly any vegetation growing upon it; while on the north side, which is

A Chief in his Easy-Chair.

To face page 144.

less steep, there is dense tropical forest up to about 7,000 feet, of a character similar to that which grows at a rather higher level in the Mubuku Valley. Bamboos are found at about 7,200 feet—that is considerably lower than on the east side of the range—and tree-heaths also begin at a lower level; indeed, so far as we could judge in the very limited time that we were able to spend in the Butagu Valley, it would seem that all the zones of vegetation are at a lower level than on the east side of the range, and from the appearance of the vegetation and the number of constantly flowing streams it may be concluded that the rainfall is heavier than it is in the Mubuku Valley. But these very interesting questions can only be decided by the man who has the good fortune to spend a quiet time on the west side of Ruwenzori.

A short distance above Kakalongo the Butagu River is formed by the junction of three torrents. Of these, the most southern brings the water from the west slopes of Mount Luigi di Savoia and from the south side of Mount Stanley; the middle stream (Wussussa) drains the western slopes of the highest peaks (Mount Stanley); and the more northern stream (Butagu) comes down from the western outliers of the last-named mountain. In the lower part of their course these valleys are exceedingly deep, and are separated from each other by steep, knife-edged ridges.

After spending a day or two in making a camp

and putting up shelters for our porters, we sent away our chief of the escort and half of his men with instructions to return in ten days or a fortnight, and Carruthers and I, with a few porters and three soldiers to cut a track, set out for the highest part of the valley. Following, probably, the same route as that taken by Dr. Stuhlmann, we ascended by the ridge between the Butagu and the Wussussa. Though there are no huts higher than our camp at Kakalongo, we found a vestige of a track leading up the crest of the ridge, used, no doubt, by the natives on their hyrax-hunting expeditions. The forest came to an abrupt end at about 7,500 feet, and the bamboos about 1,000 feet higher, after which we entered on the heath zone, which continued as far as the highest point that we reached. The heaths were mostly in flower, and the air was filled with their scent mixed with the faint pinewood scent of podocarpus. High up among the heaths we found a curious relic of some former European traveller in the shape of fragments of a pair of breeches; they were of unmistakably English origin, but whose they can have been I have been unable to discover.

At a height of 10,400 feet we found a tolerable camping-place in a small depression on the ridge. Looking down the valley, we saw a magnificent view of the forest and the broad Semliki Valley and the distant Congo hills fifty or sixty miles to the west. Behind us towered ridge after ridge, and now and again through the clouds we caught a glimpse of one snow-peak and then of another. Though the season was getting late (it was August 3), the weather seemed to promise fairly, and we had high hopes of climbing those slopes of snow, where no white man had ever yet set foot, or, if that were not possible, we would in any case bring back photographs of extraordinary interest.

Watching a glorious crimson sunset, the first clear view to the west that we had had for many months, we were beginning to think that life was really worth living, and that there were worse places in the world than Ruwenzori, when fate descended upon us—or, more correctly, ascended to us—in the form of an anxious messenger from the camp below. The Belgian, in descending the valley, had been attacked by a large horde of natives, many of them armed with guns, and, having lost one man killed and five wounded, had retreated up the valley again to our camp, where he said it was no longer safe to remain, so we had no choice but to rejoin the rest of the party. To be compelled to turn back at the last moment, when we were within a few hours' march of our goal, was one of the most cruel pieces of ill-luck I have ever known, and I confess to having been very near the shedding of bitter tears of disappointment. Whilst an enormous Jupiter sank into the west, the full moon sailed up over the now clear snow-peaks into a sky of regal splendour, and, with better fortune, we should have been as happy as ever we were in our lives.

At dawn we scrambled up to a little above 11,000 feet, in the hope of getting a good view of the mountains ; but the clouds were already down upon them, and we turned sadly downhill to the turmoil of the camp at Kakalongo, where there were bullets to be sought for and cuts to be bandaged. One wretched fellow had two bullets in one of his lungs, and a long iron slug had gone clean through the body of another ; but though we could not do much for them until we arrived at Beni, four days later, both of them eventually recovered. It appeared that the Belgian and his party had walked un-suspecting into an ambush close to the village, where the banana shamba had been destroyed a few days earlier. In the long grass and dense under-growth it had been impossible to estimate the number of the enemy—the Belgian said he thought there were at least sixty guns, but that was probably a great exaggeration — so it was decided that discretion was the better part of valour, and a rapid retreat was made.

Our descent of the valley, hampered as we were with the wounded men carried in hammocks, and retarded by the careful skirmishing of scouts in front and on either side, was made at the pace of the slowest funeral procession, and soon it became one in fact, for we picked up the body of the soldier who had been killed the day before. His right hand had been hacked off, and is doubtless treasured somewhere as a trophy of victorious battle. As our caravan crept slowly downhill there was ample time to look back up the valley to the snow-peaks, which on that day, the day when we should have been upon them, remained unclouded for hours after the time when they were usually hidden. They seemed to be flouting us, and to be adding insult to injury, but I registered a vow that I would return to them again.

There followed three days of extremely unpleasant travelling—most of the way, in fact, it was a sort of running fight. Even the extremity of fear will not prevent a black man from loitering if he can possibly do so, and our caravan of 150 was generally straggling along a length of half a mile or more. The paths that we followed (often the wrong ones, as we had no guides) were the merest tunnels through elephant-grass and dense jungle, and if the hostile natives had had any sort of method in their attacks, they could have cut us to pieces at their leisure. Fortunately for us they contented themselves with lurking in the grass and hurling spears or shooting their little arrows when they saw a chance. Some of them, I am sorry to say, paid the penalty for their boldness, but though several of our people were hit, none were seriously injured. Two wounds made by poisoned arrows were promptly sucked, and healed up without any trouble.

Although the natives made such a poor show, it was very irritating to hear them shouting and blowing their horns close by in the bush and not to see them nor know where the next spear or arrow was coming from. And they kept up this hideous concert by night, too, which seriously interfered with sleep. Our advanced guard became quite weary of seeing so little of their enemy, so they fired volleys in the direction of every sound that they heard. Once it happened to be at a poor old elephant which was crashing about in the grass ; luckily their shooting was not very good, and the Albini rifle is not a very deadly weapon, so the animal escaped. Our miserable porters, brought from peaceful Toro into this barbarous land, were gibbering with terror most of the time. Our wounded suffered such mishandling during those days as would have killed a white man a dozen times over. The corpse of the mutilated soldier, which his comrades insisted on taking home for burial, after being carried under a blazing sun for three days, became a member of the caravan which can better be imagined than described, so that there was not one of us who was not glad enough to see the broad waters of the Semliki again, and the houses of Fort Beni upon the hill beyond.

From information which we obtained at Beni, we learnt that the misdirected attentions which we received from the Ruwenzori natives were due to the machinations of a certain Kengele, the biggest chief in the Semliki Valley, who has always been an evilly disposed person. If he is not his

In the Butagu Valley, Ruwenzori, West.

Dracænas and Wild Bananas, Ruwenzori, West.

To face page 150.

son, he is the same Tenge-Tenge whose people interrupted the expedition of Mr. Scott Elliot several years previously; and it is an interesting and note-worthy fact that, before that date, a German camp was for a long time established in his dominions. A few weeks after our departure from Beni, Lieutenant B—— and another officer set out on a punitive expedition against these people, and we were glad to hear that Kengele made a graceful and (it is to be hoped) lasting submission to the State without the shedding of any blood.

After stopping at Beni for a few days, which were variously occupied with a funeral, some surgery, and a very pleasant meeting with Major and Mrs. Powell-Cotton, who had just emerged from the Congo Forest after six months' okapi-hunting, we set our faces northwards on our rather roundabout way back to Uganda. There was formerly a fairly good road through the forest north from Fort Beni to the Ituri River, but now, owing to the attitude of the '*révoltés*' natives, it has gone out of use, and owing to the action of elephants and buffaloes, which swarm in this part of the forest, it has gone sadly out of repair. The beasts were there in such numbers that in some places the air was full of the strong and bitter odour, which one associates with the elephants' house at the Zoo. The path was pounded and churned into a sort of red cream by the feet of the monsters, and every tree-stump was polished bright and smooth, where they had scratched their huge sides, or, nearer the ground, where the buffaloes had rubbed their horns. Although there are so many—you see the bushes swaying and hear them crashing away perhaps within a few yards of you, and hear them trumpeting at night—the beasts themselves are very seldom seen.

It was in this part of the forest that the okapi was first discovered a few years ago, and it is probable that they are more plentiful, or, to be more accurate, less scarce, in the Semliki and Ituri Forests than elsewhere. Travelling in haste as we were, we had not the remotest chance of seeing one; indeed, it seems very doubtful whether any European has yet seen, much less shot, an okapi in the wild state. A Congo official informed me positively that he had shot three, but his detailed accounts of the big horns (!) of one of them showed how little faith can be placed in such statements, and probably most okapi-hunting stories are equally valueless. The okapi is an excessively shy animal, and it inhabits the densest parts of the forest, where it is impossible for a white man, move he never so silently, to approach the animal without being first seen or heard. The Pygmies, who can climb trees like a squirrel and can pass through the thickest jungle without disturbing a twig, shoot them occasionally with spears or arrows, and occasionally catch them in traps, and it is through them that most of the okapis now in Europe have

been obtained. Anyone who is anxious to procure
a specimen of this strange creature must obtain first
a special permission from the Congo Government,
and, secondly, the friendship of a tribe of Pygmies;
the latter can best be managed by a liberal offering
of salt, their most valued necessary. With reasonable luck and the exercise of patience, he might
be expected to get an okapi within a few months'
time.

The Pygmies live almost exclusively by hunting;
they grow no crops, and they do not manufacture
their bows and spears, which they obtain in exchange
for game from the other inhabitants of the forest,
who also supply them with bananas and other
produce. They have no settled dwellings, but each
tribe or family seems to have a definite hunting
district, whose bounds they never transgress; they
sleep wherever they happen to be, and we were
constantly coming across their tracks and their little
shelters, the flimsiest structures of sticks thatched
with leaves. The first Pygmy that I met greeted
me with a shout of 'Bonzoo, Bwana (sir)'; he
had been for a time in a Congo post, and 'Bonzoo'
was his version of 'Bon jour.' He was a cheerful
little person, about four feet high, and he shook
hands effusively; his was one of the most perfectly
shaped hands I have seen, but cold and clammy,
as the hands of most black men are. Now that
some of his cousins, brothers perhaps, have toured
about England and have been exhibited in music-

halls, the appearance of Pygmies is doubtless familiar to every one, and it need hardly be remarked that even in the Congo they have not all yet learnt to speak French.

The path is nearly always as bad as can be— often it is nothing but a succession of fallen trees and muddy elephant-baths ; but there is a subtle fascination about walking through the forest, which increases as the days go by. The best way to feel the forest is to walk far ahead or, as I lazily preferred to do, miles behind the caravan, far beyond the sound of a disturbing gunshot, or of the un-ceasing chatter of the porters. Sometimes there is a sound of crashing through the trees, where a herd of elephants have been disturbed in their siesta ; sometimes a troop of monkeys dash twit-tering through the tree-tops, or huge topheavy-looking hornbills fly overhead screaming uncouth discords ; but more often the silence of the forest is unbroken and complete, and you may walk for miles at a time and not hear a sound or see a sign of living creature. It may be only a result of the half-gloom and one's sense of smallness amid the vast surroundings, or it may be an instinct inherited from prehistoric forest-dwelling ancestors ; but whatever the cause may be, you find yourself walking with unwonted care, and ever on the alert for an unknown something.

It was only in the infrequent clearings, where we camped, that we realized how immense, compared

Baamba Natives, Semliki Forest.

To face page 154.

with our insignificant tents, the trees of the forest are; as a rule, their height is greater in proportion to their girth than is the case with an ash or an elm. The forest is seldom level; it is always gently rising or falling, as much one way as another, and it was not until we found one day that the streams were no longer flowing to our right into the Semliki that we realized that we had crossed the watershed into the basin of the Congo.

Wandering on, day after day, through the forest, one began to wonder, 'Shall we come out of it all some day, as one does from a tunnel?' and our coming out of it was almost as sudden as that. Without any warning, except that for a mile or so the trees had become perhaps a little smaller, the forest ended abruptly, and we found ourselves on the edge of an open hilly grass country that stretched as far as we could see to east and north.

A few miles beyond the forest is the Belgian post of Irumu, on the Ituri River, a swift-flowing cocoa-coloured stream as big as the Semliki. If one of its hundreds of tributaries was as big as this, we could but wonder what the Congo must be before it reached the sea. Irumu is a place of some importance by being on the main route from Uganda to the Congo; large quantities of supplies brought up by the Uganda Railway enter the Congo Free State from that side, notably machinery and mining apparatus for the gold-mines at Kilo, which lies three or four days' journey to the north. We tried to get information about the said gold-mines, but it was a subject about which the Belgian officials were discreetly and mysteriously uncommunicative. Urgent reasons prevented us from stopping in the Ituri Valley, and in a few days we found ourselves descending steep slopes into the Semliki Valley, not many miles from Lake Albert, and we were once more in British territory.

CHAPTER XII

' Celui qui tient la tête est un vieux chef. Son corps
    Est gercé comme un tronc que le temps ronge et mine ;
    Sa tête est comme un roc, et l'arc de son échine
  Se voûte puissamment à ses moindres efforts.

' Sans ralentir jamais et sans hâter sa marche,
    Il guide au but certain ses compagnons poudreux ;
    Et creusant par derrière un sillon sablonneux,
  Les pèlerins massifs suivent leur patriarche.'

LECONTE DE LISLE.

As in the beginning of its course, so again, where
it approaches Lake Albert, the Semliki flows
through wide plains of grass well populated with
game. The forests which clothe the northern end
of Ruwenzori are inhabited by huge herds of
elephants, which descend into the plains to feed on
the grass grown green after the rains, and to wallow
in the river. There is a curious protective resemblance between elephants and the large candelabra
euphorbias that are so characteristic a feature of the
plains. From a distance it is almost impossible to
detect an elephant standing still in a clump of these
trees, and I have often mistaken one for the other.

At the present time, when the international

boundary is so vaguely defined, there is a good deal of illicit trading between the two States ; some of the rubber and ivory of the Congo Free State leaks out on this side into Uganda, and no doubt dutiable goods find their way back in exchange.   It is obviously impossible to station customs officers at every point where a path crosses the frontier, even if the frontier itself were accurately defined, and the result is that neither State takes very urgent steps to prevent smuggling through this district—a state of things which is a most powerful argument in favour of adopting the Semliki River as the boundary.

After crossing the Semliki Valley, we climbed up the steep escarpment, down which I had looked some eight months earlier, and on arriving at Toro the British Museum Expedition came to an end, after having made the complete tour of Ruwenzori. Woosnam and Dent remained in the Toro district for a few weeks, and then made a straight journey to the West Coast.   Leaving Toro on October 8, they crossed into the Congo State to Irumu, thence through the forest by the direct road to Avakubi, on the Aruwimi River, which they descended in canoes to Basoko, where the Aruwimi joins the main stream of the Congo.   Thence they took steamer down the river, and reached the coast on December 2.   If three weeks, the time required to reach Toro from Mombasa, be added to this time, it will be seen that by following the direct routes and not halting by

Pygmies, Ituri Forest.

Pygmies, Ituri Forest.

To face page 158.

the way, it is possible to cross the continent from Mombasa to the mouth of the Congo in less than eighty days.

Legge, Carruthers, and I made a hasty dash across Uganda to Entebbe, where we arrived early in September, in time to enable Legge to catch a quick boat back from the coast to England. The clean deck and the smell of the engines of the Lake steamer, with the certainty of being in England in three weeks' time, caused us a momentary longing to be speedily quit of Africa and 'safaris'; but the distant prospect of the ocean steamer from the West Coast, even though it was at least seven months ahead of us, was more alluring still, and we set ourselves to the business of preparing for our long journey.

It was a very remarkable fact that nobody in Uganda seemed to have the least knowledge of the Congo State, or of the conditions of travel in that country. It is not to be expected that people living in England should know where Lake Tchad or Tanganyika are, but it was rather startling to find people in Uganda, whose idea of the Congo was that it started in Lake Albert Edward and flowed through Tanganyika on its way to the sea! The meagre scraps of information that we gleaned were mostly contradictory and almost invariably wrong, so we were forced to rely on our own judgment, and luckily we did not make any very serious mistakes. The greatest difficulty that we found was in calculating the necessary amount of cloth and beads to be taken as porters' wages, and payment for food in the Congo. Starting from a known number of loads of stores and equipment, you reckon the amount of beads and cloth which will be required to pay for its transport. The beads and cloth, being heavy, require a certain number of porters to carry them ; the porters require more beads and cloth, which necessitates the hiring of more porters, and so, on the principle of ' big fleas and lesser fleas,' *ad infinitum.*

The nicely calculated less or more resolved itself at length into a small caravan of forty porters, and we started from Entebbe on our long homeward way in the middle of September. Travelling south-west through the province of Buddu, we were within sight of the Victoria Nyanza for several days, and crossed several streams flowing into the lake. Near the Katonga River, which is really a very considerable river, but so much overgrown with papyrus that it was hardly to be recognized as a stream, we were for almost the only time during all our wanderings seriously worried by mosquitoes ; not content with preying upon us at night, they followed and fed upon us in broad daylight—a thing, fortunately, very rare with mosquitoes.

The province of Buddu is famous for its bark cloth, which is made from the bark of a species of fig-tree. In some places the sound of hammering may be heard coming from almost every house in a village. At the Government post of Masaka the brick walls of the fort enclose a garden of roses, which is a most pleasant little paradise in the wilderness. A very notable feature of the road through this district is the immense amount of traffic which passes along it. Every day we met scores, sometimes hundreds, of natives bearing huge loads of cotton or bark cloth, or skins of goats or cattle, on their way to Entebbe or Kampala. It is inconceivable that the natives of Uganda, as their education progresses and their prosperity increases, will be content to be always no more than beasts of burden. The supply of porters is limited and decreasing, and this form of transport is bound eventually to disappear. It is very much to be hoped that, before many years have elapsed, a system of light railways will be spreading over Uganda ; and not the least important among them will be a line to carry the rich produce from Ankole and Buddu to a point on the Victoria Nyanza, and another line connecting Toro and the south of Lake Albert with Entebbe.

As we approached Ankole, the Southern Province of Uganda, the country altered very markedly in appearance. We had left behind us the forests and swamps of the Victoria Nyanza region, and had entered an upland region of short grass and rolling hills, a true cattle country. Although the general level of Ankole is only about 5,000 feet above the sea—little more than 1,000 feet higher than the

Victoria Nyanza—the difference in the climate suggests a much greater difference of altitude. The air is dry and cool, and it may be safely predicted that, if any part of Uganda is destined ever to become the permanent home of Europeans, it will be Ankole

At Mbarara, the capital of the province, we found Mr. Knowles, the Sub-Commissioner, recovering from an almost incredibly narrow escape from death. Alone in his house one day he had been struck by a flash of lightning, which burnt him severely, fused a steel chain in one of his pockets, and ought to have killed him instantaneously. He was rendered un-conscious by the shock of the flash, which at the same time set the house in a blaze, and he was only dragged out by his boys just in time to escape an untimely cremation. Thunderstorms are, per-haps, the most dangerous feature of life in Uganda ; in some districts they occur almost daily, and are responsible for many deaths.

All the open spaces of Mbarara were crowded with herds of cattle when we arrived there, which made the place look like a gigantic cattle fair. The beasts were not brought for sale, but as payment of a fine imposed by the Government on that part of the province in which the murder of Mr. Galt had taken place the year before. The cattle of Ankole are famous for their gigantic size and for their horns, which grow to a prodigious length. Many of the chiefs are exceedingly wealthy people, and

own as many as forty or fifty thousand head of cattle. The ruling class in Ankole, the Wahima, are a pastoral people, who are supposed to have come from the North in not very remote times. Many of them are exceedingly good-looking, and have features which recall those of the Fellaheen of Lower Egypt. The King of Ankole, though quite a young man, is in height, and in every other dimension, the biggest man I have ever seen.

Going west from Mbarara we were accompanied by an escort of twenty police, not because the population of Western Ankole was hostile (we found them perfectly friendly), but because our route lay through the disputed territory between Uganda and the Congo Free State. The two Governments had agreed to leave the country severely alone, and to forbid expeditions to pass through it until the frontier had been settled; but we obtained a special dispensation from the authorities, as we were travelling for scientific purposes. It might be remarked that our own people kept most loyally to the agreement, but the same thing cannot be said of the other side. A large tract of country to the east of Lake Albert Edward, which was formerly regarded as being British territory, was in the occupation of a Belgian 'surveying expedition,' which required for its protection a hundred black soldiers, not to mention innumerable armed 'messengers,' who wandered about the country for one reason or another. The survey beacons on the top of every hill, which looked like boundary marks, and the presence of a large armed force in their country, naturally made the natives think that their country had changed hands, and we were regarded somewhat as intruders.

The descent from the highlands of Ankole into the basin of the Albert Edward Nyanza is as sudden and as steep as is the Lake Albert escarpment farther north. From a place called Kichwamba, the last village in the hills, there is a superb view across Lake Ruisamba to Ruwenzori, and of the whole extent of Lake Albert Edward, with the Mfumbiro volcanoes to the south. Near Kichwamba is a series of small lakes filling extinct craters; their steep sides are covered, some with forest and some with shambas, and the water of all of them is of the deepest blue I have ever seen. In the branches of quite a small tree which overhung the water of one of the lakes was sitting a party of pelicans— a habit of theirs which I do not remember having seen elsewhere.

Between the hills and the north-east end of the Nyanza is a plain, about ten miles wide, of acacia woods and long grass of great fertility, if one may judge from the fatness of the great herds of cattle which feed there. The plain is also the home of great numbers of antelopes, especially water-buck, which are remarkable, like the cattle, for the exceptional length of their horns. A specimen which I shot there is pronounced by Mr. Rowland Ward to be a 'record.'

The water from Lake Ruisamba flows into the Nyanza by a large river, about 200 yards wide, near the village of Kazinga, where we halted for a few days, and had a practical experience of the present unsatisfactory state of the country. The local chief, who had been until recently a subject of the Uganda Protectorate, captured and ill-treated some of our porters. I at once sent off half a dozen of our police, who brought him back artistically tied with ropes, and looking very sulky. He complained that he had been deserted by the Uganda Government, and, not unreasonably perhaps, that he did not know to what country he really did belong. In spite of his protests that he liked Englishmen and was anxious to remain under our rule, I found him a few days later taking presents to the Congo authorities on the other side of the lake. When he had been assured that it was only owing to my extreme good-nature that he was not sent a prisoner to Mbarara, he departed, and returned presently with a peace-offering of three fat goats. One of these goats was such a magnificent animal that we could never make up our minds to kill him; and he travelled with us for four months until we reached the Congo, where we left him in the care of the commandant to improve the breed of goats at Kasongo.

Kazinga stands on rising ground above the lake, and is a particularly unpleasant place, without any shelter from the fierce heat of the sun or protectior from the almost daily hurricanes, which sweep west-wards across the lake. I shall never forget one of these storms, which interrupted the course of our dinner one night. Without a moment's warning all the porters' and askaris' tents disappeared from off the face of the earth, and ours would have followed suit but for the prompt action of the askaris, who supported the poles inside and held on to every rope outside, until the storm ceased as suddenly as it began. A tremendous downpour of rain swelled the ranks of the inside pole-supporters, until there were so many people in the tent that it could not possibly have been blown down. Our beds were reduced to swamps and dinner was a failure, but we were lucky to have kept a roof over our heads.

Another unpleasant feature of our stay at Kazinga, as well as at other places on Lake Albert Edward, was the swarms of small grey flies, which emerge from the lake in immense clouds, and smother everything that they come near ; they put out your feeble candles, fill your food, and get into your lungs, so that you almost wish for a storm to drown or drive them away.

What with storms and flies and ill-mannered chiefs, we were not sorry when we were able to send back our escort to Mbarara, cross the river, and move round to the north end of the lake, and so leave Uganda for the last time.

That part of the Congo Free State which lies

immediately to the north of Lake Albert Edward
is a game reserve, and, at the time when we were
there, it was the haunt of great herds of antelopes
and elephants. From our camp upon a hill a few
miles from the lake, we saw one day a herd of
forty or fifty elephants marching abreast in a long
line across the plain towards the lake. I followed
as quickly as possible along the broad road that
they had made—it looked as if fifty steam-rollers
had been over the ground—and tracked them to
a belt of trees growing in a swamp near the lake-
shore. I climbed up into one of the trees to leeward
of the herd, and found myself within fifty or sixty
yards of the elephants, which were all packed
together within a space hardly bigger than a lawn-
tennis court. For a moment it looked like a mass
of black rocks with something loose waving about
over it; then it became possible to identify the
backs of the monsters, and to see their enormous
ears slowly flapping backwards and forwards. Sometimes one would lift up his trunk and scour his back
with a huge jet of mud and water, and sometimes
one on the outside of the herd would twist off a
branch from a tree and trample upon it. Once I
caught a glimpse of a young one playfully butting
its parent in the ribs, and being sternly rebuked
with a dig of a long tusk. It might be supposed
that one could hardly fail to see an elephant at
a distance of less than forty yards, but I had been
there for some time before I noticed a solitary old

bull apart from the rest. He was standing absolutely motionless under a tree facing towards me, and he looked exactly like a dark shadow. In spite of the thorns, with which that tree was profusely and most painfully armed, I stayed in it for an hour or more, fascinated by one of the most interesting sights it is possible to imagine—a veritable prehistoric peep.

In this connexion I might record another but less pleasant interview which we had with elephants. We were staying for a day or two in a Congo post, the name of which need not, for obvious reasons, be mentioned, when a herd of elephants was reported to be close by. I went off at once to see them, accompanied by the Belgian officer in charge of the post, who took with him a rifle 'in case of accidents' (he said). No sooner had we come within sight of them than he opened fire on the herd, and blazed away quite indiscriminately at the unfortunate beasts. There must have been more than fifty of them, and between a mad European firing at them on one side, and on the other a crowd of natives who were yelling at them and trying to drive them away from their plantations, the elephants became perfectly bewildered, and stampeded backwards and forwards between the two lines of attack. How many of them were wounded it would be impossible to say: I saw three being helped to escape by their companions, who closed round them, and one was left dead on the battlefield, when the

Water-Buck (*Cobus defassa*). Albert Edward Nyanza.

To face page 168

ammunition was at last exhausted. It was a revolting business altogether ; but even that was not the end of it, as later in the day two wounded elephants were seen wandering about not far from the post, and Carruthers and I went out and put an end to them. Not the least noteworthy feature of this incident was the fact that it took place in a part of the State in which it is forbidden to shoot game of any description at any period of the year, and, in theory at least, no Congo official is ever allowed to shoot an elephant.

With the wholesale importation of firearms and the construction of roads and railways and telegraph lines, the fate of the African elephant is sealed. Though there are still immense numbers in some remote districts, there are larger areas from which they have quite disappeared. It is to be hoped that, either in British or Congo territory, a tract of country will be proclaimed a sanctuary for elephants, where they may breed undisturbed and contribute to the future wonderment of mankind. But otherwise, brutal though it may sound, the sooner they become extinct the better ; they are exceedingly dangerous animals, they do untold damage to crops of every kind, and the traffic in ivory seems to be inseparable from cruelty and a good deal of very questionable dealing.

The Congo Government kindly lent us their steel whaleboat, in which we made the voyage to the south side of Lake Albert Edward ; it was a good deal more comfortable than the native canoes, which are made of rough planks loosely sewn together with strings of banana fibre, and are consequently very leaky. The Nyanza is about seventy miles long, with an average width of about twenty-five miles. Propulsion by long bamboo poles meant following every curve of the coast-line, and our progress was not very rapid, but in a country where nobody is in any hurry two or three days more or less are a matter of no moment.

The Belgians have instituted an excellent system of rest-houses down the west side of Lake Albert Edward. At intervals of a day's canoe journey— that is, from ten to twenty miles—they have built good mud-houses in a cleared space near the shore, and round some of them they have even made a garden, where tomatoes and sweet-potatoes are grown for the use of travellers. There is a custodian, generally an ex-soldier, in charge of the place, and he keeps a flock of sheep and goats, one of which a State official is entitled to take in case of necessity. The inhabitants of the village, if there happens to be one near by, are required to provide water and firewood for passing travellers, and to carry their baggage between the canoes and the camp. Travellers are few and far between, so this tax, which they pay in labour to the State, cannot be called very oppressive.

After crossing the outlet of the Semliki, which is inconspicuous and might easily be overlooked if

attention were not drawn to it by the great herd
of hippos which always guard it, we passed down
the west side of the lake. Mountains 3,000 or
4,000 feet high slope abruptly to the lake, so
steeply that it is only in a very few places that
there is any space for cultivation on the lake-shore.

From one of our camping-places we saw a
wonderful view of the highest peaks of Ruwenzori in
the far distance to the north :

> '. . . far off, three mountain-tops,
> Three silent pinnacles of aged snow,
> Stood sunset-flush'd.'

It was a view not to be forgotten—our last glimpse
of the range—and it was some small compensation
for the ungenerous way in which we had been
treated before by Ruwenzori.

CHAPTER XIII

THE MFUMBIRO VOLCANOES

' At my departure I had won his confidence enough to beg his advice how I might carry myself there without offence of others or of mine own conscience. " *Signor Arrigo mio*," says he, " *I pensieri stretti ed il viso sciolto* will go safely over the whole world." Of which Delphian oracle (for so I have found it) your judgment doth need no commentary.'—SIR HENRY WOTTON.

THE range of mountains which bounds the western banks of Lake Albert Edward runs almost directly north and south, and in the latter direction forms the western wall of the great Central African trough, in which Lakes Kivu and Tanganyika lie. As we approached the south end of Lake Albert Edward, we found the shore-line trending away towards the south-east, and the character of the country becoming more like that of the east side of the lake. The shore is low and flat, and the water exceedingly shallow ; sand-banks are seen miles out in the lake, covered with countless thousands of gulls and pelicans and wading birds, and hippos abound everywhere. Along the water's edge is a barrier of papyrus and yellow-flowering ambatch-trees, in the branches of which are perched egrets

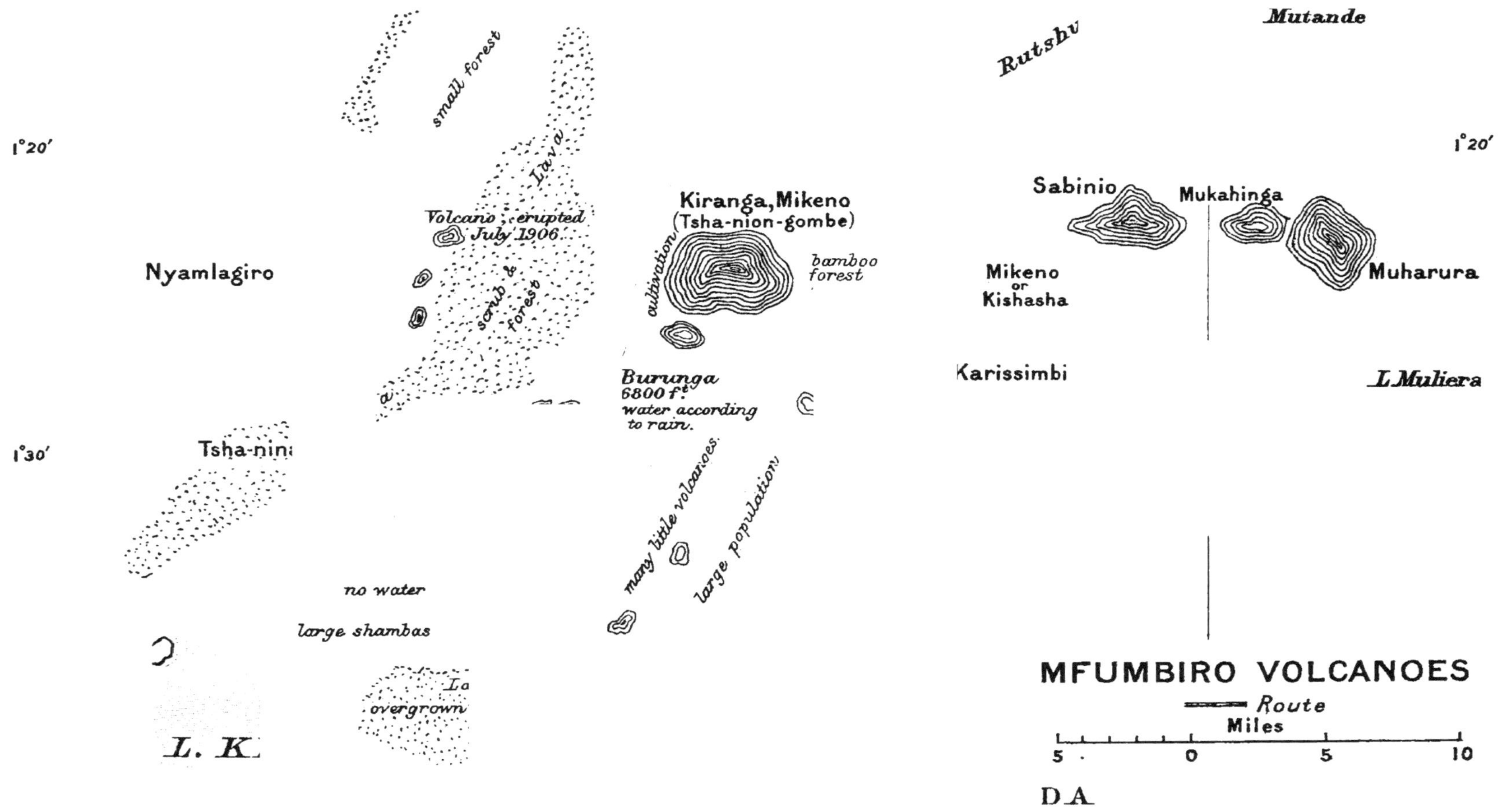

MFUMBIRO VOLCANOES

Route
Miles

5 · 0 5 10

D.A.

Mutande

Rutshv

Sabinio   Mukahinga   Muharura

Mikeno
or
Kishasha

Karissimbi

L.Muliera

1°20'

bamboo
forest

Kiranga, Mikeno
(Tsha-nion-gombe)

cultivation

Burunga
6800 ft.
water according
to rain.

many little volcanoes   large population.

Nyamlagiro

Lava

small forest

Volcano erupted
July 1906.

scrub & forest

Tsha-nini

no water

large shambas

overgrown

L. K.

1°20'

1°30'

and herons and little bitterns, and cormorants with their wings spread out to dry in the sun, and darters sitting disdainfully with their chins in the air.

Beyond this swampy barrier is a rolling plain of short dry grass, where antelopes are almost as numerous, though there is not so great a variety of species, as on the Athi Plains of British East Africa. One of the commonest is the topi, or Senegal hartebeeste,* an ungainly red beast with sloping shoulders and a long, serious face. I was stalking one of these animals one day when I disturbed three wart-hogs, the first I had ever seen. The wart-hog is the most grotesque-looking beast that lives, with a facial expression like those of the bull-dog and the hippopotamus combined, and an absurd little tail with a short tuft of hair at the end, which stands straight upright like a little flag when the animal runs. The sight of them as they trotted away caused me such merrimentt hat the topi owed his life to those three wart-hogs.

Another antelope, which is very common on the Albert Edward Plains is the reedbuck, which was often a welcome addition to our larder. It is not difficult to approach a reedbuck on open ground, but where the grass is long the animal progresses by a series of prodigious bounds, and trying to hit one is about as easy as potting at a tennis-ball with a pea-shooter.

The few inhabitants of the district seem to be

* *Damaliscus corrigum.*

almost wholly a water-side people, who live entirely by fishing. At the south-east corner of the lake are some curious colonies of lake-dwellers whose huts are built several yards from the shore, with the object, presumably, of escaping the attack of the lions, which are always in attendance on large herds of game. At Vichumbi, a small village at the extreme south end of the lake, our camp was surrounded by a high reed-fence for the same purpose, and only a few days before we arrived there a man, who incautiously went outside the fence after dark, had been carried off and eaten.

We had intended to stop for a few days at Vichumbi to shoot some antelopes and visit the villages of the lake-dwellers, but in that we had reckoned without the spirillum.* There is a species of tick (*Ornithodoros moubata*), a frequenter of native houses and old camping-places, which carries in its blood a micro-organism called *Spirochæta duttoni*. When it is introduced into the blood of a man by the bite of one of these ticks, the spirochæta is the cause of a particularly unpleasant relapsing fever. An ordinary attack lasts for two or three days, and recurs again after an interval of a week or more ; in severe cases the attacks may be continued for months. Hitherto no satisfactory remedy has been discovered for the fever, and all that can be done is to take steps to avoid being bitten by the tick. There are some districts in

* See Appendix.

Albert Edward Nyanza, West Shore.

To face page 174.

which the fever is so prevalent that it is difficult to induce porters to travel through them. It is useless to tell them that if they sleep in the old shelters they will get fever ; they smile indulgently but incredulously at the crazy European, and unless they are turned out of the old shelters and compelled to make new ones, tick-bites and spirillum fever are the speedy results. The Uganda Government has ordered the destruction of the camp shelters along the roads in the worst infected districts, and it is hoped that in this way the disease will be kept within bounds.

In spite òf all our precautions, Carruthers and I fell victims to it and to malaria, and our designs upon the big game near Vichumbi were frustrated. It was bad enough to be fever-stricken both at the same moment, but when our ' boys ' succumbed too, and we had no one to do anything for us, we were in a poor way indeed. Those ten days were a perfect nightmare, and the few recollections that I have of Vichumbi are among the least pleasant that remain of our time in Africa. If one of us was slightly better one day, the other was sure to be worse, and there seemed to be every chance of our remaining at Vichumbi for the rest of our natural lives ; so a change of climate was decided on, and we had hammocks made and ourselves carried slowly and uncomfortably away from the pestilential spot.

It was a very grievous disappointment to us to

be compelled to pass through that most interesting country without seeing anything of it. The waters of the Rutchuru River, where we crossed it a few miles above the lake, were most distinctly warm from receiving some hot springs a little higher up its course. No doubt there were beautiful views of the volcanoes which we were approaching, but a temperature of 103° is enough to make one disregard utterly even the most wonderful scenery; and my only recollection of the country is of a monotonous jogging up and down for seven or eight hours a day, my feet often higher than my head, when, as they preferred to do, the tallest porters took the front end of the pole, and often a sudden bump on to the ground when they stopped to eat or rest.

Ascending steadily all the time, we arrived in three days at the Belgian post of Rutchuru (altitude about 5,000 feet). The officers at the post had heard that there were two Englishmen in the district, and when they saw the slow approach of our caravan they thought that their hospitality to us was going to begin and end with giving us a funeral. They told us afterwards that they hardly altered their opinion when they saw us emerge from our hammocks; but they welcomed us most kindly, installed us under a weather-tight roof, and did everything that was possible to restore us to health.

Rutchuru was only recently established as a Congo post, and it now ranks as one of the most important stations on the eastern frontier of the State. It stands on high ground above the right bank of the Rutchuru River, between Lake Albert Edward and the Mfumbiro volcanoes. From the post a magnificent view can be seen of the volcanoes lying between the east and south-west. They are eight in number, and they are all visible from Rutchuru. The nearest is about seven miles distant, and Tsha-nina-gongo, the only one which exhibits signs of great activity at present, lies about twenty miles to the south-west.

The climate of Rutchuru, considering the altitude of the place and the fact that it is far removed from swamps and mosquitoes, ought to be healthy enough, but our convalescence proceeded very slowly, and Belgians who had spent long periods there all told us that the place had a bad effect upon them. If this was not merely a coincidence—if there is really something inherent in the climate which is prejudicial to the health of Europeans—it disqualifies a large tract of country which many sanguine people have marked out as a place for future colonists. Many European flowers and vegetables, sunflowers, artichokes, and potatoes, flourish exceedingly at Rutchuru, and for several months in the year strawberries bear fruit. Luckily for us, we arrived during the strawberry season, and I think they contributed as much as anything else to our recovery ; they were pale and pleasantly acid, and about the size of Alpine strawberries.

An excellent institution of the Belgians are the herds of cattle, which are attached to every post in the State except those in districts where cattle are unable to live either on account of lack of grass (in the densely forested regions) or by reason of cattle disease.   They have taught their native dairymen to make an excellent kind of cream-cheese and very passable butter, and the daily supply of fresh milk to the posts contributes not a little to the well-being of the white officials.   The grass about Rutchuru was poor, and the supply of milk was very meagre, and it says much for the hospitality of our hosts that for several days (unknown to us) they sent the whole of their supply of milk for our use.

Next to the volcanoes the most notable feature of Rutchuru are its lions.   Almost every night we heard them roaring and grunting near the post, and in the morning we often found their round footprints within a few yards of our house in the middle of the station.   When, later on, we dined with the officials, we were escorted from the mess to our house by an armed guard.   I am not at all sure that the loaded rifles behind us were not really a greater source of danger than the possible lions watching us in the darkness, but fortunately no accidents happened from either source.   Though we heard very many lions in different places, we never happened to see one.   They are chiefly nocturnal in their habits, and the country where they live is usually so

The Mfumbiro Volcanoes, from the North.

To face page 178.

densely clothed with grass or scrub that, unless you go out with the express purpose of hunting them, the chances are very much against catching a glimpse of a lion at all. In cultivated districts, so far from being a source of public danger, lions may be looked upon as the friend of the agriculturist. Like the tigers in some parts of India, their favourite food is the wild pigs and small antelopes which play such havoc among the crops, and their complete extermination would not prove to be by any means an unmixed blessing. It is only very rarely that men are attacked by them ; of course, if a man is foolish enough to walk about after dark, he offers a tempting meal, which no hungry lion would be likely to refuse ; but instances of lions, like the famous man-eaters of Tsavo, acquiring a preference for human flesh, and breaking into huts and tents to seize men, are quite exceptional.

Like most of the other posts in the east of the Congo Free State, Rutchuru exists only for military and strategic purposes. The Rusisi-Kivu District, as it is called, is a long strip of territory with a varying width of from 50 to 200 miles, and having a length of about 600 miles. It marches with German East Africa and with Uganda, and it includes the northern part of Tanganyika, the valley of the Rusisi River, the Mfumbiro volcanoes, the basins of Lake Kivu and Lake Albert Edward, and the greater part of the Semliki Valley. This, it will be seen, is exactly the strip of country which is required to unite our northern and southern possessions in Africa, and it would probably be through this district that the Cape to Cairo railway would be best constructed. Ardent Imperialists with land-grabbing instincts would like to see it added to the British Empire, but it is to be feared that such a scheme is beyond the dreams of avarice.

It is a very mountainous country, and is inhabited by many savage and warlike tribes, the great majority of whom have not yet been in any way brought into subjection to European authority. The Belgian position is at present only rendered possible by the employment of a large armed force of about 3,000 native troops, who are stationed at different posts throughout the district. With the exception of an insignificant and diminishing quantity of ivory, the district produces absolutely nothing, and the cost of its occupation must be very considerable. In addition to the large garrison, the administration numbers some sixty or seventy Europeans, whose maintenance in so remote a region is exceedingly costly. Only a very small proportion of their stores enters the country from the Uganda side; the great bulk comes from the West Coast, and the transport of material to some of the remote stations occupies as much as four months. The unproductiveness of the country would not warrant making a railway from the Congo to the middle or northern part of the district, and it is not quite easy to see why the State takes the trouble to maintain its occupation of the Rusisi-Kivu, unless it is with the object of obtaining a good price for it at some future time.

During our enforced stay at Rutchuru we had opportunities of observing the workings of a Congo post. So far as they can, the Belgian officials try to follow the ways of European barrack life. Stores and provisions of every kind are supplied by the Government, and all the officials, military and civilian, mess together, except the Commandant— a somewhat rare personage, only found in the more important posts—who has a separate establishment. The day is punctuated shrilly and discordantly by bugle-calls. The Belgian army has (it would seem) at least a thousand different bugle-calls, and the black buglers are constantly trying to vary them or add to their number. The office of bugler is one that is much sought after, and the afternoon practising of four or five aspiring buglers is a thing the very recollection of which makes one's blood run cold.

Every black soldier keeps one, and very often more than one, wife, and these women are required to do a certain amount of work for the State—light work, such as sweeping the roads and paths in the post, or weeding in the garden, if there is one. It may be objected by some people that the State has no right to make the women work; but in a country where the women are accustomed to doing the greater part of the work of the community under the critical eye of their husbands, there is much to be said for the system. It keeps them to a certain extent out of mischief, and it accounts for a good deal of useful work.

There is another aspect of women in these Congo ports, which is not quite so satisfactory. Almost every European official supports a black mistress. The right or wrong of it is a question that need not be discussed here, but the conspicuous position which the women occupy is quite inexcusable. It is not an uncommon thing to see a group of these women walking about a post shrieking and laughing, and carrying on bantering conversations with the Europeans whose houses they pass; or, very likely, the Europeans will come out and joke with them *coram populo.* The obvious rejoinder is that the same thing goes on in British African colonies, but that the perfidious and hypocritical Englishman hides his doings under a cloak of smug respectability. Even supposing that it is so, though I do not admit it, there can hardly be two opinions as to which is the better state of things. In dealing with any coloured race, and particularly with the black races of Central Africa, the European must begin by winning their respect before he can hope to make any progress with their improvement. It is impossible that natives, when they see women of their own race being treated openly and wantonly with familiarity, should feel any great degree of respect for their European masters, and when that is the case, discipline and obedience to authority are quickly lost.

Amongst the officials of the State are representatives of many nations; the majority are, of course, Belgians, but there are large numbers of Frenchmen, Dutchmen, Italians, Swiss, and Scandinavians, and a few Germans.   The official language is French, which is always spoken in public and at mess; but this rule is relaxed when strangers are present, and the result is a confusion of European tongues, with, as a rule, a strong dash of Suahili and Bangalla. Some of the Scandinavians talked English excellently well, but amongst the others it was almost unknown, and I can only think of three Belgians who had more than the most elementary knowledge of the language.

The feast of St. Leopold, which occurred during our stay at Rutchuru, was celebrated by a conclave of the neighbouring chiefs, who received presents, a review of the troops, accompanied by several newly composed bugle-calls, and a dinner in the evening, at which the toast of Great Britain was received with genuine enthusiasm, and acknowledged in my maiden French oration.   It is usual in a book of this description to reproduce at least one menu of feasts; but the various *aliases*, under which the fatted calf was (not very successfully) disguised, displayed a purely local form of humour, so I will refrain from repeating them here, and will only remark that the Congo custom of drinking 'invalid port' before dinner and sweet champagne afterwards is directly contrary to the principles of Central African hygiene.

Travelling southwards from Rutchuru to Lake Kivu, we chose the route between Tsha-nion-gombe and Tsha-nina-gongo.   There is another recognized route, which skirts the western slopes of Tsha-nina-gongo, passing between that mountain and Nyamlagiro ; but though this route is not nearly so mountainous, it is somewhat longer, and, as it follows lava streams all the way, there is even less chance of finding water than there is on the route which we followed.   After crossing the Rutchuru River to its left bank, we climbed steeply out of the valley, and reached a more or less level terrace of very great extent at the foot of Tsha-nion-gombe.   This country is inhabited by a large population, and almost the whole extent of the terrace and the slopes above it are carefully cultivated.

The first camp which we made was near a village called Bossuenda, a curious place perched precariously on the edge of the terrace.   The view from it was not the least of the many striking views that we saw in that region.   As we looked south, we saw towering up on our left hand the huge mass of the volcanoes Tsha-nion-gombe and Karissimbi, with their fertile slopes covered with cultivation ; and down below on our right hand, in striking contrast, was a scene of frightful desolation.   Between Tsha-nina-gongo and the main group of the volcanoes there is a wide valley, which slopes gradually from south to north, and widens out until it becomes continuous with the plains of Lake Albert Edward.

Tsha-nina-gongo from Lake Kivu.

Candelabra Euphorbias.

To face page 184.

The floor of the valley is made entirely of lava, most of which seems to have flowed, like a huge black glacier, from Tsha-nina-gongo. Looking down upon it from above it was easy to distinguish the courses of the different streams, and to trace them to their origin from the main crater or from various subsidiary cones, which had burst from the sides or at the foot of the mountain. It seemed as if there must have been a fairly prolonged period of quiescence, as the whole valley had become overgrown with bushes and scrub, and towards the east side, the side on which we were, even with fairly large trees. Through the middle of the valley curved a broad black band, about a mile wide and many miles in length, the track of the most recent overflow of lava. The eruption, which had taken place the year before, had continued at intervals for several months, and the glare of it (we were told) had been visible from the farther end of Lake Albert Edward.

Though we were for several weeks within a few miles of the volcanoes, we felt only one or two slight shocks of earthquakes, and the only signs we saw of present volcanic activity were a cloud of smoke that floated over the flat top of Tsha-nina-gongo, and a jet of steam that spouted from the southern slope of Nyamlagiro. There are said to be hot springs in the volcano region, but we saw none of them.

From Bossuenda, keeping parallel with the lava

stream, but always above it, we went higher up to other terraces, which were densely populated and well cultivated.   The people, so far as we could see them, looked a vigorous and healthy race, but we only saw a very few of them at close quarters; they were all provokingly shy, and retreated to the farthest ends of their fields when we came in sight. When we happened to come upon any of them unawares, they dropped their loads and made a dash for the nearest shelter, as though they had seen the devil.   Their villages are compact collections of round grass-huts, surrounded by a strong hedge of thorny bushes, and they are often perched on a prominent shoulder of the hill-side, where they can be easily defended against attack.   In some of them an additional precaution is taken by protecting the single narrow path, which leads to a village, by a strong hedge on either side, so that it is impossible for more than one person, whether friend or enemy, to enter at the same time.   It is not uncommon to see the fields themselves neatly separated by hedges. The most usual crop that they grow is a kind of dwarf bean, and sometimes a larger one which they train on sticks.   They have a great fondness for honey, and a prosperous village will possess several hundred hives of bees ; they make the hives out of hollowed logs of wood.

Some of these people are very rich in cattle, and the superstition that they live upon milk and honey has some foundation in fact, though it has a more

solid foundation of beans.   It is quite possible that
many of them drink only milk, as water is excessively scarce ; springs are very rare above
6,000 feet, and the only available water is that
which is collected in pools after rain.   We crossed
a tiny stream of running water at about 6,400 feet,
the last Nile water that we saw ; after that we saw
no sign of water until we came to Lake Kivu, about
forty miles south as the crow flies.

Above the level of cultivation, which extends to
an altitude of about 7,000 feet, the mountain-sides
are clothed with dense forests of bamboos and big
trees, which appeared to be the same as those that
occur at the same level in Ruwenzori.   The possibility of finding big forests in the volcano region
was one of the strongest reasons which had made
us choose the Lake Kivu route from Uganda to the
Congo, and it was a very bitter disappointment to
us to pass through it without having a chance of
investigating its birds and plants.   We were still so
feeble from the effects of our fever that it was the
utmost we could do to struggle along the path,
such as it was, much less could we have climbed
the steep mountain slopes above us.   Added to this
was the difficulty of obtaining water, which would
have entailed engaging a larger force of porters
than we could conveniently have compassed ; and
the Belgians said that if we wanted to wander in
the volcanoes, we must have an escort to protect
us against the doubtfully friendly natives, and

experience had taught us that that was the last thing in the world to be desired.

According to rumour, both native and European, and I see no strong reason why it should not be correct, these forests on the Mfumbiro volcanoes are inhabited by a race of Pygmies. A Belgian officer, who had spent several months surveying in the volcanoes to the east, told me that his people had once caught one of these Pygmies, but that he had escaped very soon after his capture. The natives told us that in the forests there lived ' very small, very bad people,' and, so far as we could learn, they have an ill reputation for descending from their forests and plundering the more industrious people who live below. Though they are separated by a wide distance of more or less open country from that part of the great forest where the Congo Pygmies live, it is possible that they are of the same race ; but even if they do not turn out to be of a somewhat different race, the fact of their living high up in these mountains is of great interest, and it would certainly repay somebody's trouble to make their acquaintance.

The watershed between the Nile and Kivu basins is at about 7,000 feet, and from it great streams of lava pour away to north and south. It looks as if there had once been a prodigious eruption from the east side of Tsha-nina-gongo, and the lava, having flowed across and filled up the valley between that mountain and Tsha-nion-gombe, had been deflected

The North-West of Lake Kivu.

The Northern Shore of Lake Kivu.

To face page 188.

by the solid base of the latter mountain into two
streams, of which one had flowed north to the
Albert Edward Nyanza and the other south towards
Lake Kivu. The southern lava-flow is smoother
and less broken up by secondary eruptions than is
the other, and we walked down it for many miles
towards the lake. It sloped gently downwards; it
was undulating and full of crevasses, and except
that it was black and exceedingly hot, we could
have imagined ourselves on a huge dry glacier.
To the west the long forest-covered slopes of Tsha-
nina-gongo fell away toward the north-west corner
of Lake Kivu, and to the east was a more irregular
country broken up by innumerable little conical
hills, extinct volcanoes, all cultivated from bottom
to top, and beyond that the higher hills of Ruanda.

At the end of a long day's descent we came
suddenly within sight of the blue-green waters of
Lake Kivu, with its thousand crinkled bays and
islands and steep mountainous shores, and on the
following day, after walking through miles of banana
and maize plantations, we found ourselves at the
water's edge in a beautiful little almost land-locked
cove, which would not have seemed strange in the
English lakes.

CHAPTER XIV

LAKE KIVU

'Some say they are cannibals; and then, conceive a Tartar-fellow eating my friend, and adding the cool malignity of mustard and vinegar! . . . Have a care, my dear friend, of Anthropophagi! their stomachs are always craving. 'Tis terrible to be weighed out at fivepence a pound; to sit at table (the reverse of fishes in Holland), not as a guest, but as a meat.'—CHARLES LAMB.

LAKE KIVU is interesting for several reasons. Not only was it the last to be seen by a European—Count Götzen discovered it in 1893—but it is the highest, probably the deepest, and the most recently formed of the great African lakes. Mr. J. E. S. Moore suggests that it was formed within the last 10,000 years; but a few thousand years more or less are not a matter of great moment, speaking geologically. A large number of points of evidence, which need not be detailed here, go to prove conclusively a former connexion of Lake Kivu, or of a lake somewhere about the site of the present Lake Kivu, with the Albert Edward Nyanza.

Attention has been drawn in an earlier chapter to the great Rift Valleys of Africa. The most remarkable and the most extensive of these Rift Valleys extends from Tanganyika in the south to the outlet of the Nile from Lake Albert in the north. It is a long wide trough or depression in the surrounding country, and in it lie the four lakes—Tanganyika, Kivu, Albert Edward, and Albert. It is bounded on either side by a ridge of hills, which are steep and mountainous in some places, such as the two sides of Lake Kivu, and low and insignificant in others, as the east side of Lake Albert Edward and the west side of the Semliki Valley. In former times the uplifting of the floor of the trough at the northern end of Tanganyika formed the watershed between that lake and Lake Kivu, whose waters flowed out northwards into Lake Albert Edward, and so into the Nile.

This state of things was upset by the disturbances of the earth's interior, which caused the formation of the Mfumbiro volcanoes. Starting on the eastern side of the trough, these mountains burst up, one after another, until they formed a complete dam across the trough between Lake Kivu and the Albert Edward Nyanza. The immediate effect of this was to cut off Lake Kivu from the Nile basin, and to lower the level of the water in the Albert Edward. Old lake levels can be seen now in many places along the shores of the latter lake. Another and equally important result of the formation of the volcanic dam was the raising of the level of the waters of Lake Kivu to their present extraordinary height of 4,800 feet.

It has been remarked above that the hills across the floor of the great trough to the north of Tanganyika formerly constituted the watershed between these two lakes; but as the waters of Lake Kivu were prevented by the dam from flowing into the Nile system, they rose higher and higher, probably through many centuries, until finally they overflowed the old watershed, and poured down into Tanganyika by the new Rusisi River. The remote effects of the volcanic outburst did not stop there, for Tanganyika, swollen by the addition of the Kivu water, rose until it was able to cut a channel through its western wall, by which some of its waters flow into the Congo. Thus it is seen that, by the simple damming up of the great Central African trough, two great lakes have been added to the Congo system, while the Nile has not only lost Lake Kivu, but the Albert and Albert Edward Nyanzas have been greatly diminished in size, and other lakes, which possibly lay between them, have disappeared.

It is practically certain that the formation of the mountains started in the east and proceeded towards the west, as it is only the two most western volcanoes which exhibit signs of activity at present. This latter fact tends to prove that the actual cutting off of Lake Kivu from Lake Albert Edward took place in quite recent times, as the western slopes

War-Dance, Lake Kivu.

Fisherman, Lake Kivu.

To face page 192.

of Tsha-nina-gongo, which touch the walls of the trough and thus complete the dam, are made of newly erupted lava, and are, in one place, only a few hundred feet above the level of the water of the lake.

The Mfumbiro volcanoes have been very incompletely explored, and are still, to a great extent, *terra incognita.* Only one of the mountains—Tsha-nina-gongo (11,350 feet)—has, so far as I know, been ascended, so there remain several virgin peaks to be climbed. There is no permanent snow on any of the mountains, though it is often seen lying on the top of Karissimbi, the highest peak, which rises to a height of about 14,000 feet. The name 'Mfumbiro' seems to be the name by which the Waganda know these mountains; locally they are called Kirunga or Virunga. The names which I have used for the peaks are those by which they are known to the natives in the Rutchuru district, and these names have been adopted by the Belgians. Mr. E. S. Grogan named the volcanoes Mounts Götzen, Sharp, Chamberlain, etc.; but as the right of naming peaks belongs properly to the man who first climbs them, it seems preferable to retain the native names, unwieldy though they are, by which they are already known.

In many of the maps which show the straight line of the frontier between German East Africa and Uganda, there will be seen at its western extremity a southward curve, which was designed to bring the Mfumbiro volcanoes within our territory, in part consideration of the cession to Germany of Heligoland and Kilimanjaro.   Latterly we seem to have given up all claims to the district, doubtless for some good reason ; but one cannot help regretting the fact, as the possession of the group would have given us access to the waters of Lake Kivu, and so would have greatly reduced the distance dividing our northern and southern possessions in Africa. Except for the seventy or eighty miles which separate Lake Kivu from Tanganyika, it would have been possible, by using the lakes as water-ways, to travel under the British flag from north to south in Africa.   It is, perhaps, not being over-sanguine to hope that, when the Congo Free State is put upon a permanent footing, we shall be able to secure this strip of territory.   I can see a day, in the not very distant future, when Messrs. Cook will issue through tickets to Kivu and Tanganyika ; there will be a funicular railway up one of the volcanoes to an hotel on the top, and very likely a hydropathic establishment near one of the hot springs.

At the time of our visit in 1906—and it is probably in the same condition still—we found Lake Kivu a bone of contention between the Congo and Germany, in the same way that Lake Albert Edward is between the Congo State and Uganda.   Formerly the two States agreed that the geographical line, by which these territories are divided, ran from north to south through the middle of Lake Kivu, so that Germany took possession of the east side and the Congo State of the west side of the lake. Subsequently it was found that a mistake, similar to that which was made on the Uganda frontier, had been made here in Kivu, and the Belgians claimed that the whole of the lake belonged properly to the Congo State.

Pending the result of a new survey and the report of a Commission which was appointed to settle the difference, the two States agreed to hold their hands and do nothing on the east side of Kivu or in the strip of territory to the south of it, which is also the subject of disagreement. In this disputed territory there are three German posts, one at the north and one at the south end of Lake Kivu, and another in the Rusisi Valley, and the Germans, so far from showing signs of giving up their occupation of the country, were strengthening and improving their posts in a way that suggested the intention of remaining there permanently. As a rather feeble countermove to this, the Belgians had established a temporary post opposite to, and within a mile or two of, each of the others, by way of asserting their authority, and keeping an eye on the doings of the Germans. If there was one officer and thirty men in the German post, there would be the same number in the corresponding Congo post; if the Belgians increased their garrison by three men, the Germans would follow suit. According to the terms of their agree-

ment, neither side profited in the least by remaining
there, and it seemed an absurd and very expensive
thing for them to be sitting there doing nothing,
when they might just as well have retired until the
question is settled.

Close to the place where we first came down to
the north shore of the lake was the temporary
Congo post of Ngoma. We found there a small
garrison and one Belgian officer living in miserable
grass huts on a tiny patch of cleared ground between
a plain of solid lava on one side and the lake on the
other. What purpose they could possibly serve by
being there it was difficult to imagine.

A couple of miles along the shore, near the north-
east corner of the lake, was the German post of
Kissegnies. A more complete contrast to the Congo
post it would have been impossible to find. The
Germans had settled upon a beautifully fertile piece
of land, which they had cleared and cultivated; they
had made roads and planted trees. The brick-built
house of the commanding officer was a miracle of
solid walls and of coolness inside, and the houses of
the askaris were better than many houses of the
Europeans which we had seen in posts of the Congo
State. The whole place had a thoroughly well-
ordered appearance, as though nothing had been
forgotten and no expense spared; if Kissegnies is
typical of the posts of German East Africa, it may
be supposed that the Colonial bill is no small matter.
The soldiers whom we saw were fine-looking men,

and compared well with the Uganda police. Each man has his own house and garden, wives, and boys to attend to him. Their wages are absurdly high, according to our standard ; a private receives twenty, a corporal forty, and a sergeant fifty rupees a month. It might be expected that desertions would be numerous from the Congo forces to the higher pay across the border, but this does not appear to be so ; perhaps they are deterred by the rumours of the 'kiboko,' which is said to play an even more important part in German posts than it does in the Congo.

In making their post at Kissegnies the Germans wisely selected one of the few places on Lake Kivu where the shore is shallow—a very important thing in a place where most of the communications are by water. Almost everywhere round the lake the shores are rocky, and the water is immensely deep within a few yards of the bank, but at Kissegnies there is a beautiful beach of yellow sand, on which the long canoes can be pulled up with ease. The shallow water might sometimes be seen crowded with native fishermen, who angle in a way that we saw in no other place. They wade out until they are about waist-deep in the water, carrying two fishing-rods of bamboo, which they use in very much the same sort of way that we do ; sometimes they use a grass-hopper or some other insect as bait, sometimes a lump of meat.

Both the Germans and the Belgians were glad

enough, as may be supposed, when strangers came
to relieve the monotony of their existence, and we
arranged a sort of *entente cordiale* dinner of the
three nationalities at Kissegnies, in which a long-
treasured bottle of Munich beer played a prominent
part.   Calculations of the probable cost of trans-
porting that bottle of beer from Munich to the
north of Lake Kivu ended in pity for the over-
burdened German taxpayer, whose health we drank
with acclamation.

There is a mission station of the White Fathers
in the Ruanda Mountains a few miles from Kissegnies, but we had no opportunity of visiting it.   The
Fathers distil a very excellent liqueur from the juice
of the banana, and they make very fair cigars from
the tobacco for which Ruanda is famous.   In contrast with the Congo stations, where such people
are not encouraged to stay, there are settled near
Kissegnies a number of native traders—Suahilis,
Zanzibaris, Arabs, and one Greek.   So far as I could
find out, their trade consists chiefly in an illicit business in ivory and rubber, which is brought out from
the Congo in large quantities, and finds its way by
devious routes down to the coast.   Nobody seems
to mind very much, or to attempt to put a stop to
the smuggling.   During our stay near Kissegnies it
was known to the Germans and the Belgians that
several canoe-loads—about two tons—of rubber had
arrived one night in a trader's storehouse from the
Congo side of the frontier.

Kivu Native making Fire.

After spending a few days on the north shore of the lake, we crossed over to the north-west side, where the Congo State has a post at Bobandana. The lower slopes of the mountains, which descend steeply into the lake on the west side, are uncultivated, and covered with thick grass and bush for a few hundred feet. Above this there is a very dense population, and an enormous amount of cultivation ; banana shambas stretch for miles and miles along the hill-sides, and there are numerous fields of beans and mealies. The natives are fine, well-set-up people of a very independent character, according to the reports of the Belgians, who have as yet very little authority over them. Almost all of them have the unsightly habit of filing their teeth to sharp points, which is generally supposed to be a sign of cannibalism. There is no doubt that cannibalism is still exceedingly common in those regions, but there are few things about which it is more difficult to get direct information from the natives themselves, unless it is by actual personal experience. Luckily for ourselves, both Carruthers and I are of a lean habit, and, made even more so by attacks of fever, we offered no temptation to even the least fastidious anthropophagist.

Bobandana is well perched upon a hill a few hundred feet above the lake, and it well deserves its other name—Kilima-Mungu—the hill of the Deity—by which it is commonly known among the natives. Looking north, beyond the head of the lake, we saw the vast black plain of lava sloping down from the truncated cone of Tsha-nina-gongo, and, farther away, the jagged line of the other volcanoes; to the east, across fifteen miles of green water, the beautiful outline of the hills of Ruanda ; and stretching far away into the south lay Kivu, with its wooded islands and rocky bays, and innumerable headlands.

When we came to Bobandana, we found that the officer in command was absent, and the place was in charge of a youthful *sous-officier*, aged about twenty, who had five months' experience only of Africa. This hopeful young person gave an instructive exhibition of the high-handed way in which it is still possible to behave in these out-of-the-way places. One of his boys cracked a drinking-cup one evening, and was sentenced to a punishment of twenty-five strokes of the 'kiboko,' to be delivered on the following morning. During the night the boy ran away, and the whole garrison was sent out to scour the country for him, which they did without success. A day or two later the chief of a neighbouring village, bribed by the offer of a piece of cloth (a half of the boy's monthly wage), brought back the boy, whom he had no doubt been concealing. The boy received his promised twenty-five lashes, and so also did a wretched soldier, who had been unlucky enough to search unsuccessfully near the village in which the boy had been hiding. Curiously enough, the boy appeared to bear no ill-will for his harsh treatment, but went about his work as cheerfully as if nothing had happened. A rumour of this most scandalous treatment reached the ears of his commanding officer, and I was glad to hear subsequently that the young man found himself in considerable trouble. I have related this episode as an instance of the danger of leaving the young and uneducated *sous-officiers*, who have no experience of the country, in positions of authority and responsibility. The number of the staff of the Congo State is so wretchedly inadequate, that it is not uncommon for a youth to find himself in sole charge of a large district before he has had time to learn the language of the country. In the hands of commissioned officers the natives are safe enough, but the same cannot always be said of the *sous-officiers*, who are seldom of higher rank than corporal in the Belgian army, and are not accustomed to the proper exercise of authority.

We were detained by illness at Bobandana for several days, during which the *sous-officier* tried to bribe our Uganda boys to enter his service, thinking that, being so far from home, they would not be able to run away ; but though they accepted his bribes, they elected to stay with us. I did not hear of this till I was on my legs again, and then I spoke words to him which made me feel a great deal better, and gave him food for thought. On our departure from Bobandana, he presented us, by way of a peace-offering, with the weaklings of his flock of sheep—little skeleton creatures hardly

bigger than rabbits. We tried to resuscitate the
poor beasts; but when they were lifted out of the
canoe at the other end of the lake, they could
not walk, so we made a present of them to the
paddlers.

Our voyage down the sixty miles of Lake Kivu
occupied four days. It was a time which, when
I look back upon it, gives me a greater pleasure
than any other period of our wanderings in Africa.
Lake Kivu is a thing of many and different moods,
but beautiful in all of them. At one moment the
sun is blazing out of a brilliant sky on the glassy
surface of the green water, in which the outline
of the hills and the trees on their ridges are perfectly
reflected. At another, the sudden south wind comes
racing up the lake in a long black line, and the
waves grow big as if by magic. And again,
black clouds of thunderstorms pour down from
the volcanoes; terrifying peals crash and re-echo
from one hill-side to another, and the heavens let
loose a flood of waters, and the surface of the
lake seethes and hisses like a boiling cauldron.

The scenery of Kivu is strangely reminiscent of
many other places. Our first view of it reminded
me, as I have said before, of the English lakes.
There was a place which reminded me most forcibly
of the Island of Miyajima in the Inland Sea; and
at yet another place I could easily imagine myself
on one of the sea lochs on the west coast of Scotland.
And the climate (or, to be more accurate, the

weather) is curiously fickle too. In three weeks
we had every variety between the sultriness of
tropical African heat and the bright chill that might
have been a day from an English April.

The native dug-out canoes are not so long as
those on the Congo, but of the same pattern, and
many of them are built with thwarts, upon which
the paddlers sit. There are few more delightful
ways of travelling than to sit in the bow of the
canoe (there are excellent reasons for sitting in
front of the Kivu paddlers) and to feel the regular
rise and fall of the craft, as it is urged powerfully
forwards. The paddlers sing almost continually,
while they work, a number of curious and pleasing
songs. The steersman, who sits in the stern,
generally fills the office of choragus; he sings a
long recitative in a high-pitched nasal falsetto, and
then the others join in, and sing in unison a very
melodious chorus. The general scheme of most
of their songs is somewhat that of a scale, in which
they descend by semi-tones and quarter-tones and
many complicated turns, until they arrive at a pitch
which the profoundest European basso would find
difficult to reach. They sing with marked expression and admirably together, and many of them
have voices of extraordinary richness.

Until we had gone about half-way down Kivu
we followed the west shore, and then we crossed
over to the Island of Kwijwe, which is separated
from the mainland by a channel four or five miles

wide. Kwijwe is the largest island on Lake Kivu ;
it is about thirty miles long, mountainous, and partly
covered with forest. There is a large population,
who are at present in the happy position of belonging
neither to the Belgians nor the Germans. At one or
two of the places where we stopped on the island
we were evidently the first white men the natives
had seen, and we caused them some alarm ; but they
soon overcame their shyness, and were perfectly
friendly.

These people, and the other natives of the Kivu
region, still retain the primitive method of obtaining
fire from wood. The apparatus is simple enough,
and consists of a slender stick of hard wood, a flat
piece of soft and partly charred wood (often a seg-
ment of a bamboo), and a scrap of inflammable
material, such as rag or bark. The slender stick
is placed upright upon the soft wood and is rotated
very rapidly between the palms of the hands ; the
tinder, placed close to the point of contact, smoulders
in a few seconds, and can easily be blown into a
flame (see illustration, p. 198). Many of them were
glad enough to sell their fire-machines for a small
box of Swedish matches. In districts where this
method of obtaining fire is not employed, the natives
have a convenient habit of carrying fire secreted
somewhere about their persons. If he is a person
who wears a rag of some sort, he probably has a
fragment of smouldering wool or fibre tied up in a
corner of his garment. If he is very scantily attired,

Paddlers, Lake Kivu.

To face page 204

his fire will be carefully folded up in a piece of banana-leaf and attached to his spear or stick, as the case may be.

One of the drawbacks to travelling on Lake Kivu is the scarcity of water. The water of the lake itself is salt and undrinkable, and though there are numbers of streams running down the mountain-sides, they are lost before they reach the lake. It is probably this extreme saltness which explains the absence of crocodiles from the lake, though they are plentiful enough where the Rusisi runs into Tanganyika. Nor are there any hippos in the lake, but one would not expect to find them, as the shores are almost everywhere steep and rocky, and there are none of the shallow mudbanks and papyrus swamps in which hippos delight. Otters, which are always as much at home in salt as in fresh water, abound, and you may often see a dozen or more playing together when the water is calm. They are much less nocturnal in their habits than the otters in Europe, and not nearly so timid. They utter a number of different sounds—barks and grunts, and a shrill whistle, which is very like the whistle of a widgeon.

Towards its southern extremity the country about Lake Kivu changes in character. The hills become much lower and less mountainous ; and trees, except for a few palms along the water's edge, disappear almost entirely, and are replaced by luxuriant grass, on which large herds of cattle and sheep are seen grazing. To the south of Kwijwe there is a group of smaller islands, which seem, as you approach them, to be the end of the lake ; but there is a narrow channel between them leading to a large southern extension of the lake, which is so well separated from Kivu as almost to deserve another name. We landed at Nya-Lukemba, where the Belgians were making a post near the outlet of the Rusisi River from the lake.

CHAPTER XV

FROM KIVU TO TANGANYIKA

'Allons ! we must not stop here,
However sweet these laid-up stores, however convenient
   this dwelling, we cannot remain here.
However shelter'd this port and however calm these
   waters, we must not anchor here.
However welcome the hospitality that surrounds us, we
   are permitted to receive it but a little while.'

WALT WHITMAN.

IN an earlier chapter I mentioned the fact that, when we started from Uganda to travel through the Congo State, we had to increase our caravan by porters laden with cloth and beads. We took with us several loads of ordinary white trade-cloth— 'Americani,' as it is called—and the best beads that Entebbe could produce. The Indian trader who supplied them said that they were good enough for Congo savages, and we were foolish enough to believe him.

In the old days of African travel no doubt any kind of cloth and beads of any size or colour were welcomed everywhere, but the old order has changed. It is true that our beads went like hot cakes round the shores of Lake Albert Edward, but when we came to the Volcanoes and southwards, the natives

207

turned up their noses (or made an equivalent grimace) at our beautiful blue glass beads, and would have nothing of them. They said they must have red beads—small red beads—or none at all. In other places they wanted small blue beads, or large red beads, and so on. It was the same with the cloth ; one district had a preference for blue cloth, another for white, and another for spotted cloth. There are as many different fashions in beads and cloth in Central Africa as there are in ladies' hats and gowns in more civilized countries.

At first sight this may seem to be a small matter, but it is, as a matter of fact, the outward and visible expression of one of the most fundamental errors which the Congo Free State has made. By means which I do not profess to understand, the State has succeeded in ousting all private traders from the Congo,* and, except in those districts that are leased to concessionary companies, has become the sole trader and the sole employer of labour. Under these circumstances the authorities have, naturally enough, not seen the necessity of going to the expense of establishing a currency which would be universal throughout the country, but they have adhered to the antiquated and doubtless more profitable method of paying for everything in trade goods. In one

* The only exception to this statement, in the Upper Congo, is Stanleyville, where there were (in 1907) two or three trading firms. In the Lower Congo there are traders at Leopoldville, Matadi, Boma, and Banana.

Paddler, Lake Kivu.

To face page 208.

district they pay the natives in cloth, in another in brass wire, in another in beads or salt, and so on. Very often the native has not the least desire for the piece of cloth or the handful of beads—his wife may have half a dozen flowing robes or head ornaments already—but he must take what he is offered or go without payment altogether. If there were traders settled in the country, the native could go and exchange his useless cloth for something more to his liking, or, better still, if he were paid in coin, he could go to the trader for what he wanted, and he would be sure of getting better value for his money than he could by exchange of goods.

The policy seems, at the best, a short-sighted one. The natives of Central Africa, speaking generally, are not always merely lazy beasts ; many of them are greedy and exceedingly covetous, and I cannot help feeling convinced that if they were paid in money, with which they could buy sheep and food and wives and all that they most desire, they would find the incentive to work, which they certainly have not at present, and the State (not to mention the natives themselves) would be very greatly the gainer.

It stands to reason that this state of things adds immensely to the difficulties of travelling in the Congo State. It is impossible, before you enter the country, to find out what kinds of trade-goods are necessary in the districts through which you propose to travel, and it is equally impossible, when you are in the State, to buy the goods you want, because there are no traders, and the officials at the State posts are not allowed to sell to travellers. The consequence is that you take a great many unnecessary things and omit to take many that would have been useful, and trust to luck to get through somehow. We were fortified with powerful recommendations from Brussels, and we were fortunate in keeping on friendly terms with some of the officials, who occasionally strained the law a little in matters of exchange, so that we had not any very serious trouble; but there was always the uncomfortable feeling that we were there only on sufferance, as though we were walking in somebody's private property.

There is another feature of modern travel in Central Africa, which does not compare favourably with the ways of the old times of twenty or thirty years ago. Formerly travellers, who entered the country from the east, used to engage at the coast Suahilis or Zanzibari porters, who were paid by the month and continued for the whole of the journey. Each porter knew his own load, and quickly learnt his duties in the caravan, and when once their own country was left well behind them, there was no risk of the men running away. There was, of course, a chance, if they were not kept well in hand, of their causing trouble by looting the people of the countries through which they passed, and there was the business at the end of the journey of sending them home; but these drawbacks were more than made up for by the convenience of recruiting porters once and for all. Nowadays, owing to the diminished supply of available Suahilis and the expense of bringing them up from the coast, you have to engage your porters for short distances as you go along. They will not pass beyond the bounds of their own country, for the excellent reason that, if they do, they run a very good chance of being captured and eaten on their way home again. The result is that your progress is a series of short journeys, sometimes as little as three days, and seldom longer than a fortnight, interrupted by the delay (generally a matter of days) and the worry involved in constantly hiring a fresh batch of porters.

The Belgians have taken advantage of this disinclination to travel on the part of the natives, and I saw a curious instance of it at Stanley Falls. The canoe of the judge at that place was manned by a crew of twelve stalwart natives of the Lower Congo. All of them were murderers, who had been sentenced at Boma to long terms of imprisonment, and had been sent up the river to Stanleyville. It was impossible for them to attempt to pass through the many strange tribes which lay between them and their own country, but to all intents and purposes they were as free as anybody else, with the difference that they walked up to the prison every evening and locked themselves in. The chiefs of the various districts in the Congo are supposed to be responsible for procuring porters for travellers, but they are often disagreeable people, and they are seldom in a hurry to help you if you do not wear the uniform of the State official.

Between the Albert Edward Nyanza and the Congo we changed porters no less than seven times, and I can only remember one occasion when we had no difficulty about it. That was at Nya-Lukemba, at the south end of Lake Kivu, where, within a few hours of our request for forty porters, at least 150 presented themselves and clamoured to be engaged. We selected forty magnificent giants, and the few days during which they carried our loads were about the pleasantest part of the journey ; they picked up the loads as if they weighed nothing, trotted off with them, and invariably arrived at the camping-place long before we did. Those were a brilliant and much-appreciated exception to the rule among Congo porters, who are generally quite as slow and as disinclined to work as the Uganda variety.

Most of the porters in the Congo carry spears, and many of them, particularly in the Kivu district, carry also long, narrow-bladed knives in wooden sheaths ornamented with copper wire. They are truculent-looking ruffians, and appear to be quite capable of any villainy ; but luckily they are arrant cowards, where white men are concerned. I very well remember one day walking, as I fondly imagined, miles behind the caravan, and coming suddenly on the whole crowd of porters sitting on the path and eating bananas, which they had stolen from a neighbouring shamba. I attacked them furiously with my umbrella, and they picked up their loads and fled precipitately, though any single one of them could easily have made a hole in me with his spear, and the rest would have had great pleasure, but very little satisfaction, in picking my bones. It was a 'regrettable incident,' because my weapon was disabled by coming into violent contact with a black head, and I have been unable to boast of having crossed Africa armed only with an umbrella.

It is their ungovernable greed more than anything else which gets them into trouble ; offers of increased pay will not rouse them to energy, but they will march all day long if there is a prospect of eating as much as they can at the end of it. On one occasion in the Mfumbiro district our porters, who had distinguished themselves by loafing along on the previous day, took wings to themselves and went an immense distance, quite double an ordinary day's journey, and mostly in the wrong direction. They might have made a short march to a place where there was a little cultivation, but they preferred to go miles out of their way—and by so doing increased the next day's journey, too—in order to indulge in an orgy of beans and bananas. I hit upon a very salutary punishment for that little escapade by depriving the 'headman' of his spear (a gross indignity), and cutting it in two in his presence ; the shaft made me a new handle for my butterfly-net, and the blade is now a very service-able paper-knife.

Unlike the Uganda porters, who always carry their loads upon their heads, in the Congo, and more particularly in the mountainous districts, the porters carry loads upon their backs suspended by a rope, which passes across the forehead. It does not matter if your supply of rope fails, as it is sure to do, for the porters very soon manufacture some more. Tear up an armful of coarse grass, not so long as barley straw, and try and twist it into a rope that will not fall to pieces at a touch. I have tried it and have failed ignominiously, and I doubt if one white man in a hundred can do it ; but a Congo porter will make in a couple of minutes a rope which will support the heaviest load and will never break.

The usual scale of payment of the porters in the Congo is one '*brasse*' (two metres) of cloth for a journey of three or four days, or a '*doti*' (two *brasses*) of cloth for a journey of a week, and so on in proportion to the length of the journey. The value of one *brasse* is calculated in the Upper Congo to be one franc fifty centimes, so that the payment of three francs a week compares favourably with the average payment of four rupees (equal to about six and a half francs) which the Uganda porter receives a month. In addition to this the Congo porter is paid a daily '*posho*' (ration) of beads to the value of fifteen centimes ; the usual

Natives of Kwijwe Island, Lake Kivu.

To face page 214.

measure is a small 'Liebig' pot, and the porter always takes good care to see that it is well pressed down and running over.

The above digressions were suggested by the splendid physique of the porters whom we engaged at Nya-Lukemba; and when we left that place and passed through their country, we saw the reason of their good health. The Rusisi River wriggles out of Lake Kivu in a most unpretentious way, and immediately plunges down a narrow valley, where it becomes a huge mountain torrent, and is exceedingly difficult to follow. The route which we took led us away to the west of the Rusisi through a hilly, rather than mountainous, country, at an altitude of between 5,000 and 7,000 feet. Everywhere there were villages, and every hill-side was covered with cultivation—splendid crops of beans and maize and millet—and where the slopes were too steep for cultivation, or in the valleys, where the ground was wet and marshy, there were grazing great herds of fat cattle. The people, who were working industriously everywhere in the fields, seemed to be a splendidly healthy race, and the children, who swarmed round every village, were the fattest and sturdiest little milk-fed creatures it would be possible to see.

When, if it ever does, the eastern part of the Congo Free State becomes accessible by railway, there can be hardly any doubt that these highlands between Kivu and Tanganyika will be occupied by European settlers.   The land is amazingly fertile, and the natives, who are industrious, lack only training to become excellent agriculturists.   The Belgians, for some reason, have a strong prejudice against the district, and officials very much resent being sent there, perhaps because a few people have died there of 'blackwater' fever, but the disease was almost certainly contracted elsewhere. The country is high, the rains are not very severe, and the climate ought, on the face óf it, to be perfectly healthy ; personally, I felt more 'fit' there than I had done at any time since we left Ruwenzori. Sheep and cattle thrive extraordinarily all over the district; the former are so cheap that at Nya-Lukemba we bought twelve for six *dotis* of calico—that is, at a cost of about one shilling and threepence a piece.   Congo officers returning from Kivu generally take a flock of sheep with them, and if only as many as 10 per cent. of them survive the journey, they are sure to make a large profit by selling them when they reach the Congo, where sheep are rare and costly.

As we went south from Lake Kivu, we found the hills becoming steeper and less cultivated, until they culminated in a succession of knife-edged ridges at the top of slopes covered with grass and flowers, and in the valleys were roaring torrents.   About thirty miles from the lake the hills end abruptly, and fall away steeply into the Tanganyika plain. Coming over the last of the ridges, we saw the end of another stage of our journey. Far below us at our feet lay the wide, tree-covered plain, where once the lake used to be, and over it, like a streak of silver, curled the great Rusisi River. On the horizon, forty miles away, the sunshine sparkled on the waters of Tanganyika. Though everything there was on such a vastly greater scale, the view at once suggested to me a view from the Cotswolds of the winding Severn, and a glimpse of the sea beyond.

The descent of those 3,000 or 4,000 feet was another of the swift changes, almost theatrical in their suddenness, to which one is so often treated in Africa. On the whole, I think it is not a very good arrangement ; ninety-nine days' journeys out of a hundred are so monotonously alike that it seems a pity to concentrate all the excitement of a change into the hundredth. It is a waste of emotions, and one would like to prolong the pleasure over a few days ; but perhaps the sudden and unexpected changes are better impressed upon the memory. In a few hours we exchanged a cool European climate for the roasting heat of tropical Africa, and mountain meadows filled with flowers for the typical euphorbia- and acacia-covered plains, which had become so familiar to us in the Albert Edward country. A few miles before it leaves the hills, the Rusisi flows (we were told) through a long natural tunnel, probably through the debris of a landslip ; but the sultriness of the plains was demoralizing, and we did not summon up energy enough to go and see it. Soon after it emerges from the hills, the Rusisi is joined by some big streams from either side, and it is a great river—bigger than the Rhone at Geneva—before it flows into Tanganyika.

Our route took us along the west side of the valley, which is there about fifteen miles wide, close to the foot of those mountains which I have described before as forming the western wall of the great Central African trough. The valley itself is densely covered with bush, and has but few inhabitants, except elephants and antelopes, but the lower slopes of the hills are thickly populated, and we often saw a crowd of natives perched upon a point of vantage to watch us as we passed. These people are famous for their skill as blacksmiths—their knives and spears are exceedingly well wrought—and for their tobacco, which they smoke and chew and use as snuff in prodigious quantities. They have a curious device to assist them in their habit of taking snuff; their noses are of the *retroussé* type, and their nostrils are large and round, so, in order to prevent a waste of the precious snuff, they fix a neat little bamboo clip over the end of the nose, which compresses the nostrils and prevents the snuff from falling out. When it is not in use the clip is carried fixed on to the ear (see illustration, p. 218).

Though there are hardly more than forty miles between the foot of the hills, which we had left, and

Kivu Native, showing Snuff-Clip in Ear.

To face page 218.

the northern end of the lake, African paths pursue a
winding and uncertain course, and when we had
been dawdling along the valley for six days, I began
to think that Tanganyika must be a myth. But, as
we came over a little hill, there it was, not half a
mile away. I said at once to myself: 'Lago Maggiore!' There was no doubt about it at all : it was
as though we had been coming down from Bellin-
zona to Locarno. The hills on either side were the
same in form and height ; there were clusters of
villages scattered along their sides ; there were deep
gorges and mountain torrents. There was a dark
promontory pointing out where Canobbio lay, and
the bluest water I had seen since I saw the Lago
Maggiore, with here and there a patch of purple,
where there was a puff of wind. A long dark line
to the south showed, not the 'sirocco' blowing up
from Italy, but the daily south wind coming up from
Rhodesia and Nyassaland. The black euphorbias
took the place of cypresses, and at Uvira, where we
arrived a few hours later, the illusion was strength-
ened by the gardens of lemon-trees laden with golden
fruit.

A violent storm a few weeks earlier had swamped
most of the available canoes, and there was difficulty
in finding a sufficient number to transport us and
our belongings down the lake, so we had to stop at
Uvira for a few days, but we were not altogether
sorry to have an excuse for loafing in such a pleasant
spot. Uvira is the chief post of the Rusisi-Kivu

district, and it lies on the west shore a few miles from the head of the lake. The shore is low and sandy, and there is about a mile of fairly level ground between it and the foot of the hills. At Uvira the lake is more than fifteen miles wide, but the atmosphere is so clear that it looks not half that distance, and the houses at Usumbura, which lies almost directly opposite to Uvira, can always be most clearly seen. Usumbura is a German East Africa post of some importance. There is a good road from there to Bukoba on the Victoria Nyanza, which is the easiest and most direct route between Tanganyika and Uganda. There is another road from Usumbura to Dar-es-salaam, the port of German East Africa; the journey takes about five weeks: and it is also reached by a German steamer, which makes the voyage (when it is in working order) up the east side of the lake once a month, and it is thus in direct communication with the road to Lake Nyassa and the Zambesi.

One of the most striking features of Tanganyika is the wonderful regularity of the daily wind. In the morning there is not a ripple on the water until about eleven o'clock, when a strong wind comes roaring up from the south, and in an amazingly short time the lake becomes a heavy sea, and big waves break upon the beach. At four o'clock the wind falls, and by sunset it is as calm as ever. In the shallow waters near the head of the lake is a great abundance of fish, which the natives kill with spears by night, and it is a pretty sight after dark to see a score or more of brilliant lights gliding over the lake.

Christmas fell during our stay at Uvira, and 'Noel' was celebrated by a banquet, in which *conforts médicaux* played a prominent part. In a party of eight Europeans there were representatives of six different nationalities, and towards the small hours of Christmas morning, when the '*Schnick*' had made a few journeys round the table, the conversation was a polyglot mixture of at least eight different languages. It is to be recorded with sorrow that that dreadful engine, the gramophone, had penetrated even to the farthest end of Tanganyika. But (to be honest) either because the vulgar tunes of Brussels are less offensive than those of London, or because one's senses had become blunted by the climate—or it may have been an effect of the '*Schnick*' —the wheezy 'music' was not quite so objectionable as it generally is ; and the singing by the Swiss member of the party of the ' Ranz des vaches ' was the best thing that had happened for many long months.

After we had waited for a week or more, some battered relics of canoes were fished up from the bottom of the lake ; we crammed lemons into the holes to stop the leaks, and left Uvira and our hospitable hosts. Generally our crew punted the canoes with long poles, and we followed every curve of the shore, but when we came to a very deep bay they rowed across with absurd little paddles, which looked like elongated salt-spoons. If you do not travel by night on Tanganyika, you must start betimes in the morning, as the daily wind quickly raises a sea, which is very dangerous for the clumsy dug-out canoes. Two or three times we were caught unawares in it before we had reached a convenient camping-place, and six inches of water in the bottom of the canoe, in spite of the manful baling of the paddlers, irretrievably spoilt a quantity of valuable plants and butterflies. Our paddlers were merry fellows and enthusiastic fishermen, which is always a sign of grace. At every camp they armed themselves with bamboo rods and lines and little metal hooks, which they baited with banana or manioc, and spent the afternoon at their favourite amusement. They waded into the shallow water and cast most dexterously, but though they whistled softly all the time, a sure way (so they said) of attracting the fish, I never saw them catch anything larger than a minnow.

The scenery of the western shore of Tanganyika is exceedingly beautiful, and the lake itself is an unending joy with its quickly changing moods of sunshine and storm. The few evenings of our short voyage, when we dined by the water's edge under the gorgeous moon, are among my happiest recollections of Africa. On the whole, I am inclined to place Tanganyika before all the other lakes I have seen in Africa for beauty, perhaps excepting my first

The Western Hills of Tanganyika.

Cattle near Tanganyika (North-West).

To face page 222.

love, Naivasha.   Kivu is beautiful enough with its mountainous shores, its islands and bays and winding channels, but in Tanganyika there is a spaciousness and a grandeur which belong to a higher order, and for magnificence of colour its equal does not exist.

CHAPTER XVI

‘ Through many a dark and dreary vale
They passed, and many a region dolorous,
    *   *   *   *   *
Rocks, caves, lakes, fens, bogs, dens, and shades of death—
A universe of death, which God by curse
Created evil, for evil only good ;
Where all life dies, death lives, and Nature breeds
Perverse, all monstrous, all prodigious things,
Abominable, unutterable, and worse
Than fables yet have feigned or fear conceived.’

MILTON.

ABOUT seventy miles down the west shore of Tanganyika is the wide inlet known as Burton's Gulf, near the head of which is Baraka, where we landed. It would have been more interesting to continue down the lake to the Lukuga, the river by which a small portion of the water of Tanganyika finds its way into the Congo ; but such a journey would have been a matter of weeks, and it was out of the question to attempt it with the miserable canoes at our disposal. To more fortunate travellers, provided with better boats than we had, I would suggest coasting down the west side of the lake as far as the Lukuga, and then following that river, as far as possible, towards the upper waters of the Lualaba ; the latter part of the journey could not fail to be of exceptional interest. Another reason which determined us to leave the lake at Baraka was that there is from that place to Kasongo, the nearest point on the Congo, a well-recognized route, on which we should probably be able to find porters without any great difficulty. This was formerly one of the principal routes by which slaves were brought from the Upper Congo; when they arrived at Tanganyika they were shipped across in dhows to Ujiji, on the east side of the lake, whence their Arab owners sent them down to Zanzibar and the east coast towns. Though it looks but a short distance on the map—it is, in fact, only about 170 miles in a straight line—the road wanders most irritatingly in very nearly every direction, and the journey from Baraka to Kasongo took us exactly a month.

The country around Baraka has been almost entirely depopulated by sleeping sickness,* which was unknown on the shores of Tanganyika until the year 1903. Whole villages have been wiped out, and huge tracts of fertile land along the lake, which were formerly cultivated, have become impenetrable jungle. Between Uvira and Baraka we passed the deserted relics of a mission station, which had been the centre of a large settlement ; the people had all died or had migrated to a less cursed country,

* See Appendix.

and there were no pupils left to be taught by the Fathers, who had, therefore, gone elsewhere. Almost daily, as we walked westward from Tanganyika, and, later on, in the Manyuema country, we passed corpses by the roadside, dead of the terrible sickness ; and it was no uncommon thing for the caravan to make a wide detour to avoid some unspeakable horror. The people are brutally inhuman to the victims of the disease. So soon as a man becomes incapable of supporting himself, he is turned out of the village to subsist for a short time on loathsome garbage and soon to starve like a dog. So long as I live I shall be haunted by the recollection of one of these miserable creatures, who came crawling about our camp not far from Tanganyika. The porters—' our black brothers,' as some people would call them—were stuffing themselves on the fat of the land at the time, and though he was one of their own tribe, they jeered at his infirmities—he could not walk, but dragged himself along the ground with his hands—and refused to give him a scrap of the food for which he begged. Heartrending spectacles of this sort can be seen on the outskirts of almost every village between the Congo and Tanganyika.

The Congo State is making strenuous efforts, by the establishment of lazarettos in which infected people are confined, to check the spread of the disease ; but it is a task beset with innumerable difficulties, and the medical staff of the State is hopelessly inadequate in numbers. Thus, for the

A Tattooed Beauty from the Lower Congo.

To face page 226.

A Rough Sea on Tanganyika.

To face page 226.

whole of the Rusisi-Kivu District. which is about as large as England without Wales, there are two doctors ; for the Manyuema District, which is roughly the size of Ireland, there is one doctor. So it frequently happens that an unfortunate official, who falls ill in a remote station, is twelve or fourteen days' journey from the nearest doctor, who arrives only in time to find him either recovered or in his grave. It is only fair to say that the doctors, who are mostly Italians, work most nobly and perform wonderful feats of travelling by day and night ; but it is manifestly impossible for them to devote much time to the study of native diseases, or to take very active steps towards preventing the spread of sleeping sickness. On our way down the Congo I visited three or four of the State lazarettos, which (with one exception) were well conducted ; but with such a splendid highway as the river itself forms, it is excessively difficult to check the movements of infected but unrecognized individuals, who are a constant source of danger wherever they go. It is a lamentable fact, but one which cannot be gainsaid, that civilization must be held responsible in no small degree for the spread of sleeping sickness during the last few years. In the old days, when every tribe and almost every village was self-sufficient, and had no intercourse with its neighbours, except in the way of warfare, it might very well happen that the disease became localized in a few districts, where its virulence became diminished. Nowadays, with the rapid opening-up of the country, the constant passage of Europeans travelling from one district to another, and the suppression of native warfare, it is becoming increasingly easy for natives to move beyond the limits of their own countries, and by their means sleeping sickness is spread from one end of the country to another. The prevention of the disease is by far the most serious problem which confronts Europeans in Africa, and the outlook at the present time is at the best a gloomy one.

For the first few days after we had left Tanganyika, we occasionally saw behind us magnificent views of the lake lying in its great trench among the hills. This mountain country to the west of Tanganyika is an exceedingly beautiful country, but very little populated and apparently infertile. The mountains are a continuation of the same range which we had followed all the way from Lake Albert Edward, but much lower than they are farther north, and little more than 5,000 feet high at the point where we crossed them. The descent on the west side of the range is as sudden and unexpected as the ascent on the other side is slow and gradual. After climbing, almost without noticing it, through hills and valleys for six days, we came without any warning to the top of a slope of about 3,000 feet— so steep that I experienced the same feeling of a desire to throw something into the abyss, which (I confess it with shame) comes over me on the tops of cathedral towers and other high places. It was a day of grief and pain for me, as I was suffering from an ill-conditioned leg, and was forced to travel in a hammock ; but the porters and the hammock and I would have been picked up in fragments at the bottom if they had tried to carry me down, so I had to crawl down as best I could. At the top of the last steep pitch of about a thousand feet, I remember thinking of Tom in 'The Water Babies,' when he looked over into Vendale. Far below was a clear stream and a hut where the camp was, but a group of naked black figures instead of the old woman with the red petticoat. After the lapse of time and with many groans I arrived at the bottom as dirty in body and as sore in spirit as was Tom.

Although Tanganyika and Lake Kivu do actually form a part of the Congo system by the connexion of the former lake with the Congo through the Lukuga River, it was not until we crossed the mountains to the west of Tanganyika that we entered the Congo basin proper. From the foot of the mountains to the river, a distance of about 120 miles, there is a hideous country of unspeakable dreariness, without a single landmark or physical feature of beauty. As we looked down upon it from the hills, it seemed to be an almost level plain covered with trees, but we soon found that it was a rough, undulating bush-country, in which it was seldom possible to see more than half a mile in any direction.

After crossing the Luama—a large tributary which joins the Congo a little south of Kasongo—we entered the Manyuema District, an immense country over which the Belgians have at present a very precarious hold. Most of the natives that we saw were miserable, half-starved creatures, rotten with disease, and it was difficult to believe that they belonged to the race which was for so long a time the terror of Central Africa. In two or three places we crossed the telephone line which the Belgians have established between Uvira and the Upper Congo. More often than not, through the agency of elephants, or storms, or of natives in need of metal ornaments, it is out of gear, and it is hardly likely that it would be of the least use for military purposes in the event of a native rising.

Many parts of the Manyuema country, particularly the swamps and plains about the Luama River, are well stocked with game, and we saw the tracks of antelopes in many places ; but with the consistent ill-luck which always dogged our footsteps, we found ourselves there at the wrong time of the year : it was the wet season, and the country was overgrown with tall and impenetrable grass. Leopards abound throughout the Manyuema District, and are very much feared by the natives, whom they not infrequently snatch out of their huts at night ; they are particularly fond of lying in wait for the women and children, when they go to fetch water in the evening. I remember being waked one night by a loud, rasping sound, like the sound of sawing wood ; it was the horrible grunting of leopards, and there must have been fully half a dozen of them prowling about within a short distance of the camp. But we saw neither antelopes nor leopards, and there was nothing to relieve the monotony of the journey except some unlucky collisions which we had with the natives.

Near a village called Muniemboka, Carruthers, who had been, unfortunately, suffering from fever at intervals ever since we left Lake Albert Edward, became too ill to walk, so, as there was a Congo post at Kabambare only two days' journey distant, we decided to push on at once to a place where he would have a chance of recovering in tolerable comfort. I accordingly sent the 'headman' and the 'boys' into the village to engage at least four porters, so that we could start as quickly as possible. After waiting for more than two hours, as they did not return, I went into the village—a wretched collection of about half a dozen huts—and found them with three willing recruits and a fourth, the only other able-bodied man in the place, who was bellowing like a spoilt child and insisting on being paid a quite exorbitant amount of cloth. I told him to make less noise, but as he still continued to shout and insult me, I gave him a slap on the face with my left hand, after which he came like a lamb and worked splendidly at carrying the hammock. But that was only the beginning of the incident. A

few miles along the road we met Captain E——
the police-officer of the Manyuema District, who
was making a tour of inspection. The man stopped
and told his story to Captain E——, and I explained
the circumstances apparently to his satisfaction. He
told me that the judges had long ears in the Congo,
and he advised me to be more careful in the future;
I apologized, and we parted good friends. It might
have been supposed that the affair had ended there,
but when we arrived at Kasongo, three weeks later,
I was met with a request to call on the Deputy-
Judge, who was armed with a *procès-verbal* that
occupied some eight or ten sheets of folio. It
appeared that Captain E——, on arriving at
Muniemboka, and having presumably nothing better
to do, had inquired into the matter, and had examined various 'witnesses.' It happened that all
the actual witnesses of the occurrence were with me
at the time, but plenty of willing and imaginative
volunteers presented themselves, and told the most
monstrous collection of falsehoods, all of which
Captain E—— had embodied in his *procès-verbal.*
The Deputy-Judge at Kasongo found the case too
difficult to be dealt with there, so it was referred to the
Judge at Stanleyville, the head-quarters of the Province Orientale. At Stanleyville I spent a pleasant
afternoon discussing it with the Judge, but he again
found the case beyond his powers, so the papers, which
by this time had grown to formidable proportions,
were forwarded to Boma, the chief town of the

State. At Boma I interviewed a legal luminary of a still higher rank, and that functionary, being a person of intelligence and having less time at his disposal than had his legal brethren higher up the river, became convinced of my innocence after a couple of hours of cross-examination, and I was allowed to leave the country without paying the fine of twenty-five francs to which I was liable.

I have mentioned this very trifling incident in order to illustrate, for the benefit of the uninformed, the lengths to which protection of the natives has been carried in the Congo Free State. My offence was not that I had compelled the man to work for me, which I had done, but that I had hit him. I treated the obstreperous person in the same way in which stern parents used to (and possibly do still) treat unruly children, and found myself liable to punishment in consequence. *Correction paternelle* is supposed to be legally permissible in certain cases, and if a left-handed slap on the face is not *correction paternelle* I cannot imagine what is, but it was not allowed in my case. The judicial authorities, whom I consulted, informed me that my proper course was to go to the nearest State post and lodge a formal complaint against the man for being noisy and insolent. It is true that in this case the nearest post was only two days' march distant, but it might have been fourteen days' march, and in any case such a course was quite impracticable in the face of necessity. I am not for a moment defending harsh treatment of the natives—I never punished either of our 'boys,' though they often enough deserved it—but I very much deplore the existing system, the result of which is that natives, whom you pay to work for you, can drive you to the last pitch of desperation by their laziness and insolence without your being able to lay a finger on them, the only kind of punishment which they appreciate. They are quite clever enough to seek for trouble, and they know perfectly well that they have only to run off and tell their tale to the nearest judge, who will probably, as in my case, give a better hearing to a black than to a white man.

Kabambare, where we spent a few days pending Carruthers' recovery from his fever, is one of the most hideous and forlorn places I have ever seen. There are half a dozen houses and stores enclosing a square space of bare mud, where the soldiers do their daily drill; the whole space is cut up by deep channels to carry off the floods of water that fall in the daily thunderstorms. A hundred yards outside the post is a howling wilderness of bush and swamp. There were two officials at Kabambare at that time, and if they had not been constantly occupied with the thousand and one reports and red-tape regulations with which the Congo Government burdens its servants, they must have died of depression. The *Chef de Poste*, a Belgian, was a genial lieutenant of a Line regiment, who had missed his proper vocation by not becoming a market-gardener. He had about half an acre of potatoes, which he used to visit at every spare moment of the day. I am sure he knew every single plant by sight, and at each visit he made a note of those that were to be dug in the evening or the next morning. We used to have bets in tobacco as to the probable number of potatoes which each plant would bear, and on the rare occasions when I won, he would hurl abuse at the head of his grinning gardener for having under-fed or over-fed the plant, as the case might be. He also grew cabbages of colossal dimensions, and admirable lettuces. His salad-making occupied a long interval between the cabbage-soup and the *chou farci*, which was the invariable dinner, and was an art that would have been worth a fortune to him in an European restaurant. His other recreation was singing, and his repertoire was extensive and peculiar. For an hour or two every evening we used to sit out in the square and sing songs of all nations to the listening earth and the wondering natives. He nearly wept for joy when he found that I knew the round 'Frère Jacques,' and thenceforward it became a regular number in the evening concert.

From Kabambare to the Congo is a march of twelve or fourteen days, which we hoped to make in peace, but there was trouble still in store for us. Near a place called Piana Lusanghi, a large village, or, rather, a collection of large villages, with a very dense population, nine of our porters ran away. It was their own country, and presumably they could not resist the temptation of uninterrupted leisure and unlimited food, though by so doing they forfeited the pay which they had already more than half earned. The prospect of an immediate feast was more alluring to them than to work for a few days more and receive payment which would suffice to keep them in luxury for months; but such is the unreasoning nature of the black mind. Piana Lusanghi was a horrible place, and our camp was in the midst of a collection of hovels which reminded me of a very squalid Irish village; sheep and goats and dogs and fowls and children swarmed every-where, and the noise that they all made was inde-scribable. It was obviously not a place to stop in longer than could be helped, so I called on the chief, Lusanghi, and requested him to find me some porters, that being part of his duty as chief. He met me with a direct refusal, saying that he did not like white men. I then tried the move, which was sometimes successful, of saying that I was not 'Birighi'' (Belgian), nor 'Gerrimani' (German), but 'Ighirees' (English) from Uganda; but his ill-mannered reply to that was an order to one of his attendants to fetch a gun, a long and dangerous-looking gas-pipe weapon, with which he threatened to shoot me. It was then time to send a 'boy' to our camp for a chair and some food and a gun, which he brought, but forgetting the cartridges. The above exchange of courtesies took place in the open square in the village in front of the chief's

Near Kibombo, Upper Congo.

To face page 236.

house ; in spite of his gun and his fierce looks he kept at a reasonable distance from me, thinking probably that I carried a revolver in my pocket. I installed myself as comfortably as the circumstances would allow in the verandah of his house, and patiently awaited events from seven o'clock until after mid-day, when the affair ended ludicrously enough in rain. Lusanghi paid me visits at intervals, and looked unutterable things and uttered things that cannot be published ; but when a deluge of rain came down and threatened to spoil his many-coloured garment, he gave in at once, and the porters were forthcoming in five minutes.

I have related this incident at some length to show the kind of difficulties which the foreign traveller may expect to encounter in some parts of the Upper Congo. Such a thing could not possibly occur to State officials, because they never go anywhere without a certain number of soldiers as escort, and an insolent person would very soon find himself in trouble; but people travelling, as we were, without any outward signs of authority, are abso-lutely at the mercy of the chiefs of the countries through which they pass.

From inquiries that I made about my friend Lusanghi, it appeared that he had very materially assisted the Government in quelling the Arab revolt a few years before. The Belgians had very unwisely shown their gratitude for his services by making him chief paramount over many minor chiefs and an enormous population, of whom, it was commonly reported, ten thousand possessed guns. The natural result was that he had come to consider himself a very great personage indeed, and quite justified in bullying any European who came without force at his back. I lodged a formal complaint against him with the authorities, but he was an awkward person for them to deal with, and I doubt if the Belgians took any steps to lessen his power. In the meantime he, and people of his kind, are a common danger; at the time of my interview with him Lusanghi was less than half sober, and it is quite possible that in a fit of drunken madness he might treat the next inoffensive traveller to the contents of that prodigious gun, if he did not blow himself up in the attempt.

Our first glimpse of the Congo, or, to be more accurate, the Lualaba, as it is called there, was of a streak of grey water seen through a blinding storm of rain—ugly enough, but it was a very welcome sight. Though we were almost exactly in the middle of the continent, and there were about 1,700 miles of river between us and the sea, it was for us practically the end of our journey. Henceforward there would be no more stifling swamps, no more elephant-grass, no more weary hills and valleys, and, best of all, no more quarrelling porters. The hour in which we paid off and said good-bye at Kasongo to our last batch of porters was one of the happiest of my life; paddlers going downstream, at all events, could not possibly rouse one to frenzy in the same way as porters can.

At Kasongo we fell into the kind hands of the commanding officer of the Manyuema District, Commandant Moltedò, a distinguished Italian officer, who had fought in Abyssinia, and cherished as his most valued possession a British decoration. He supplied us with newspapers less than three months old, and on parting he presented me with a lump of rubber and a beautiful ivory trumpet, which, considering the labour represented by the one, and the approaching extinction of the other, he appropriately called *Travail et Progrès.**

* The motto of the Congo Free State.

CHAPTER XVII

'Erret, et extremos alter scrutetur Iberos.
Plus habet hic vitæ, plus habet ille viæ.'
CLAUDIAN.

AMONG the many agreeable recollections that I have of travelling in Africa, two stand out pre-eminent above the rest. One is of coming suddenly into the comfort and luxury of the Sudan Railway, after jogging on the back of an evil-tempered camel for many weary days over the burning desert; the other is of the almost intoxicating sense of restfulness which we felt in gliding down the Congo in canoes, after trudging over the hideous wilderness of Manyuema. It is likely enough that, if we had been going in the other direction, we should have been just as much relieved to land after paddling for weeks up against the current; but we were going downstream, and we were not in any hurry —two things which mean comfort in travelling.

The canoes on the Upper Congo are very long dug-out canoes, some of them nearly 100 feet in length. There is usually a little roof of leaves, supported on four posts, in the middle of the canoe, under which the European sits on his long chair, while the paddlers stand at either end, and the baggage occupies the intervals. A big canoe will carry forty or fifty loads, half a dozen 'boys,' and about twenty paddlers. Going downstream, the current is usually so swift that it is enough if the paddlers give a stroke now and again to get steerage way on to the canoe; but when they really work— and they do sometimes, particularly when they come in sight of the village where you intend to camp— it is amazing how the clumsy-looking craft travels over the water. As a rule the paddlers are merry fellows, more cheerful and of finer physique than the average Congo porter. They have a good musical ear, and they love to sing at their work. I reproduce here one of their most easily remembered songs, which may be heard almost anywhere between Kasongo and Stanley Falls :

The solo is sung by the steersman to extempore words, which generally treat of the character and personal appearance of the European in the boat.

The words of the chorus are 'A—a—a' twice repeated, and are accompanied by two tremendous strokes with the paddles. Sometimes we saw another canoe ahead of us, and a furious race would ensue; if we won, the victory was celebrated in song for the rest of the day.

At Kasongo the width of the river is hardly as much as half a mile; but it increases rapidly, and at Nyangwe it is more than a mile from bank to bank. In this part of its course the banks are steep, and covered with a dense tangle of bushes and long grass. Twenty years ago, when the country was in the occupation of the Arabs, Nyangwe was an enormous place with a population of about 100,000 people. Now the Arabs have almost completely vanished, and the population is perhaps a twentieth of that number; but traces of the Arab influence can be seen there and in all the villages along that part of the river. The houses are square mud huts, with a verandah on one or more sides, and many of the people affect a sort of semi-Arab costume.

Canoes going upstream creep laboriously along the banks or wherever the current is slowest; but we went royally down mid-stream when the course was straight, or, as was more generally the case, in the swift water under the outside bank of a curve. There was always something to be on the look-out for—a village in the distance, or a crocodile, or a flock of geese and ducks on a sand-bank, or a school of hippos asleep in a backwater. Near a large village that we passed, we saw crowds of canoes all converging towards one point. On the top of the bank was a yelling multitude surrounding a hippo, which had just been killed and dragged ashore, and the whole population had turned out to get its share of the meat. We followed their example, and I went ashore with our cook to replenish the larder. There must have been fully 500 men and boys crowded about the dead beast, all of them armed with magnificent knives, with which they, or as many of them as could get within reach, were cutting off the skin as if it had been paper. I was given a front place in the middle of the throng while the cook cut off a fillet, and was then glad enough to escape from the smell and the din, which surpassed anything I have ever known. The meat of the hippopotamus, be it noted, is not at all bad eating—in Africa.

Whilst we were going down this part of the Congo in canoes, we came across a good illustration of the wonderful wireless telegraphy which the natives employ to send news about the country. On the third day after starting on our voyage from Kasongo, we arrived at the Belgian post of Kibombo. Though there was no means of communication by land, and no other canoe had gone ahead of us down the river, the officer in charge of the place had known of our coming ever since the evening of the day that we left Kasongo.

Not only did he know that we were coming, but he knew exactly how many loads we had and how many 'boys.' The only mistake in his information was that we were Germans; Englishmen are unknown in those parts of the Congo, and the European who is not a Belgian is a German. The telegraphic apparatus is simple enough, and consists only of a drum, very often a hollowed piece of wood, the sound of which, when it is beaten, carries for an immense distance over the water. The interval between the last two villages above Kibombo was between three and four miles, but news was drummed from one to the other without a mistake being made. After seeing a practical illustration of the art, I began to be less sceptical of the truth of the story, which the Belgians at Rutchuru told us, of news having been sent from Fort Beni in the Semliki Valley to Rutchuru in the Mfumbiro volcanoes in a single night; that was a distance of about 150 miles, and probably a good deal farther by the way that the news travelled.

Between Nyangwe and Kibombo the Congo enters the Great Forest, which is as sharply defined at its southern boundary as we had found it to be at the east, and thenceforward, for 1,400 miles without a break, the river runs through forest.

In the Upper Congo every big village on the river bank is required by the State to furnish a certain number of paddlers in proportion to the

Making a Fish-Trap, Upper Congo.

To face

population, who work between their own village and the next above or below, and are paid a monthly wage. They naturally like to return to their own villages as soon as possible, so it happened several times that when we met another big canoe going upstream, the two would come alongside of each other, and in half a minute, and with what sounded like the most bitter recriminations, though probably they were really expressions of joy, the crews of the two canoes would exchange places and return whence they came. It is true that in certain instances this paddling tax weighs very heavily on a small village where there is much traffic. In many other instances it weighs very heavily on the feebler individuals, for they are forced to work continuously by the stronger and lazier ones, who stay all the time at home. At many villages you are met by the distressing announcement that all the paddlers who have not died of sleeping sickness are out working for the State ; but the offer of a little extra payment has a magical effect in raising the dead and recalling absent brothers from a distance. The unexpected visit, which I witnessed myself, of a State official to pay their monthly wages produced the full complement of paddlers in a village, which had just declared that there were none to be found for two or three days.

Except at two places—Kibombo and Kamimbi (or Sendwe), where there are some rather dangerous rapids, the river is navigable for canoes from a point a little higher up than Kasongo to the head of Stanley Falls, a distance of more than 400 miles. We stopped for a few days at Kamimbi, as it looked a promising place for birds and butterflies, and we were the guests of the *Chef de Poste*, Lieutenant de Rossi, who had a wonderful faculty of taming the birds and beasts with which his house was filled. The latest addition to his menagerie was a young half-grown chimpanzee, which had taken an extraordinary affection for him, and would hardly let him go out of its sight. It used to sit on a chair at the dinner-table and drink its soup with a spoon in the most ludicrously grown-up manner. If it behaved badly, a message would be sent for the sentry and a whip, and at the mention of the word ' fimbo ' (whip) Joseph would scream with rage or terror, and fling his arms round his master's neck. If he woke up during the night, the only way to stop his crying was to put him in Lieutenant De Rossi's arms until he fell asleep, and then a boy would carry him off to bed again. It was a horrible exhibition, and a painful caricature of humanity, and I was not at all sorry when we no longer dined with Joseph.

We also spent a few days at Sendwe, a place at the lower end of the Kamimbi Rapids, where the Congo Government has established an experimental botanical station. The undergrowth in the forest had been cut down, and in long narrow strips, where the ground had been cleared to the bare earth, various rubber-producing vines had been planted at intervals of about 15 feet. Altogether there were about 100,000 plants growing at the time of our visit, and they seemed to be making good progress, though it was as yet too early to judge which kind of vine was likely to be most profitable. Rubber plantations have been started in several places in the State, and with proper management they ought to take the place of the indiscriminately collected forest rubber. Working in these gardens is the kind of work that the natives really like. At Sendwe there were 300 labourers, the full number authorized by the State, about half men and half women. They are paid very fairly, and there were constant applications every day from people asking for employment at the gardens.

The official in charge of the gardens at Sendwe was a painful example of the ill-effects of long residence alone in the tropics. He was an Italian-Greek of an artistic temper, and he knew almost every note of every modern Italian opera; but after two years of solitude his uncongenial surroundings had so worked upon his mind, that he firmly believed that all his neighbours were cannibals and that there was a leopard behind every bush. He could hardly be persuaded to move a yard from his house, and when he did he carried a revolver in his pocket, and was accompanied by five men armed with rifles, as well as by his 'boys' and his cook! It was like wine to him to meet some one who could share a little in his interests, but I do not like to think of his state of depression after we had gone away.

A, few miles below Sendwe is Kindu, the starting-point of the railway from the Congo to Tanganyika and the Katanga District. At that time (February, 1907) about three miles of the railway were completed, and for about thirty-six miles the track had been cleared and partly constructed. The work was being rapidly hurried on by a staff of about sixty Europeans and an army of between 2,000 and 3,000 native labourers, and it was expected that the line would be completed in three years. Notwith-standing the good wages which were being paid —about double what labourers receive for any other kind of employment in the Congo—work on the railway was very unpopular, and desertions were frequent, owing (presumably) to the pernicious system of payment in trade goods, for which the natives had not the slightest desire. It is most earnestly to be hoped that the line will be com-pleted before very long, as it was having the effect of reducing the country to a state of absolute starvation. Sheep and goats, fowls and eggs, rice and flour, had already reached almost prohibitive prices, and there was every prospect of the supply becoming altogether exhausted, for the simple reason that the State has never thought it worth while to teach the people even the elements of stock-rearing and agriculture. In spite of the extraordinary natural richness of the Congo, the railway authorities were in the deplorable position of having to feed their workmen on preserved beef from America and dried fish from Norway!

At Kindu we found one of the steamers which bring up material for the railway, and it took us in two days down the 200 miles of navigable water between the Sendwe Rapids and Ponthierville, at the head of Stanley Falls. In this part of its course the Congo receives some very important tributaries, notably the Elila, the Ulindi, the Lowa, and the Lilu, all from the east, and from being a rapid stream barely half a mile wide at the Sendwe Rapids it swells out into a large lake four or five miles wide above Ponthierville. The natives inhabiting the villages where we stopped in this part of the Congo were, without any exception, the most miserable I have ever seen. Sleeping sickness had destroyed a very large proportion of the population, and those that were left were diseased and famine-stricken, and were little more than skeletons. The few men that we saw sat stolidly on the bank, while the women—wretched, naked creatures—brought wood for the steamer. We were told that they did this voluntarily, and that they received no payment for their trouble—a very exceptional state of things if it was true.

At Ponthierville we found ourselves at the beginning of regular communication by rail and steamer with the coast, and so with Europe, and there, so far as the uncertainties of travel went, our journey came to an end. We spent a very pleasant week with the chief of the district, Commandant Van der Creuyssen, under whose kindly rule Ponthierville has less of the appearance of the military post, and more of the appearance of a colonial settlement than any other place that I saw in the Congo. He had established a school—a very primitive one, it is true —for orphan children, and he encouraged the people to become carpenters and gardeners, ideas which never seem to enter the heads of the ordinary officials, as they certainly do not enter into the programme of the State.

During our stay at Ponthierville I spent an interesting day at the copper mines at Bamanga, about twenty miles down the falls, or, rather, cataract. The ore is exceedingly rich in copper, and Dr. David, the Swiss engineer in charge of the works, was very sanguine of the success of the mines. Not the least pleasing part of the place was the evident healthiness and the apparent contentment of the native labourers, men taken from the surrounding district, who presented a striking contrast to the half-starved wretches that we had seen higher up the river. Dr. David lent me twenty of them to reinforce my crew in going upstream again, and we went up the cataract as if it had been still water. The moon rose, and they began to sing when we came out into the open water above the rapids, and my last voyage in a Congo canoe was a pleasure which I shall not quickly forget.

At a River-side Village, Upper Congo.

Formerly the only way to go from Ponthierville to the lower navigable waters of the Congo was to go in canoes down Stanley Falls, a long series of cataracts, which begin at Ponthierville and extend for about 120 miles to Stanleyville. It was a tiresome journey, as there were four or five places where the canoes could not descend, and baggage had to be transported overland, and there was always a chance of being shipwrecked. Nowadays, since the year 1906, there is a line of railway from Stanleyville to Ponthierville which cuts straight across the bend of the falls, and the journey of eighty miles is accomplished in about six hours. The line is almost straight, and it passes through magnificent forest. The terminus is on the left bank of the river, opposite to Stanleyville, to which place we crossed in canoes. The river there is very narrow, less than a mile across, and the current is very strong. The falls end about two miles above Stanleyville, and the sound of them at night is like the sound of the sea, and is very pleasant to hear. We were received by the Commissaire-Général of the Province, M. Sillye, and his wife, who entertained us most hospitably during the few days that we stayed there.

Stanleyville is the most important place in the Upper Congo, and it is comparable in many ways with Entebbe, though it falls very far behind that place in one important respect. Whereas at Entebbe one of the most characteristic features of the place is the great number of native and Indian traders,

who do an immense business with the native population, not to mention their trade with the Europeans,
at Stanleyville there are no native traders and only
three European firms, of whom at that time one was
bankrupt, another was on the verge of the same condition, and the stock of the third consisted almost
exclusively of cigars and lager-beer.

I found myself at Stanleyville, without either
desiring it or deserving it, in a position of very un-
enviable notoriety. A letter, which I had been
unfortunate enough to write to England describing
our disastrous attempt to explore the western slopes
of Ruwenzori, had been published in the *Times* with
an anti-Congo purpose for which it was never
intended. The Congo Defence Society had seized
upon this letter, and in the last number of their
journal, *La Verité sur le Congo*, which had just
arrived at Stanleyville, it appeared in French,
German, and English, with vehement vituperations
against the writer of it. Most of the Belgians with
whom I discussed the subject were exceedingly
polite, and were quite ready to admit any fair criticism, but it had an unpleasant sequel, which came
near to prolonging my stay in Congo territory against
my will. When we arrived at Boma I was met by
the Commissioner of Police, who invited me to call
without delay on the Procureur-Général. As we
were going ashore he showed me a warrant for my
arrest, which he would have used if I had declined
the invitation. My interview with the Procureur-

EXPERIENTIA DOCET 253

Général was long and difficult, and I only emerged from the rather awkward situation by assuring him that, whatever my opinion might have been, I should not have been fool enough to write and publish an attack on the administration of a country through which I was just about to travel. One learns only by experience, and the lesson which I learnt from this—and I mean to follow it in future—was never to write letters from strange countries, but to go provided with an abundance of picture-postcards on which nothing may be written.

There is a regular service of steamers which ply three times a month between Stanleyville and Leopoldville, or ' Falls ' and ' Leo,' as the two places are more usually called. The voyage upstream is made in from twenty to twenty-eight days, and the voyage down in from twelve to sixteen days, varying with the amount of water in the river. The departure of the boat from Stanleyville is one of the few excitements that the people there have, and the whole white population, to the number of about seventy, turns out in parade uniform and wearing medals and orders—nearly every man in the Congo has a decoration of some sort or another, and many of them have four or five.

The steamers are large, shallow-draught sternwheel boats of about 150 tons, with accommodation for twenty passengers. Except on the newer boats, the cabins are bare, and each man provides his own bed and furniture. There is an open space on the upper deck where the passengers live by day, and a table at which they consume the not very luxurious food provided by the State. Passengers who are not State agents pay for their meals a daily sum, which ensures, I should imagine, a very substantial profit to the State.* The officers and engineers are almost without exception Scandinavians, who can talk a certain amount of English. A fluent captain may be heard addressing his crew in a barbarous mixture of Swedish, French, English, and Bangalla, which might be expected to bewilder the uneducated native, but the tone of his voice is generally a sufficient indication of his meaning. The lower deck is a crowded chaos of wood for the engines, native passengers, soldiers on their way from one post to another, and parrots and monkeys on their way to Europe.

Progress is not very rapid, as the steamer is always stopping at a wood post to take in more fuel, or at a State post to load cargo. We took as much cargo as we could carry, more than 100 tons, in the first seven days after leaving Stanleyville; about 15 tons of it was elephants' tusks; there was a small quantity of palm kernels, and the rest of it was rubber, which is loaded in large wicker baskets, each holding about 80 pounds. It is impossible to travel during the night, and at sunset the steamer makes for the next village, if there is one in sight, or, as more often happens, for the nearest point

* See Appendix.

Near Sendwe, Upper Congo.

Dug-out Canoes, Upper Congo.

To face page 254.

of the bank. One of the crew jumps overboard and swims ashore with a steel rope, which he ties to a tree, and the steamer is secure for the night. The native passengers are not allowed to sleep on board; they scramble on to the bank, and the forest is soon alive with shouts and laughter and the sound of chopping wood, and the air becomes heavy with the smoke of their fires. At eight o'clock the ship's bell rings the 'Cease talk,' and it is pleasant to sit on deck in the cool silence and watch the great river sliding by to the tune of the crickets and the tree-frogs in the forest behind you.

The river is immensely broad, reaching a width of twenty-four miles from bank to bank between Basoko and Nouvel Anvers, but it is so much interrupted by islands that the whole expanse can never be seen at one time. Navigation is exceedingly difficult on account of the sand-banks, which are constantly shifting their position, and steamers frequently spend a week or two firmly embedded on an unsuspected shoal. We spent twenty-four hours stuck on a bank, and as the river was falling rapidly, it was a question whether the cargo could be landed in time to lighten the ship, before we were hopelessly aground until the next rainy season. Happily, when 50 tons of rubber had been laboriously dumped ashore on the nearest island, half a mile distant, we floated off, and then wasted another day in loading up again.

One day was very much like another, and every mile was extremely like the last and the next—an endless panorama of forest and water and islands. Some excitement was caused one day by a native prisoner on his way to trial at Coquilhatville, who jumped overboard and swam to an island. It was a marvel that he was not snapped up by one of the many crocodiles which swarm there; but luck was with him, and as we were steaming down a dangerously narrow channel, he was left in peace.

One of the most interesting things to be observed in a voyage down the Congo is the remarkable differences in the colour of the river. The water of the main stream from Stanley Falls is of a chocolate-brown colour until below Nouvel Anvers, where it receives some big rivers from the Equator District on the south—the Lulongo and others—whose waters are a clear black. Farther on it is joined from the north by the great volume of the Ubanghi, whose waters are a milky white, and these three streams, the black, the brown, and the white, flow along together for an immense distance without mixing, until they finally become churned up together in the narrow passage of the 'Channel,' where the river is less than a mile wide. Below the 'Channel,' in the course of which it is joined by the yellow waters of the Kasai River, the Congo widens out into the lake known as Stanley Pool. On the north side of Stanley Pool is a long escarpment of white cliffs, well named

Dover Cliffs. After passing Brazzaville, the chief station of the French Congo on the right bank, we crossed over to Leopoldville, and came to the end of our sixteen days' voyage from Stanley Falls.

There is a railway from Leopoldville to Matadi, a distance of 240 miles, but I was so much engrossed with my mails of the last six months, which I had found waiting for me at Leopoldville, that I can remember but little of the journey, except that it was exceedingly dusty and that the fare was excessively high. The train stops for the night at a place called Thysville, where the State passengers are told off to quarters allotted to them, but the accommodation for 'outsiders' is scanty and indifferent. For the last few miles down to Matadi the railway goes through a magnificent gorge, with the Congo swirling along hundreds of feet below. At Matadi we found the Elder Dempster s.s. *Albertville*, called by courtesy and in virtue of a subsidy the Belgian Mail, though there was nothing Belgian about it except the flag. But, Belgian or English, it mattered not at all so long as there were baths on board, in which we could wallow from Banana Point to the English Channel, and wash off some of the grime of Africa.

To wait while the ship finished loading at Banana, and for reasons of State which I have mentioned above, I went ashore at Boma, and stayed there for two days. Like every other place in the Congo Free State, with the possible exception of Matadi, where there is at all events an appearance of business activity, Boma has a painfully official aspect. There are a few private trading firms, of which the most important is the English firm of Hatton and Cookson, but practically all the business is in the hands of the State. The number of officials in the place is about 200, and all of them seemed to be prodigiously busy, but what their business is it would be hard to say. In paying our debt to the State for the Ponthierville Railway and the steamer fare to Leopoldville, I interviewed nine officials in the course of an afternoon, and was eventually referred back to and paid the official I had visited first. It was only through the kind offices of two Commandants and one Judge that I obtained permission to carry out of the country the ivory horn which Commandant Moltedo had given me at Kasongo. The most ludicrous piece of officialdom that I saw was their regulation which requires time-expired officers to call on the Governor-General in the full uniform of Europe before leaving the country. On a roasting afternoon, when the temperature was 98° F. in the shade, I saw a weary little party climbing up the steep hill to the Residency, all of them buttoned up tight in thick black frock-coats with stiff collars up to their chins. Half of them were already invalids after their three years' service in the Congo, and I should think that that afternoon call must have put the finishing touch to the rest of them.

Baskets of Rubber, Congo.

Chain-Gang Road-Making, Congo.

To face page 258.

Boma is a depressing place, and I was glad enough when the steam tug took us down the last forty miles of the Congo to Banana, where we found the *Albertville* with steam up and ready for home. As we rounded the Point, the last thing we saw was the Congo flag, the yellow star on the blue ground, waving above the palm-trees, and the last sound of the Congo that we heard was the bugler sounding the call of 'Cease work.'

> ' You cannot see the land, my land,
> You cannot see, and yet the land is there—
> My land, my land, through murky air—
> I did not say 'twas close at hand—
> But—land, ho ! land.'

CHAPTER XVIII

THE CONGO FREE STATE

' I cannot fall out, or condemn a man for an error, or conceive why a difference in opinion should divide an affection :
for controversies, disputes, and argumentations, both in
philosophy and in divinity, if they meet with discreet and
peaceable natures, do not infringe the laws of charity : in all
disputes, so much as there is of passion, so much there is of
nothing to the purpose ; for then reason, like a bad hound,
spends upon a false scent, and forsakes the question first
started.'—SIR THOMAS BROWNE.

WHEN I first contemplated writing an account of
my wanderings in Africa, nothing was farther from
my thoughts than to enter on the thorny paths of
Congo controversy ; more than that, indeed, it was
my fixed intention to avoid the question altogether.
During the last few months, however, the subject
has been brought forward to such a point of pro-
minence that it is impossible to be altogether silent,
and I am assured by people whose opinion I value
very highly that silence on my part might be very
seriously misconstrued, or at the best that it might
be taken as a sign of indifference to the gravity of
the situation. A misconstruction of silence would
be unpleasant ; a suggestion of indifference would
be infinitely worse. So it is inevitable that I should

record, as plainly as may be, my opinion of the present state of things in the Congo Free State.

I do not think I can be accused of undue haste in giving expression to my opinion. I have read with great care most of the letters and articles and White Books which have been written on the subject during the last few years, and I am writing this twelve months after I quitted Congo soil.

At the outset I am confronted with an almost insuperable difficulty in the prejudice—it is honest and very praiseworthy, I admit—which exists in the minds of a great majority of the British public. For instance, a daily paper of the highest repute, in reviewing a book* of travel in Africa, in which the author, one of the most observant and fair-minded explorers of modern times, deliberately records a favourable opinion of the administration of the Congo, says: 'We suppose it is useless to try to open the eyes of explorers to the futility of this sort of thing and the egotism it displays. Even if the system of administration in the districts on the edge of the Congo State visited by Lieutenant Boyd Alexander were above criticism—and Lieutenant Alexander himself affords evidence that such is not the case—it would not affect the testimony of other eye-witnesses in other parts of the State as to the conditions prevailing in time as recent as Lieutenant Boyd Alexander's own journey.'

* 'From the Niger to the Nile,' by Lieutenant Boyd Alexander (1907).

The 'testimony of other eye-witnesses' is, of course, of great value, and worthy of all consideration, but it is not quite easy to understand why greater credence should be given to the testimony of vice-consuls and missionaries than to that of disinterested travellers.

Part of the reason may be found in that side of the human character which formerly sent people in their thousands to witness an execution, and is now represented by the doubled sale of newspapers at the time of a particularly revolting murder. So long as it does not occur in his own respectable house and cannot bring discredit upon himself, the ordinary citizen feels a certain sense of smug satisfaction in hearing of the misdeeds of other people, whether it is atrocities from Bulgaria or the Congo, or from the divorce courts, and he is secretly not at all sorry that these things should happen. To the majority of people it is the 'atrocities' which constitute the chief point of interest in the Congo. It is always more pleasant to believe what you wish to believe, and I was quite prepared to be treated with open incredulity, when I answered inquirers about atrocities in a way not quite to their satisfaction. But I confess I was astonished (being ignorant of that trait of humanity) at the genuine and hardly concealed disappointment with which many good, and otherwise right-minded and kind-hearted, people have received my remarks.

During the last three years three English travellers

—Lieutenant Boyd Alexander,* Mr. A. H. Savage Landor,† and the late Mr. Marcus Dorman‡—have travelled widely in the Congo Free State, and have recorded favourable reports of what they saw in three different parts of the country. None of those gentlemen had the smallest personal interest in the State, and it is impossible to believe that any one of them was influenced in his report by other than the purest motives. It may be objected that the opinions formed by travellers in passing through a country must be merely impressions, and cannot be of any great value. Such a charge might fairly be brought against the impression of a country caught from the windows of a railway-carriage, but it cannot hold against the experience which you get of a country, when you travel through it at a foot's pace with frequent halts of days and weeks, and when you are constantly in touch with the native inhabitants and very often with the officials of the Government. It may also fairly be maintained that a passing traveller sees many things, faults and merits alike, to which the man who sees them daily is blind.

It is as easy to fall into the snare of exaggeration on one side as on the other. One tells us that the Congo is a shambles swimming in blood, and another that it is the negro's paradise. But, it need hardly be said, neither of these pictures is the true one ;

* 'From the Niger to the Nile,' 1907.
† 'Across Widest Africa,' 1907.
‡ 'A Tour in the Congo Free State,' 1905.

since the coming of the white man the flow of blood in Africa has steadily diminished and is almost staunched, and since the coming of the white man there has been no longer a paradise for the negro, who has been made to pay taxes and work for the white man, and can no longer pursue his ideal existence of endless idleness.

No one, who has taken the trouble to study the question, can remain in doubt for a moment of the wholly indefensible position which the Congo Government has assumed with regard to the Act of Berlin. The signatory Powers have been openly defied, every article of the Act has been set at naught, and the freedom of trade for all nations, which (it was supposed) was ensured by the Act, is a dead letter. When they endeavour to secure the re-establishment of free trade, the Congo reformers can be sure of the sympathy of all thinking people. But the real issue, which is this question of the freedom of trade, has been obscured by the popular cry of oppression and 'atrocities.' Very few of us are likely to profit materially from the opening of the commercial door in the Congo, and a crusade with that object would not find many enthusiastic supporters ; but when there are direct accusations of robbery and murder, we are honestly shocked at the criminal behaviour of our neighbours, and secretly glad of the chance of attending another execution. Clergymen and ministers of every denomination (all honour to them) inveigh against the iniquities of the

Congo dragon in impassioned sermons; Bishops and Lord Mayors appeal to the Foreign Secretary in the name of humanity and philanthropy, and all of them serve the purpose of the disappointed trader.

Bordering on the Congo Free State is the Portuguese territory of Angola, a country about as large as France and Switzerland and Italy combined. For every thousand people who have heard of the Congo it is possible that two have heard of Angola, and perhaps one of those two knows that from a time some score of years before the inauguration of the Congo State, there has existed in that country a system of slavery which is only comparable with that of the Spaniards in the West Indies. Slaves are brought down from the far interior, often as far as 800 miles, by agents who think they have done well if one-half of their drove survive the journey. At the coast, knowing that it is impossible for them to return home, the slaves bind themselves to a term of service, which never ends, in the cocoa plantations of the islands of S. Thomé and Principe.

My object in mentioning Angola is not to excuse the faults of the Congo on the grounds of the infinitely worse condition of things in Angola—a great evil was never a justification of a less evil—but to point out the disinterestedness (or otherwise) of the Congo reformer. The great difference between the two countries, though they are so close together, is briefly this : Angola is a poor country, poor in natural products of the soil and poor in minerals, but still moderately rich in men, in spite of having been squeezed for generations by the Portuguese. It is not worth anybody's while to start an agitation for the suppression of the present state of slavery which exists there; in fact, it is better to leave it alone, as the end of 'indentured labour' in S. Thomé would mean an immediate rise in the price of cocoa. The Congo, on the other hand, is in natural pro- ducts by far the richest part of tropical Africa, and it was only to be expected that our merchants should bitterly resent being excluded from it, particularly when they have a legal right of entrance. Small wonder that they are annoyed, and are prepared to provoke an European conflagration in order to secure their undoubted rights.

It was hardly likely that an agitation, which aimed only at the rights of traders in a remote country, would find any great measure of popular favour; but when it appeared that the wealth of the Congo was being exploited under a system of the most diabolic cruelty, and that our neighbours were growing rich at the price of the last drops of the natives' blood, we lost sight of the real question at issue, and were filled with a righteous indignation. A chorus of protest went up against the iniquities of the dragon, and sermons were preached and meetings held from one end of the country to the other.

It is far from my intention to insinuate that the organizers of this agitation have been actuated by any than the highest motives in conducting their campaign. I am sure that in their own hearts they have been honestly satisfied of the truth of the charges which have been brought against the Congo State, and so long as the multitude was determined to redress this crying evil and to remove this blot from the face of the earth, there was no reason why they should be more properly instructed in the foundations of the question.

Nor will I deny that numerous cases of atrocities and oppression have occurred in the Congo Free State. It is a deplorable fact, but a fact none the less, that such things have accompanied the early stages of the occupation of a savage country by white men in nearly every instance. One has only to study the present condition of the German African colonies and of Angola (though it can hardly be said that Angola is in the early stages of occupation), to know that this is true.

To look the question broadly in the face, what does this charge of ' atrocities ' involve ? It means that we are prepared to believe that a civilized European nation, many of whose citizens are near akin to ourselves in blood and in language, supports some 2,000 villains and murderers in the Congo, where they commit the most barbaric atrocities for the purpose of filling the pockets of a monarch, who happens to be a relation of the King of England. It will be objected that I am wrong when I charge the Belgian nation with the responsibility; but the central government of the Congo is entirely Belgian, and nine-tenths of the agents of the State are Belgians, so Belgium must bear the brunt of the attack. It may also be objected that only a small minority of the 2,000 are murderers and villains; but if it were true of only one in every hundred of them, the rest of them would stand condemned for being associated with such a system of outrage. It will also be objected that I insist too strongly upon the word 'atrocity'; but it is through the stories of atrocities that this agitation has grown and prospered, and it is safe to say that, without 'that blessed word,' the Congo would have been as unfamiliar a name as Angola or the Kamerun.

Leaving out of consideration for the moment that large host of well-intentioned but rather hysterical people, whose favourite intellectual food is scandal and the halfpenny newspaper, is it to be supposed that the solid balance of educated and thinking people, who form public opinion in this country, really believe that these Belgians are the blackguards they are said to be? I can hardly doubt that the common sense and the prevailing generosity of the majority render the question unnecessary.

In the minds of most of our countrymen a Belgian is a sort of inferior Frenchman, and a Congo official is a scoundrel who has made his own country too hot to hold him, and has taken service as a licensed murderer in Africa. As a matter of fact, the average

Belgian is quite as enlightened a person as the average Englishman, and the majority of the Congo officials are officers in the Belgian army, who have been moved by the same spirit of adventure that has sent Englishmen into every corner of the world. Being a small nation, they have been compelled to enlist a large number of foreigners for the Congo service; but though this has possibly diminished to some extent patriotism and *esprit de corps*, many of the foreigners, notably the Scandinavians and Italians, have filled the highest posts in the Administration with conspicuous success.

When I first went there I was, I confess, prejudiced against the Congo State, as most Englishmen who read their newspapers would probably be ; nor was my first experience calculated to give me a very favourable impression of the State. In the preceding pages (Chapters XI. and XIV.) I have recorded fully, perhaps even at too great a length, the two instances of ill-treatment of natives which came under my personal notice. In both of these cases the individual at fault was a *sous-officier*, who was enjoying temporarily a position of exceptional authority, and I believe that the chance of airing his authority in the presence of strangers had not a little to do with his behaviour. In any case, the policy of placing people of that sort in positions of responsibility is most strongly to be condemned ; but I believe that such incidents are rare.

In other chapters I have expressed sufficiently

strong opinions with regard to the Belgians' treatment of native women, to the judicial treatment of natives and Europeans, and to the question of a money currency. The attitude of the Belgians towards native women—and the same thing is often seen in their dealings with servants and native soldiers of non-commissioned rank—shows generally an error in the direction of over-familiarity rather than of severity. I have seen natives interrupt and join in a conversation between Europeans in a manner which would certainly not be tolerated for a moment in any of our African colonies. The fault arises, probably, from their lack of experience in dealing with native races ; they have not the advantage of centuries of colonizing habits in their blood, but there is no reason to suppose that they are not eager to profit by the mistakes that they have made.

With regard to the functions of the judges, the Government has made the grievous mistake of conceiving too many laws and regulations, and leaving too little to local circumstances and the initiative of the man on the spot. The result too often is that the harassed official or the learned judge (often a very youthful person) finds himself perplexed by conflicting rules and unable to carry them out, and his lack of authority loses him the respect of the natives. Utter savages though most of them are, they have been accustomed to receive in times past from their native or Arab rulers a certain rude justice, often harsh enough, no doubt, and it is justice they want rather than laws.

Though I have searched diligently through most of the recently published accounts of the Congo and its administration, I have failed to find a single recorded instance of actual ill-treatment of natives witnessed by an European, and I believe that no one has seen anything more serious than that which I have seen myself, as set forth in the preceding pages. This is not to say that instances of injustice and 'atrocities' (if the word be insisted on) have not occurred. It is a truism that there is never any smoke without fire, but a very small smoulder often produces a vast volume of smoke.

There is a Boer maxim, which applies as well in Central Africa as in the South—'In Africa believe nothing that you hear and only half that you see.' There must be some subtle influence in the climate, which affects the minds of Europeans in Africa, so that their imaginations sometimes play strange tricks with them; but no more of them, for fear of causing offence. It would be an injustice to the natives of Central Africa to say that you can never believe a word they say, but they have a disconcerting habit, which is not altogether unknown amongst more civilized races, of answering a question in the way that they think you would like best, and it is not easy to get at the actual truth.

As an instance of the difficulty of finding out the true circumstances of a story, I will mention a case which came within my own experience. At the village of Muhokya, in Uganda, where the Ruwenzori Expedition spent some months, there lived a man who had lost his nose, one hand, and one ear. Taking a somewhat surgical interest in him, I asked him, through an interpreter, how he had come to be mutilated, and his story was that the parts had slowly withered. So far as the hand was concerned his tale was an obvious lie, but he was shrewd enough to give an explanation which he thought would have a professional interest for the dispenser of medicines. Shortly afterwards he came with me to Toro—he was exceedingly strong and a good porter in spite of his deformity—and there I got two Europeans to question him independently and on different occasions. One of them he told that it had been cut off by the soldiers of the big Englishman (Captain Lugard, presumably) after the fight at Muhokya a few years before. To the other he said (and this was probably the truth) that it was done by the people of Kabbarega, the King of Unyoro, who was for a long time the terror of the country. Had I been a Belgian in search of 'atrocities' committed in British territory, he would doubtless have told me the story which was most likely to please me, and I should have accepted it without hesitation.

A curious instance of the way in which native rumour spreads, and loses nothing in the telling, occurred when the Ruwenzori Expedition left the Congo on our return to Toro. At the first village we came to on the Uganda side of the boundary, we found that it was commonly reported that the whole Expedition had been massacred by the natives on the west side of Ruwenzori, with the exception of two of the Europeans (Carruthers and myself, I suppose), who had fled with ten porters up into the mountains. Belief in the rumour was so well established that our porters were welcomed as though they had returned from the grave.

On another occasion, when we were staying for a day or two in a small Congo post, tenanted by one Belgian officer, the cook and the 'boy' of our host absconded with half a sheep. Our own 'boys' (Waganda) informed us, with every appearance of telling the truth, that they had run away because the Belgian had put the finishing touch to his usual ill-treatment of them by slitting their ears with a long knife. On the following day, however, the truants returned with ears intact, but crying out for medicine for their stomachs, which were grievously disordered by a surfeit of mutton.

It would be easy to multiply such cases indefinitely, but I think enough has been said to show how careful one must be in examining native testimony.

In travelling from one side to the other of the Congo Free State, I had exceptional opportunities for observing the relations which exist between the natives and the agents of the State, both when travelling by land or water, and in the posts of the State, where we unavoidably spent more time than

18

we had intended. Here the critic will object that of course I did not see any ill-treatment of the natives, because the officials were on their good behaviour, when they knew that the watchful, and probably hostile, eyes of Englishmen were upon them. Such a suggestion is to credit them with a degree of duplicity which I find it impossible to concede. They have little enough reason, Heaven knows, to feel much liking for Englishmen, but the kindness and consideration with which we were invariably treated, and the manner in which many of them went out of their way to help us in difficulties, make it inconceivable to me that these people can be guilty of the crimes with which they are charged. I have been present when the natives have brought in their tax of rubber ; I have come unexpectedly upon an official paying the paddlers of a village their monthly wages ; I have seen them travelling with porters or in canoes along the rivers ; I have been present at the Sunday ' palavers ' with the chiefs, and, as a rule, the prevailing spirit has been one of *bonhomie* and good-nature.

With regard to the taxation of the people, if the taxes were spread uniformly over the whole population they would not be unduly heavy, but in the majority of cases they affect the few rather than the many, and unquestionably entail a large amount of hardship. For instance, a village has to supply, say, fifty kilos of rubber a month. If the whole adult population saw fit to bestir them-

To face

The Congo above Stanley Falls.

selves, they could easily procure the amount in a couple of days' work ; but such a system is quite foreign to their ideas, and the result is that a few servants of the chief, who are to all intents and purposes slaves, do the whole work of the community, while the rest stay at home at ease.   The same thing occurs, as I have pointed out in an earlier chapter, in those villages whose tax is paid by the labour of paddlers on the rivers—a few unfortunates are unceasingly at work, whilst the rest do nothing.

Until a universal currency has been introduced, and a tax in money has been substituted for the tax in labour, there can be no end to the unfairness of the taxation as it exists at present.   It should always be borne in mind—and it is a fact which is not generally known, or, if it is known, it is forgotten—that the householder in Uganda who fails to pay his annual hut-tax of three rupees, or the taxpayer whose poll-tax of two rupees is not forthcoming, pays an equivalent in one month's compulsory labour for the Government.

With regard to the payment of natives as hired labourers, I have remarked above (Chapter XV.) that the porter in the Congo Free State, and to a somewhat less extent the paddler, is paid at a higher rate than the porter in Uganda.   The only injustice here is that the labourer in the Congo is paid in the objectionable 'trade goods,' and this, again, can only be remedied by the establishment of a currency.

I have to some extent compared the conditions of labour and taxation in the Congo with those which obtain in Uganda, because the two countries are so close together geographically, but it must not be forgotten how fundamentally they differ from each other in the nature of their peoples. In Uganda we found a docile people, already with a certain civilization of their own, who were ripe for the introduction of European methods of government. In the Congo the Belgians found an immense population consisting of a great number of different tribes, most of whom were cannibals and most of them at war with their neighbours. The signal success which has crowned their efforts in unifying these very antagonistic elements and in opening up an immense country must be recognized by any unprejudiced observer. It is no part of my purpose to enter into the vexed question of the appropriation by the State of the fruits of the soil; that is a subject which may be as legitimately discussed by people who have never been within a thousand miles of the Congo as by people who have visited the country.

In conclusion, I would say that I have not lightly nor without deliberation appeared to range myself on the side of what very many people consider to be a criminal régime. I recognize most fully the honesty of the motives of the people who wish to redress evil, and I recognize most fully the existence of many evils in the Congo Free State.

We are already looked upon with suspicion, both in Belgium and France, as having not altogether disinterested motives in this Congo agitation. I would venture to suggest that, from our own colonial experience, we can afford to treat generously the shortcomings of others, and, above all things, we can assure ourselves absolutely of their truth before we bring serious accusations against a friendly nation.

APPENDICES

APPENDIX A

NOTES ON THE ZONES OF VEGETATION IN RUWENZORI

[I am indebted to Dr. A. B. Rendle, of the Natural History Museum, for permission to take these notes from his paper on the plants collected in Ruwenzori by the British Museum Expedition. The plants were examined, and the new species named and described by Dr. Rendle, in conjunction with Messrs. E. G. Baker and S. Le M. Moore, also of the Natural History Museum. The paper was published in the *Journal of the Linnæan Society* (Botany), vol. xxxviii., January, 1908.]

THE first botanical collection of any extent made on the Ruwenzori range was that of Dr. Stuhlmann in 1891. He ascended the valley of the Butagu on the west of the chain to a height of 13,326 feet. Mr. G. F. Scott Elliot, in 1895, made five excursions towards the central ridge, approaching it on the east by the valleys of Yeria, Wimi, Mubuku, and Nyamwamba, and on the west from the Butagu Valley. In the last he reached 13,000 feet. Later, Sir H. Johnston reached a height of about 15,000 feet on the east slopes of the peak, which he named Kiyanja. On this expedition some plants were collected by Mr. Doggett and presented to the Royal Gardens, Kew. Collections have also been made recently by Dr. Roccati, who accompanied the Duke of the Abruzzi in 1906, and by Mr. Dawe, of the Botanic Gardens at Entebbe.

The plants obtained by the British Museum Expedition were mainly collected from two camps: one at about 3,500 feet altitude on the south-east slopes of the range, between the mountains proper and Lake Ruisamba; the other at an altitude of 6,500 feet in the Mubuku Valley, the most important valley on the east side of the range. Expeditions were made to intermediate and higher altitudes, the highest camp being at about 12,500 feet, whence plants were collected to the snow-level, which may roughly be said to be at 14,500 feet on the east side of the mountains. The time of year was from January to July. January was a month of fine weather; February, March, and April were very wet in the mountains. From the middle of April, when a move was made to the lower camp near Lake Ruisamba, the weather was almost continuously fine. Most of the flowering plants had ceased to blossom by the end of May, and butterflies, which were exceedingly abundant during the latter part of April and May, were almost absent from the lower slopes in June.

The following is a brief summary of the general aspect of the country and the more striking forms of the vegetation seen at various altitudes:

3,000 to 4,000 feet: Beyond the wide belt of papyrus and swamp, which surrounds Lake Ruisamba, is a park-like country of shortish grass, with scattered trees, mostly acacias, and intersected by deep ravines, in which is found a thick jungle of two species of fleshy euphorbia, a large-leaved fig (*Spathodea campanulata*), with magnificent clusters of scarlet flowers, a tangle of vines and asclepiads, and a conspicuous white, sweet-scented jasmine (*Jasminum Schimperi*). Two species of epiphytic orchids were found in these jungles.

The plants collected include a number of wide·

spread tropical species. *Acacia Catechu* and *Ipomœa Wightii* are of Eastern affinity, occurring in Tropical Asia, but not passing into West Tropical Africa. Others are more or less widely spread Tropical African or Tropical South African species, as *Pavonia macrophylla*, *Vernonia cinerascens*, *Ruellia patula*, and *Ornithogalum Eckloni*. Other species are East Tropical African, such as *Grewia similis* and *Hibiscus æthiopicus*; while *Hibiscus crassinervis*, *Jasminum Schimperi*, and *Barleria grantii* are more northern 'Nile Land' types, and *Mellera lobulata* and *Lissochilus Livingstonianus* of more southerly distribution (Uganda, the Mozambique District, and British Central Africa). A western affinity is represented by *Spathodea campanulata*, a West Tropical African species, which finds the eastern limit of its distribution on Ruwenzori; *Thunbergia fasciculata*, a Cameroons plant; and *Mucuna Poggei*. *Schizoglossum eximium* is restricted to Ruwenzori, and the following are new species: *Aloe Wollastoni*, *Chlorophytum ruwenzoriensis*, and *Baphia Wollastoni*.

4,000 to 5,000 feet: About this level there is a good deal of native cultivation, chiefly bananas, manioc, Indian corn, and beans. At this altitude the huge 'elephant-grass,' growing from 10 to 15 feet high, is the most important feature of the vegetation, and conspicuous among it are the pretty little trees of *Erythrina tomentosa*, with tufts of crimson flowers.

The following were collected at 5,000 feet: *Tephrosia paniculata* (Angola and Uganda); *Fleurya podocarpa*, a widely spread Tropical African species; *Crinum scabrum*, a more northern type (Abyssinia and the Nile Valley); and a new composite, *Guizotia collina*.

5,000 to 6,000 feet: Cultivation and elephant-grass still continue, with species of *Ipomœa* climbing about the stems of the grass, and the very handsome red-and-yellow *Gloriosa virescens*, which is found up to

7,000 feet. A few small patches of forest, with a good many ferns, polypodiums, and others, fill the bottom of the valley at this level. The plants collected at 6,000 feet include some widely distributed tropical species, such as *Vigna luteola*, *Ageratum conyzoides*, and other composites, with a new variety of *Laggera alata*, a common Tropical African and Asiatic species; some widely spread Tropical African species, such as *Desmodium Scalpe* (also India), *Melanthera Brownei* (also South Africa), *Platystoma africanum* (also India), *Cyathula cylindrica* (also South Africa and Madagascar), and *Crinum giganteum*. A marked east tropical affinity is shown by *Eriosema montanum*, *Osbeckia densiflora* (Mozambique), *Helichrysum fœtidum*, and *Indigofera longebarbata* (Abyssinia); *Brillantaisia patula* is a Cameroons plant, also found in Uganda. *Isoglossa runssorica*, *Triumfetta ruwenzoriensis*, and *Gynura ruwenzoriensis*, the two latter also collected at 7,000 feet, represent an endemic distribution; and the following are novelties: *Thunbergia oculata*, *Coleus gracilentus*, and *Pentas pubiflora*.

6,000 to 7,000 feet: The banana is not cultivated much above 6,000 feet, and the 'elephant-grass' ceases at the same level. Above this is a zone of shrubs, conspicuous among them being *Acanthus arboreus* with mauve flowers, two or three yellow-flowered papilionaceæ, and a handsome *Solanum* with prickly leaves and a large yellow fruit. The first of the tree-lobelias (*L. Giberroa*) is found in the open places on sunny slopes. Wild bananas are found in shady places up to 7,000 feet and beyond. Dracænas, reaching a height of 30 feet and upwards, are found in groups beside the streams. Millet and colocasia are cultivated up to 7,000 feet, above which level cultivation ceases.

A large number of species were collected at 7,000 feet, the majority of which are more or less widely distributed in the highlands of Tropical Africa. Of these a minority occur on both sides of the Continent; such are *Pavonia Schimperiana* (Abyssinia to Cameroons and Angola), *Cassia didymobotrya* (East Africa and Angola), and *Plantago palmata* (Kilimanjaro to Cameroons). Twice as many are restricted to Eastern Africa, including the Central Lake district. Of these, some have a northward range, generally as far as Abyssinia, while others have a more southern or restricted distribution, and there are also the endemic species, *Vernonia ruwenzoriensis*, *Lissochilus ruwenzoriensis*, and *Satyrium crassicaule*. At this altitude were also collected the north temperate species, *Sanicula europæa* and *Orobanche minor*. The following novelties were found: *Begonia Wollastoni* (allied to *B. Johnstoni*, from Kilimanjaro and Kenia), *Pentas pubiflora*, var. *longistyla*, *Pavetta ruwenzoriensis*, *Grumilea megistosticta*, *Vernonia Wollastoni*, *Conyza scariosa*, *Senecio Wollastoni*, *Plectranthus Wollastoni*, *Peperomia ruwenzoriensis*, and *Polystacha bicarinata*.

Between 7,000 and 8,000 feet is found the biggest forest of Ruwenzori. A large *Dombeya* with clusters of white flowers is very noticeable, and one of the finest trees, though not very numerous, is a *Podocarpus*. A sweet-scented begonia (probably *Begonia Meyeri-Johannis*) is found climbing about the lower trunks, and tree-ferns occur in shady places and on the banks of the streams.

At 8,000 feet were collected the widely spread Tropical African highland species, *Stachys aculeolata* (Cameroons, Fernando Po, and Abyssinia) and *Habenaria Rendlei;* also *Hibiscus diversifolius*, var. *granatensis*, a Tropical South American variety which is also recorded from Uganda.

8,000 to 9,000 feet: The slope of the mountains becomes much steeper, and the forest thins out into open spaces covered with bracken and occasional big trees, having very much the appearance of the higher slopes of the New Forest. This gives way to a belt of small tree-heath (*Erica arborea*) and *Podocarpus*, and so to the zone of bamboos, which begin on the east side of Ruwenzori at about 8,500 feet, and continue up to 10,000 feet, while on the western slopes of the range they begin at 7,000 feet.

9,000 to 10,000 feet: The big tree-heaths begin about 9,500 feet; their branches are covered with long wisps of grey lichen. A good many terrestrial orchids were found at this level (*Epipactis africana*, *Cynorchis anacamptoides*, *Satyrium crassicaule*, and *Polystachya gracilenta*), all endemic species; while the epiphytic *Angræcum Scotellii*, and two new species of *Polystachya*, were also collected. A big bushy *Impatiens*, the endemic species *I. runssoriensis*, was found at this altitude. Ferns, notably polypodiums and a long, narrow-leaved hart's-tongue, are numerous, and the biggest of the alchemillas, *A. ruwenzoriensis*, forms large silvery beds. A *Helichrysum* (*H. argyrocotyle*, sp. nov.) in the moist places and a small yellow orchid (*Polystachya Doggettii*) on the rocks contribute agreeable touches of colour.

In addition, the following novelties were collected at 9,000 feet: *Senecio jugicola*, *Coleus latidens*, *Pycnostachys Elliotii*, and a remarkable amaryllidaceous plant which seems to represent a new genus (*Choananthus*), combining in some respects the characters of *Hæmanthus* and *Cyrtanthus*. At 10,000 feet were found *Thalictrum rhynocarpum*, a species widely spread on the mountains of Tropical and South Africa; a variety of *Cotyledon umbilicus*, known also from the mountains of Abyssinia and Kilimanjaro; several endemic species (*Rubus*

Doggettii, Solanum runsoriense, Mimulopsis Elliotii, etc.);
and a new species, *Coleus clivicola.*

10,000 to 11,000 feet: This is the zone of moss *par
excellence.* It forms round cushions on the trees (most
of them *Erica arborea*), and masses 2 feet deep on the
ground and amongst the fallen logs, where the hyraxes
make their burrows. Two tree-lobelias (*L. Deckenii*
and *L. Stuhlmanni*) appear at this level, also a fine
tree-hypericum with a big yellow flower. A blue
violet (*Viola abyssinica*) is found in the more open
spaces. At 11,000 feet were found two new species,
Conyza montigena and *Calamintha parvula,* and the
widely spread northern temperate *Cerastium vulgare.*

11,000 to 12,000 feet: Helichrysums (including a new
species, *H. Wollastoni*), tree-lobelias, tree-heaths, and
tree-senecios, are the most conspicuous plants at this
altitude, though the two latter attain their greatest
growth above 12,000 feet. A handsome *Rubus* (*R. runssorensis*) with a pink flower and a large but tasteless
fruit is fairly abundant, and a small *Sedum* (*S. ruwenzoriense,* sp. nov.) grows on the rocks. The plants
found at 12,000 feet include *Alchemilla geranioides,
Alchemilla argyrophylloides* (a new species), *Senecio
sycephyllus,* the tree-senecio *S. adnivalis,* and several
Alpine species, which have been found on the mountains
of Abyssinia and Kilimanjaro—*Ranunculus oreophytus,
Cardamine obliqua,* and *Hypericum keniense.*

12,000 to 15,000 feet: The tree-heaths cease about
12,500 feet, but the senecios continue much farther,
in some places above 14,000 feet. A fourth species of
Lobelia (*L. Wollastoni,* allied to *L. Rhyncopetalum* from the
mountains of Abyssinia) appears at about 12,500 feet,
and is found growing on the steepest slopes almost up
to the snow-line. *L. Deckenii,* which grows only on
the level terraces in very moist ground, does not occur
above 13,000 feet. Helichrysums, sometimes forming

bushes 4 or 5 feet high, grow most luxuriantly in this region, one species (*H. Stuhlmanni*, var. *latifolium*) being found nearly up to 15,000 feet. A small *Arabis* (*A. alpina*) was found at 14,000 feet, and a rush (*Luzula Johnstoni*), a grass (*Poa glacialis*), and mosses were found growing up to the level of permanent snow.

To this zone belong the following plants : *Galium serrato-hamatum*, sp. nov. (at 12,500 feet), *Helichrysum Stuhlmanni* (at 13,000 feet), *Senecio gymnoides*, sp. nov. (at 12,500 feet), *Rubus runssorensis*, *Sedum ruwenzoriense*, *Carpha Emini*, and *Carex runssorensis*. At 14,000 feet was found an interesting new alchemilla (*A. subnivalis*).

When it is remembered that all the plants which have hitherto been brought from Ruwenzori have been collected in the Mubuku Valley on the east side, on the southern foot-hills, and (a very few) in the Butagu Valley on the west side, it will be seen that there still remains a very large portion of the range in which future explorers may expect to make botanical collections of the greatest interest.

APPENDIX B

SLEEPING SICKNESS

SLEEPING SICKNESS, properly so-called, is the name applied to the terminal stages of trypanosoma infection, or trypanosomiasis.

Trypanosomes belong to the *Hæmoproteidæ*, a group of the *Hæmoprotozoa*, organisms which inhabit the blood of many vertebrates, fishes, birds, reptiles, and mammals. The disease has been known in Africa for more than a century, but its connexion with the trypanosome was not recognized until 1902. In that

year Dutton, in the Gambia Colony, found a trypanosoma, which he called *Trypanosoma gambiense*, in the
blood of a native suffering from fever of a non-malarial
character. In the same year Castellani, in Uganda,
discovered trypanosomes in the blood and in the
cerebro-spinal fluid of cases of sleeping sickness. He
suggested that the parasite is the cause of sleeping
sickness, and this has been fully proved by the
researches of Bruce and others, who have also shown
that the infection is transmitted by the tsetse-fly.

Trypanosoma gambiense has been found in West
Africa from about 15° North to 15° South latitude;
it is widely spread in the Congo basin, reaching a
point about 11° South in the Lualaba River; it is
found in the Tanganyika region and in Uganda, and
along the Nile as far as 6° North latitude. But its
distribution is not uniform over this vast area; it
corresponds with the distribution of a tsetse-fly, and
is thus confined to the banks of rivers and lakes, and
even along these it is not absolutely ubiquitous. One
stretch of shore is for some reason more favourable to
it than another. Though the trypanosome is not at
present found in all the districts in which the tsetse-
fly occurs, there is, unfortunately, no reason to
suppose that it has yet reached the limits of its distribution. By a strange irony, the opening-up of these
countries by Europeans, the spread of civilization, and
the consequent improvement in intercourse between
the different native races, have unquestionably been
largely responsible for the great increase of the disease
in recent years.

Nothing is known of the life-history of the trypanosome, and it is impossible at present to make a dog-
matic statement as to the relations which exist between
it and the tsetse-fly. It seems probable that the tsetse-
fly ' serves as an alternative host in a truly biological

sense, and not as a simple mechanical transmitter; that the trypanosome, after entering the intestinal canal of the insect, undergoes developmental changes requiring a considerable space of time for their completion, developmental changes which enable it subsequently, when the opportunity occurs, to effect a lodgment in the human or other vertebrate host. Considering the bionomics of *Glossina*, it seems not improbable that the trypanosome, after undergoing certain unknown changes, enters the larva, and is thus transmitted by heredity to the vertebrate host' (Manson).

It has been proved beyond question that the infection is transmitted by a species of tsetse-fly (*Glossina palpalis*), but it is not definitely known that it is never transmitted by other species as well. It has been stated that a species of mosquito (*Stegomyia*, sp.) is also capable of transmitting trypanosomiasis.

The disease affects individuals of all ages and of both sexes. Males, perhaps, more often contract the disease than females, because they are more constantly exposed to the attacks of tsetse-flies during the course of their occupations as paddlers, fishermen, etc.

The *incubation period* of trypanosomiasis has been found experimentally in animals to be two or three weeks, and it is probably the same in man.

The *symptoms* usually begin with a fever of an irregular and indefinite character. In some cases it lasts for a few days, and recurs after a longer or shorter interval; in other cases it may last for weeks, with an equally long interval between the periods. The degree of fever is also exceedingly variable. The patient becomes enfeebled by the attacks, and becomes anæmic. The cervical and other glands become enlarged and sometimes tender. Occasionally they resume their normal size either temporarily or permanently; in others they remain enlarged, but seldom suppurate. Local œdemas and affections of the skin are frequently seen; the latter commonly take the form of papular eruptions and of large patchy erythemas, of a curiously fleeting character. Some of the eruptions are painfully irritating, and lead (in negroes) to scratching, which produces large and very intractable sores.

The later symptoms of trypanosomiasis—those which constitute the condition known as *sleeping sickness*—probably indicate the beginning of the infection of the nervous system. There may be an interval of years—as many as seven years (it is said)—between the primary infection and the commencement of the sleeping sickness symptoms; but in the majority of instances the period is probably much shorter. The duration of the sleeping-sickness stage varies from three or four months in some cases to three or four years in others. In these latter cases there are often prolonged intervals, during which the patient seems to have recovered his normal health; but sooner or later a relapse occurs, and in every case, whether it is acute or chronic, it is terminated by death.

The onset of the sleeping-sickness symptoms is indicated by an accentuation of the symptoms of trypanosomiasis already existing. 'The physical languor finds expression in disinclination to exertion; a slow, shuffling gait; a morose, vacant expression of countenance; a relaxation of features; a hanging of the lower lip, and a puffiness and drooping of the eyelids; a tendency to lapse into sleep, or a condition simulating sleep; a slowness in answering questions; a shirking of the day's task. Dull headache is also generally present. Later there may occur such symptoms as fibrillary twitching of muscles, especially of the tongue, and tremor of the hands, more rarely of the legs, indicating a definite implication of the motor centres. By this time the patient has taken to bed, or he lies about in a corner of his hut, indifferent to everything going on about him, but still able to speak and take food if brought to him. He never spontaneously engages in conversation, or even asks for food. As torpor deepens he forgets even to chew such food as is given to him, falling asleep, perhaps, in the act of conveying it to his mouth, or with the half-masticated bolus still in his cheek' (Manson).

Later on he begins to lose flesh; convulsions and temporary local paralysis occur; bed-sores tend to form and spread rapidly. As the lethargy becomes more continuous, he wastes quickly from lack of nourishment, and the end is brought about either by coma or by the increasing weakness. In some cases all or most of these symptoms may be seen, but different cases exhibit a wide range of different symptoms, and it is impossible to define the exact course of the disease.

The *mortality* of the disease must be reckoned as 100 per cent. It is possible—but there is no definite knowledge on this point—that recovery may take place in the very early stages of trypanosomiasis, but when once the sleeping-sickness stage of the disease has been reached, it is probably invariably fatal. I have already drawn attention (see Chapters III. and XVI.) to the appalling destruction of human life that has taken place in the last few years in a corner of Uganda and one small district of the Congo Free State; but this represents but a fraction of the havoc which has been wrought in Central Africa by sleeping sickness.

Not longer ago than September, 1907, Professor Koch, in reporting on his investigations made in Lake

Victoria, added yet another terror to the already gloomy outlook on sleeping sickness. He found a large number of cases in districts where the tsetse-fly was absent. The majority of the cases were undoubtedly imported, occurring in people who worked in the rubber industry in forests along the lake-shore, where tsetse-flies abounded. But fifteen of the cases could not by any possibility have been imported. All were women, and all were wives of men employed in the rubber industry in a tsetse-fly area. Assuming that no other biting insects than tsetse-flies are capable of transmitting the disease, the only tenable hypothesis is that these women contracted it from their husbands by the act of coitus. If Professor Koch's observation is correct, the prospect of eradicating sleeping sickness is a sufficiently remote one, as not only can the disease be transmitted by a widely distributed fly, but it also belongs to the category of venereal diseases, and experience of many centuries has shown the difficulty of stamping out diseases of that class.

The *diagnosis* of sleeping sickness is best made microscopically. It may be confused with beri-beri, but the latter is a disease of the peripheral nervous system, and is non-febrile, while sleeping sickness is a disease of the central nervous system and is febrile. Microscopically, it is often difficult to find the trypanosomes, which are always rare, and occasionally absent from the peripheral circulation. It is better to puncture a lymphatic gland and examine some of the aspirated lymph.

The *treatment* of sleeping sickness is a subject about which there are widely different opinions, but it is impossible to speak very hopefully at present of any of the therapeutic methods which have been suggested. The greater number of authorities have more or less confidence in the potent arsenic compound, 'atoxyl' (a sodium salt of paramidophenylarsenic acid), and all agree that it is the best drug yet known. More recently its use has been combined with that of bichloride of mercury, and the results seem to promise well. There seems to be no question that the disease may be held in check for a time by the use of atoxyl, and it is possible that complete cures have been obtained by this means; but relapses are exceedingly common. In any case the treatment must be continued for a long time and energetically, until the patient has been free from all symptoms for a long period and no sign of trypanosomes can be found (by injection into susceptible animals) in the blood. The attempts that have been made in serum-therapy have hitherto been failures.

It is to the *prevention* of sleeping sickness that the most strenuous measures must be directed at present; but even here there are very serious drawbacks in our ignorance of the complete life-histories of the tsetse-fly and the trypanosoma, and of the exact relationship between the parasite and its carrier. Nor do we know what are the normal hosts of the trypanosome under natural conditions. It is true that a great deal can be done in this direction. The tsetse-fly lives near water; villages must, therefore, be moved away from the banks of rivers and lakes. The fly requires rank vegetation; much can be done (as has been done successfully at Entebbe) in the way of clearing the bushes and undergrowth from the lake-shore. But there still remains the absolute necessity of following the waterways for purposes of transport, fishing, etc., and in these occupations the natives must inevitably be exposed to the bites of tsetse-flies. If they could be induced to wear some sort of light garment, they would obtain a certain measure of protection; but water-side populations in Africa usually go even more naked than others.

It is obviously a desirable thing to avoid infected areas, and, if possible, to prevent natives from inhabiting them; it is also desirable to prevent infected natives from entering uninfected districts, but this latter measure is beset with almost insuperable difficulties. Even in civilized countries whose frontiers are well defined and not easily crossed without detection, the establishment of systems of quarantine has been excessively difficult; how much more so would it be, therefore, in savage countries with ill-defined boundaries, and where the number of officials competent to enforce the regulations is necessarily very small. It has been suggested that all natives showing enlarged cervical glands should be isolated; but this would involve the detention of a certain number who were not suffering from sleeping sickness, whilst a still larger number would escape detection by reason of the very insidious nature of the disease in its early stages.

The most recent recommendation is that of Professor Koch, who asserts that in the neighbourhood of the Victoria Nyanza the tsetse-flies subsist almost entirely on the blood of crocodiles; he therefore suggests the extermination of these reptiles by the destruction of their eggs. It is difficult to take this suggestion really seriously. The numbers of crocodiles are so immense, their distribution is so wide, and their powers of reproduction so great, that it is doubtful whether the best-conducted campaign against them would have any appreciable effect. And it is only too probable that, if they were deprived of crocodiles' blood, the tsetse-flies would find some other food, as they undoubtedly must do in those districts—e.g., the shores of Lake Ruisamba and the Albert Edward Nyanza—

where sleeping sickness is found, but crocodiles are absent.

In the present absence of complete knowledge respecting the trypanosome and the tsetse-flies, the best that can be done is, so far as is practicable, to close infected districts, to prevent the passage of infected individuals into uninfected areas, and, by clearing the rank vegetation along the banks of rivers and the shores of lakes in the vicinity of villages, to destroy the breeding-grounds of tsetse-flies in the places where they are most likely to have an opportunity of infecting human beings. If, however, Professor Koch's suggestion of *mal de coit* is proved by subsequent investigations, and 'transmission of the disease between the sexes in the human subject is possible and reciprocal, it is obvious that comparatively little good is likely to be effected by measures directed against what may prove to be only an occasional alternative method of infection. Should such be the case, the outlook is indeed dark, for it is difficult to see what general measures can be suggested that offer any hope of preventing the spread of the disease in actual practice' (*Journal of Tropical Medicine*).

The tsetse-flies (*Glossinæ*) comprise ten species, which are confined to Africa. They are sombre-coloured, narrow-bodied flies from about 8 to 12 millimetres long, with a thick proboscis projecting horizontally in front of the head. When the fly is at rest the wings overlap each other, crossing like the blades of a pair of scissors. *Glossina palpalis* has been found from Senegal to Angola on the west, through the Congo and Lualaba to Tanganyika and the Victoria Nyanza, and northwards along the Nile to the Uganda-Sudan border. The flies are seldom, if ever, found above 4,000 feet, and always near water. A swampy shore is not much to their taste; they are most commonly found along those stretches of river bank or lake-shore where there is a beach of mud or sand, overhung by trees or bushes. There must certainly be some reason for this preference on the part of the fly for a certain type of ground; it may be, as has been suggested by Sambon, that there is some relation between the flies and certain air-breathing fishes, but our knowledge on this point is at present only fragmentary. More complete information may perhaps lead to some more effectual means of dealing with the flies.

Tsetse-flies do not lay eggs, like most Diptera, but larvæ, which turn into the pupa condition almost immediately after extrusion. The perfect flies, both male and female, are blood-suckers. They feed during the day, and by reason of their exceedingly rapid flight and the extraordinary softness with which they alight on their victims, it is very difficult to detect them until after the mischief has been done.

APPENDIX C

AFRICAN TICK FEVER (ALSO CALLED 'AFRICAN RELAPSING FEVER,' OR 'SPIRILLUM FEVER')

TICK FEVER is an acute specific fever due to the presence of spirochætæ in the general circulation. The spirochætæ are conveyed by the bite of a tick; they can also be communicated by inoculation with infected blood.

Fever due to the bite of a tick was first described by Dr. Livingstone. In 1873 Obermeier discovered the spirochæta, which causes the relapsing fever of Europe, and in 1897 it was discovered that the parasite

and the disease are communicated by the common bed-
bug. In 1903 Dr. Philip Ross found spirochætæ in a
case of fever at Entebbe (Uganda), and succeeded
in infecting a monkey from the case. In 1904 Dr.
Milne found spirochætæ in the blood of eight cases
of fever, which the patients themselves (natives of
Uganda) ascribed to the bites of ticks. In the same
year Dutton and Todd, in the Congo State, discovered
that the spirochæta was communicated by the bite
of a naturally infected tick, *Ornithodoros moubata ;*
they also found that they could infect monkeys with
the disease by feeding newly hatched ticks upon them,
and thus proved the hereditary transmission of infective
powers from the parent tick to the offspring through
the egg.

There are differences of opinion as to the exact
nature of spirochætæ, and biologists have not yet
decided whether they should be regarded as bacteria
or as protozoa. The spirochæta of African tick fever,
on account of its great length, its somewhat different
appearance (it is often seen arranged in a circle or
coiled like a figure of eight), and on account of the
shorter febrile period to which it gives rise, has been
differentiated from the spirochæta of European relapsing fever, and has been named *Spirochæta Duttoni.*
The spirochætæ may be found in the blood during
the attacks, and they become less numerous with
each relapse. The most convenient method of staining
them, in a tropical country, is with Leishman's stain.

The *incubation period* is from two to eight or ten days.

The *onset* of the disease is usually quite sudden.
The patient feels not quite well, the temperature begins
to rise, and in a few hours he is in a state of prostration.

The *symptoms* are fever, vomiting, and headache.
The temperature rises to 103 to 105° F., and remains
fairly constant, though it is rather lower (perhaps 101°)

in the morning than in the evening. There may be very severe headache, and pains in the back and limbs. One of the most distressing symptoms is the vomiting, which is often exceedingly severe and difficult to stop. Diarrhœa is not infrequent. In some cases after forty-eight hours, but more commonly after three or four days, the temperature falls rapidly to below the normal, and the symptoms are immediately relieved. After a varying interval of from four days to a week, and sometimes longer, there is a recurrence of all the symptoms, occasionally as severe as in the first instance, but generally less severe. The relapse lasts for two or three days, and after another interval it is followed by a third. There is a tendency for the duration of the attacks to become shorter, and for the intervals between them to become longer, until they cease altogether. Five or six relapses is not an uncommon number for an European to suffer; occasionally there are as many as twelve. Amongst natives there is not always a relapse, and there is seldom more than one.

Although tick fever is not a very fatal disease—the mortality is usually below 6 per cent. (Manson)—it is a very disagreeable disease for Europeans in a tropical climate, which is itself a hindrance to complete convalescence.

The *diagnosis* is not always easy, unless a microscopic examination of the blood can be made. It may be very suggestive of malaria, but the fact that it does not respond to quinine ought to help the diagnosis in this case; and the persistent vomiting is unlike malaria. Some of the cases in which intestinal symptoms are prominent somewhat resemble enteric fever.

The *treatment* must be confined to treating the most distressing symptoms, so far as is possible. There is no drug which is known either to stop the disease or to prevent the occurrence of relapses. In the course of time probably a serum-treatment will be possible.

Prevention consists in avoiding the places where the ticks are found, such as old rest-houses and native huts, and in enforcing absolute personal cleanliness on the part of native servants, in whose clothes the infected ticks are often carried. The ticks move about and feed at night, and it is most important, by means of a well-arranged mosquito net, and by taking care that no bedding touches the ground, to prevent their gaining access to the bed.

The tick of African tick fever, *Ornithodoros moubata*, is exceedingly common throughout Tropical Africa from the East Coast to the West. 'Its body is flattened from above downwards, and is oval in outline. Its colour, when alive, is greenish-brown. The integument is hard, leathery, covered with close-set granules or tubercles, and marked both above and below with symmetrically arranged grooves. The females may attain about 8 millimetres in length, by 6 to 7 millimetres in breadth' (Manson).

The ticks live in the huts of the natives, and hide during the day in cracks in the walls, or in the thatched roof, or in the grass on the floor. They move about at night in search of food. In some districts the natives have learnt to protect themselves against the ticks by frequently plastering the walls and floor of their huts with fresh cow-dung; but as a rule, especially in rest-houses along the roads, they take no trouble to avoid their attacks.

APPENDIX D

APPROXIMATE TIMES AND COST OF TRAVEL IN
UGANDA AND THE CONGO FREE STATE

THE number of days given is the number of days
actually occupied in travelling between the various
places. Considerable allowance should be made for
delay occasioned by recruiting porters, getting provisions, and so on. The cost, except in the case of
steamers and railways, varies locally and from time
to time.

In Uganda the average rate of payment of porters
is equivalent to about 5s. 4d. per month. A native
cook receives from 20s. to 25s. per month, a 'boy' from
16s. to 20s. per month, and a headman' about 20s.

In the Congo Free State the average payment of
porters is from 8s. to 10s. per month, and of paddlers
rather less. A cook receives about 15s., and a 'boy'
from 8s. to 10s. per month.

Where it is not otherwise stated, it should be under-
stood that travelling is done with porters.

FROM MOMBASA TO ENTEBBE, 3 DAYS. FARE £10.
(FIRST CLASS RAIL AND STEAMER.)

1. Direct Route from Uganda to the West Coast.

From Entebbe to Toro, 14 days.
From Toro to Irumu (Ituri River), 6 days.
From Irumu to Mawambi, 11 days.
From Mawambi to Avakubi (Aruwimi River), 8 days.
From Avakubi to Basoko (Congo), 11 days. Canoe.
From Basoko to Leopoldville, 12 days. Steamer.
From Leopoldville to Matadi, 2 days. Rail.
From Matadi to Boma, ½ day. Steamer.

II. Route from Uganda to the Congo by way of Lake Kivu and Tanganyika.

From Entebbe to Mbarara (Ankole), 13 days.

From Mbarara to Kasindi (Albert Edward Nyanza), 8 days [or from Entebbe to Kasindi, *via* Toro, 19 days].

From Kasindi to Vichumbi (south end of Albert Edward Nyanza), 5 days. Canoe.

From Vichumbi to Bobandana (Lake Kivu), 7 days.

From Bobandana to Nya-Lukemba (south end of Kivu), 4 days. Canoe.

From Nya-Lukemba to Uvira (Tanganyika), 7 days.

From Uvira to Baraka (Burton Gulf), 4 days. Canoe.

From Baraka to Kasongo (Congo), 28 days.

From Kasongo to Kindu, 7 days. Canoe.

From Kindu to Ponthierville (head of Stanley Falls), 7 days. Canoe [or, by steamer, 2 days].

From Ponthierville to Stanleyville, 1 day. Rail.

From Stanleyville to Leopoldville, 14 to 16 days. Steamer.

From Leopoldville to Boma, 2½ days. Rail and steamer.

The price of tickets on the railway from Ponthierville to Stanleyville was not fixed in 1907. We paid 25 francs each.

The steamer fare from Stanleyville to Leopoldville is 110 francs. Besides this there is a charge of 5 francs per diem for the use of a cabin, and 12 francs per diem for food. Baggage to the amount of 200 kilogrammes may be taken by each passenger.

From Leopoldville to Matadi the price of the railway ticket is 200 francs. One hundred kilogrammes of luggage may be taken, and extra luggage is charged at the rate of 1 franc per kilo, so it is advisable to get rid of superfluous baggage at Leopoldville.

We found that the cost of transport from Entebbe to Stanley Falls, by the Kivu-Tanganyika route, was almost exactly 25s. per load.

APPENDIX E

BIG-GAME SHOOTING IN WESTERN UGANDA AND THE CONGO FREE STATE

It is not likely that anybody will visit these districts for the sole purpose of shooting big game, as there are many other regions more easily reached, where there is a greater abundance and variety of game. It was not a part of the object of the British Museum Expedition to shoot large mammals in the neighbourhood of Ruwenzori, and the small number of antelopes, etc., which were obtained there by members of the Expedition, and subsequently by Carruthers and myself in our journey to the Congo, were shot mainly for purposes of food. For the benefit of future travellers who may find themselves in some of the places visited by us, I will mention the districts where we came across big game, and the species which they may expect to find.

In Uganda the licence to shoot big game costs £50, and is valid for twelve months. The licence includes the right to kill two elephants, the ivory of which should, with moderate luck, more than cover the cost of the licence. In the Congo Free State the big-game licence costs 200 francs, with the right to kill one elephant. There is a theoretical close-time from October 15 to April 15, but it does not seem to be very rigidly enforced.

In Uganda, the districts where we found the greatest abundance of game were : The plains at the south end of Lake Albert, on either side of the Semliki River; the forest and grass country near Fort Portal (elephants); the plains between Ruwenzori and Lake Ruisamba; numerous parts of the province of Ankole, particularly the neighbourhood of Mbarara, and the eastern shores of Lake Albert Edward.

In the Congo Free State the best big-game countries that we passed through were : The northern shores of Lake Albert Edward and the upper part of the Semliki Valley; the plains at the south of Lake Albert Edward as far as the Mfumbiro volcanoes; scattered districts in the Manyuema country between Tanganyika and the Congo, especially along the course of the Luama River.

Experienced hunters will, of course, provide themselves with different weapons, according to their tastes. As a novice, I may mention that I found a ·375 magazine rifle (J. Blanch and Co.) exceedingly satisfactory as an all-round weapon; it is heavy enough for the largest animals, and is not too big for small antelopes.

The following is a list of the species which occur in the districts that we traversed, with the localities where they may be found :

Lion (*Felis leo*): Western Toro; eastern slopes of Ruwenzori; very numerous on the east and south sides of Lake Albert Edward as far as the Mfumbiro volcanoes.

Leopard (*Felis pardus*): Everywhere; particularly common near the north of Tanganyika and in the Manyuema country.

Elephant (*Elephas africanus*): In Uganda the province of Toro is famous for its elephants, notably near Fort Portal, and all about the north end of Ruwenzori and in the Lower Semliki Valley. In the Congo State we met with them in the Upper Semliki region, in the Ituri Forest, in the Rusisi Valley, and within a short distance of Kasongo.

Buffalo (*Bos caffer*): The Uganda buffalo is not uncommon about the eastern foot-hills of Ruwenzori, and in the province of Ankole, where 'record' specimens have been obtained. We met with the Congo buffalo (*Bos nanus*) in a great many places; it is especially numerous in the Semliki Valley, in the Manyuema country, and near Sendwe on the Upper Congo.

Eland (*Taurotragus oryx*) is found in the province of Ankole in Uganda.

Roan Antelope (*hippotragus equinus*) occurs in the Manyuema country in the Congo State.

Lesser Koodoo (*Strepsiceros imberbis*) : We saw the horns of a specimen of this antelope, which had been found floating in the Luama River in the Manyuema country.

Puku (*Cobus vardoni*) is widely distributed between Tanganyika and the Congo.

Topi, or Senegal hartebeeste (*Damaliscus corrigum*), is found in the province of Ankole, in immense numbers on the plains to the south of Lake Albert Edward, and fairly numerously in the Manyuema country.

Water-buck (*Cobus defassa*) is found in many places in Uganda, particularly on the plains about Lakes Ruisamba and Albert Edward; in the latter district they bear horns of remarkable size. The measurements of my 'record' specimen are : length of horns, $36\frac{3}{4}$ inches; spread from tip to tip, 36 inches; circumference at the base, $9\frac{7}{8}$ inches. In the Congo State we found water-buck at the south of Lake Albert Edward, in the Semliki Valley, and at one or two places in the Manyuema District.

Uganda Kob (*Cobus thomasi*) occur commonly on the plains about Lake Ruisamba and the Albert and Albert Edward Nyanzas; at the south of the last-named lake they attain an unusual size.

The *Sittatunga* (*Limnotragus spekei*) occurs in most of the papyrus swamps of Uganda, but it is exceedingly difficult to obtain.

Bushbuck (*Tragelaphus scriptus*) occur almost everywhere where the country is suitable; they are particularly numerous in the Rusisi Valley.

Reedbuck (*Cervicapra arundinum*) may be seen in hundreds on the plains at the north and south of the Albert Edward Nyanza.

Wart-hog (*Phacochœrus œthiopicus*), near Mbarara (Ankole), and at the south of Lake Albert Edward.

Hippopotamus (*Hippopotamus amphibius*) is found in every river and lake that we visited, with the exception of Lake Kivu. In the Congo below Stanley Falls the hippopotamus is becoming less numerous than it was formerly on account of the frequent passage of steamers.

APPENDIX F

A FEW HINTS FOR AFRICAN TRAVEL

In many of the books which treat of travel and exploration in Africa and other tropical countries, there may be found exhaustive lists of the necessary stores and equipment, and valuable suggestions towards promoting the greater comfort of intending travellers. I will, therefore, only mention some of the things which are omitted from the ordinary lists, and suggest a few points which I have found useful in a tolerably wide experience of travel in tropical countries.

A very sound guiding principle is to take, so far as is possible, all the more important things *in duplicate*. This, of course, does not apply to such bulky things as tents, beds, etc., but to smaller things, such as washing apparatus, watch-glasses, mosquito-nets, razors (if used), umbrella, hat, inkpot, knife, boot-laces, and other things which the reader can imagine for himself.

Loads should be made up, if possible, before leaving England, and none should exceed 60 pounds in weight —50 pounds is better.

Double loads—i.e., loads which require two porters for their transport—should be avoided at all costs. They cause frequent delays to the caravan in a rough country, and are an endless source of worry and irritation to black and white.

Tents should be made of green Willesden canvas, waterproof and rot-proof. A wide extension of the outer 'fly' at the front of the tent is an advantage. In countries where white ants abound, it will be found useful to have a spare supply of *iron pegs* in addition to the wooden ones.

Bed: The ordinary × pattern folding-bed is by far the best.

Wolseley valise: This is, in my opinion, almost indispensable. For short expeditions away from your base-camp you can carry in it all your personal luggage as well as your bedding, and you can use it as a makeshift tent, or as a sleeping-bag. They are made by Messrs. Silver and Co.

Chair: A comfortable chair is a necessity. The canvas 'deck-chair,' which most people use, has a disadvantage in that it must be carried on the top of a load, where it often gets wet. I prefer a square chair of wood and canvas, which is readily taken to pieces and packed in my bed.

Umbrella: Many people will scoff at the idea of taking an umbrella to Mid-Africa, but I am prepared to uphold its use. Where the path is wide enough to admit of it, it is pleasanter to walk in the shade than with the sun beating down on your back, and on the too frequent occasions when the heavens are opened, an umbrella will keep part of you dry, at all events for a time. This becomes increasingly important towards the end of a long journey, when your clothes, like everything else, have begun to rot. I should like to take also a long and light *waterproof cape*, if such a thing can be made to withstand the ill effects. of a hot and damp climate.

Boots : Twice as many boots should be taken as are at first thought to be sufficient. I have a preference for long boots which reach almost up to the knee. They are invaluable in soft country, and save the trouble of leggings or puttees.

Mosquito-boots : Soft leather slippers with long ' tops ' reaching well up the legs are a luxury, which conduce largely to the comfort of evenings in camp· Mosquitoes have an evil habit of searching out unguarded ankles under the shadow of the table, and the result is either (very possibly) malaria, or the discomfort of putting boots again on to your weary feet. A very good pattern of mosquito-boot is made in Madeira.

Basin : An aluminium washing-basin in a leathern or canvas cover, which holds all the other washing apparatus, is strongly to be recommended.

Mosquito-nets are made in various patterns, and most of them are unhandy. Perhaps the best is the square type, which is attached to a framework of sticks or canes jointed like a fishing-rod. A simpler pattern, which I always use, is like a large wide petticoat, which can be tied to the roof of the tent, or the branch of a tree, or any suitable fixed object, and the free edge tucked underneath the bedding. It should be remembered that the mosquito-net must never trail upon the ground. If it does, it affords an easy means of access

20

to the bed for beetles, ticks, scorpions, and other undesirable creatures.

Filters : A great deal of ingenuity has been devoted to the construction of filters which have been recommended for use in tropical places, but I would strongly dissuade anyone from taking a filter, at all events to a country where negro servants are employed. The more efficient a filter is, the sooner it becomes clogged with dirt and requires cleaning. Unless it is kept constantly clean by boiling, under the supervision of the European, the filter becomes a splendid breeding-ground for bacteria, and is a source of danger rather than of safety. Except in high mountain regions, above the highest habitations, all water for drinking-purposes should be *boiled* as a matter of routine. In order to clear very muddy water, the addition of a small quantity of *alum* (sulphate of alumina) will be found useful.

. *Dubbin,* or some equivalent, should be taken in large quantities. Except in places where hippos can be shot, it is impossible to obtain fat for boots and other things made of leather. The sheep and goats and antelopes are totally lacking in fat.

Large *sacks,* made of green Willesden canvas, will be found most useful for carrying large skins and horns of antelopes and bulky curios, which would be damaged by exposure to the weather.

Naphthaline is cheap and not heavy. It is invaluable for protecting natural-history specimens, clothes, and books against the attacks of the ubiquitous ants.

Salt is in many places worth untold gold. Being heavy, it should be purchased at the last point of civilization.

A *steel tape* for measuring is a thing which ought not to be forgotten. It cannot stretch or shrink like a linen measuring-tape, and its habit of springing back into its case invests the owner with mysterious powers.

Medicines: Excellent lists of drugs suitable for the tropics have often been written. One can hardly do better than take one of Messrs. Burroughs and Wellcome's 'Congo Chests.' I will mention one drug only, and that is *Potassium Permanganate*, as a remedy for snake-bite. The method of using it is to open the wound with a knife, and rub in the crystals of the salt. As well as a considerable stock in my baggage, I took a small capsule containing the crystals, which fitted into the silver penholder that I always carried in my pocket. It was ready for immediate use in an emergency, but fortunately I never had need of it.

A *collapsible boat* is a thing which I often wished for; I should certainly take one on another occasion.

Photographic Work: Sanger-Shepherd and Co., of London, who have had wide experience of tropical photography, recommended me to take a Newman and Guardia ¼-plate 'Reflex' camera, fitted with focal-plane shutter and Zeiss convertible Double-Protar lens. This was carried in a leather sling case; an outer water-tight japanned box saved the instrument from certain damage, when it was dropped by a native one day into the Victoria Nyanza. Neither the rough conditions of travel, the continued spells of wet in Ruwenzori, nor the warm moisture of the Congo, interfered with the efficiency of the camera, and a spare shutter was never used.

Paget XXXXX Plates (backed) were used, and exposures were made in light metal single dark-slides, which worked well and were easily carried. The tropical conditions affected a few of the plates with slight markings, which had to be 'touched out,' but the majority of them gave good negatives. Sanger-Shepherd and Co. packed the plates in sealed tins, which preserved them in good condition for two years.

Head-gear: There are some fortunate people who find themselves sufficiently well protected by the light 'Terai' hat; but to most people a topee, or sun-helmet, is a necessity. The ordinary pith-helmet is an excellent thing in a dry climate, such as the Sudan; but in a rainy country it has the drawback of absorbing every drop of rain that falls upon it, and from weighing only a few ounces it speedily weighs several pounds. I have found it a good plan to cover it with a thin covering of some waterproof material, and over that a light fabric of some suitable colour.

Clothes: The 'Gaberdine' material of Messrs. Burberry is excellent in a thorny country, and it has the great virtue of resisting the attacks of mosquitoes. It has always been the custom of Europeans in the more civilized tropical places to deck themselves in white garments, following the fashion of many natives of tropical countries, but forgetting that those natives are already provided with a pigmented skin, which is a sufficient protection against the short solar rays. It is these rays which seem to be responsible for 'heat-stroke,' and, according to the researches of Dr. Sambon, white-skinned people ought to protect themselves by a covering of non-actinic colours, such as red, yellow, or black. Dr. Sambon has invented a fabric, called 'Solaro,' which contains these various colours. It has been worn by many people for several years with conspicuous success, and when people overcome this old prejudice in favour of white clothing, it will be found that 'heat-stroke' will diminish in frequency.

Books: I have already mentioned that Mr. Pepys was my faithful companion; with him was a somewhat mixed company consisting of Sir Thomas Browne, 'Don

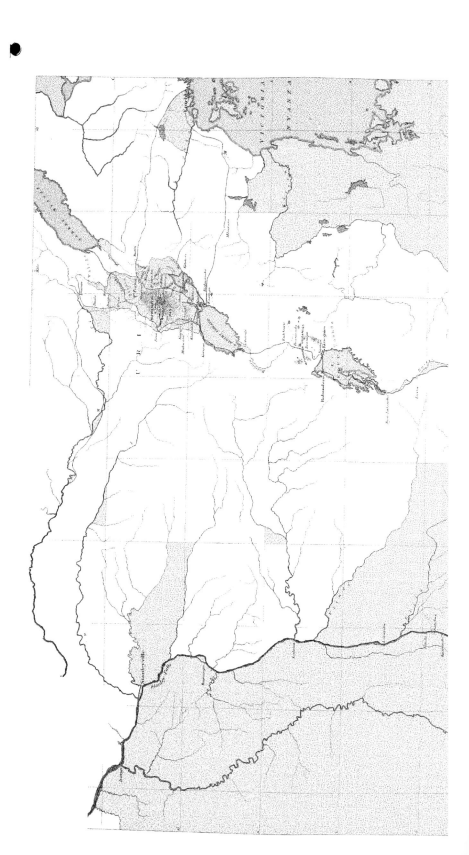

Quixote,' 'Henry Esmond,' 'The Compleat Angler,' William Shakespeare, and 'Robinson Crusoe.' But *chacun à son goût*, as was said to me by a Belgian officer whom we met in the Congo; the red-letter days in his life were those when the monthly mail regularly brought him *Ally Sloper's Half-Holiday*.

In conclusion I may remark that it is better by far to take too many things than to take too few. One porter more or less makes very little difference to the management of a caravan, and the extra load may make a vast difference to the comfort of the traveller. A tin of flour too much or an extra pound of tobacco is a thousand times better than one too few. You may throw away the things you do not want; but what you have not got, that you must do without.

As one who has failed lamentably in this respect— my journals are always pitifully meagre and frag- mentary—I would advise the keeping of a very complete journal of everything seen and heard. Nothing is too trivial to be noted, and one thing written reminds you afterwards of a score of others. The pleasure in looking back on a journey, with a memory which weeds out the disagreeable things, is in some ways even greater than the delight of the journey itself.

' No man doth safely appear abroad, but he who can abide at home.'

INDEX

THE END

BILLING AND SONS, LTD., PRINTERS, GUILDFORD.

SD - #0008 - 280721 - C0 - 229/152/24 - PB - 9781330194911